Teaching Islam

AMERICAN ACADEMY OF RELIGION
TEACHING RELIGIOUS STUDIES SERIES

SERIES EDITOR
Susan Henking, Hobart and William Smith Colleges

A Publication Series of
The American Academy of Religion and
Oxford University Press

Teaching Levi-Strauss
Edited by Hans H. Penner

Teaching Islam
Edited by Brannon M. Wheeler

AMERICAN ACADEMY OF RELIGION

Teaching Islam

EDITED BY

Brannon M. Wheeler

New York   Oxford

OXFORD

UNIVERSITY PRESS

2003

OXFORD
UNIVERSITY PRESS

Oxford   New York
Auckland   Bangkok   Buenos Aires   Cape Town   Chennai
Dar es Salaam   Delhi   Hong Kong   Istanbul   Karachi   Kolkata
Kuala Lumpur   Madrid   Melbourne   Mexico City   Mumbai   Nairobi
São Paulo   Shanghai   Taipei   Tokyo   Toronto

Copyright © 2003 by The American Academy of Religion

Published by Oxford University Press, Inc.
198 Madison Avenue, New York, New York, 10016
www.oup.com

Library of Congress Cataloging-in-Publication Data

Teaching Islam / edited by Brannon M. Wheeler.
p.   cm. — (AAR teaching religious studies)
Includes bibliographical references and index
ISBN 0-19-515224-7; ISBN 0-19-515225-5 (pbk.)
1. Islam—Study and teaching.   I. Wheeler, Brannon M., 1965–
II. Series.
BP42 .T43 2002
297'.071'1—dc21   2002071524

1 3 5 7 9 8 6 4 2
Printed in the United States of America
on acid-free paper

PREFACE

BRANNON M. WHEELER

Currently, there are roughly 1,000 undergraduate departments and programs in the study of religion in North America. Many of these 1,000 offer courses on Islam or courses (such as Western Religions or World Religions) which deal with Islam in a significant manner.[1] In part, this interest in Islam is historical and conceptual, based on the close (if not always amicable) relationship of Islam to Judaism and Christianity. This interest in Islam is also due to the growing presence of Islam in Europe, North America, and its perceived role in international affairs. Islam is now the second largest religion in the United States, with the number of Muslims surpassing that of Jews, and it remains the fastest growing religion both in the United States and worldwide.

Islamic materials have played a formative role in the study of religion. Arabic and Islamic Studies emerged within the context of Biblical Studies and Old Testament Theology just as did the modern study of religion. Examples from Islamic texts and practices were of pivotal importance in the seminal work of William Robertson Smith which, in turn, was a major influence on the work of Emile Durkheim and Sigmund Freud. Arent Jan Wensinck's close work on Islamic texts led to the development of large comparative categories on which Mircea Eliade relied for some of his most fundamental theories. Henri Corbin is well known for his work on an approach to religion based in Islamic examples represented in the Eranos papers. The historical phenomenology of Geo Widengren also draws most heavily on examples from Islamic materials, and more recently the widely influential works of Wilfred Cantwell Smith and Clifford Geertz are intimately related to the study of Islam.

Despite the growing interest in and importance of Islam in the undergraduate curricula in religion, there are currently only about 100 scholars trained in Islamic Studies and Religious Studies in North America. During the past ten years or so, this number has increased and continues to do so as institutions recognize the need to create lines in Islamic Studies. Each year new positions are created and the situation continues to improve, but without dramatic changes it will be decades until the number of positions in Islamic Studies approximates those in Jewish Studies, for example.

One consequence of this imbalance between the interest in Islam and the number of positions in Islamic Studies is a paucity of resources for the teaching of Islam in the context of Religious Studies. The majority of religion courses that focus on or include Islam are taught by scholars whose primary expertise is in another field, such as Biblical and Jewish Studies or Indian religions. This lack of expertise in Islamic Studies does not automatically entail faulty information or bad pedagogy, but there are many pitfalls which someone not well acquainted with the primary sources and current scholarship might be hard-pressed to avoid. Some of these pitfalls include uneven translations of primary texts, misplaced emphasis on and ignorance of other aspects of Islam, dubious comparisons with Judaism and Christianity, and many outright errors and mistakes which are repeated and perpetuated in introductory texts.

On the other hand, those relatively few scholars with primary expertise in Islamic Studies face significant obstacles in the teaching of Islam as a religion. Many scholars of Islamic Studies find themselves unprepared by specialized graduate study for the broad overviews of Islam they are expected to teach to undergraduates. Often, scholars are hired because of their expertise in an aspect of Islamic Studies but without any graduate training or teaching experience in Religious Studies. In addition, many scholars of Islamic Studies find themselves to be the only or the "token" Islamicist on campus, responsible for all aspects of Islam, the history of Islamic civilization, and the worldwide distribution of Muslim societies. To compound this situation, there are few exemplary attempts to combine Islamic Studies and Religious Studies in specialized research, let alone the broad theoretical categories employed in pedagogical contexts. Young scholars are left to reinvent the wheel when it comes to the nuts and bolts of designing a syllabus, selecting readings, and crafting assignments.

This book originated with the recognition of this situation by a small group of scholars concerned with their own position and that of others attempting to teach Islamic Studies in religion curricula. Earlier attempts to address the relationship between Islam and Religious Studies have not focused on pedagogical issues nor have they been entirely unproblematic.[2] While some of the essays here indirectly address the theoretical and methodological issues surrounding the relationship of Islam to Religious Studies, it is not the main goal. Nor is it our intention to retrace the history of either discipline. These are important topics that still require attention. Our aim here is to provide some first-hand advice from scholars who have learned to bridge the gulf separating their graduate specialization from broad teaching responsibilities. Moreover, all the contributions are from scholars who have chosen to take the time to focus on the pedagogical and practicable aspects of their profession.

This project began as a series of informal discussions which were organized into a roundtable discussion at the annual MESA meeting in 1994, and a similar panel discussion with different contributors at the annual AAR meeting in 1996. This culminated in an international workshop hosted by the Comparative Islamic Studies program at the University of Washington and supported by a generous grant from the Walter Chapin Simpson Center for the Humanities, in the spring of 1998, on "Integrating Islamic Studies into Liberal Arts Curricula." Not all of those who participated in these earlier conversations chose to include their work in this volume, but their contribution is still an important part of what is produced here, including Jack Renard, Steven Wasserstrom, Juan de Campo, and Richard Martin.

The contributions here represent a variety of perspectives, all of which are concerned with aggressively integrating Islamic Studies into Religious Studies. All the contributors are researchers with active records of publication in the particular textual and ethnographic traditions of their specializations, ranging from classical Arabic and the Middle East to Persia, India, Africa, and America. The contributors represent a range of different institutions, from small liberal arts colleges to large research universities, many of the contributors having taught in a variety of different pedagogical contexts. Different approaches to Religious Studies are represented in the diversity of the graduate programs from which the contributors received their degrees, including Chicago, Harvard, McGill, Princeton, Temple, Toronto, and Yale. We have purposefully not drawn on scholars who have published introductory texts on Islam or other works in which their pedagogical perspective and approach is clear.

The book is divided into three sections, roughly corresponding to different types of pedagogical concerns. Section one addresses theoretical and pedagogical frames for presenting Islam in the Religious Studies classroom. The essays raise salient issues regarding the teaching of Islam in the context of Religious Studies, questioning the pedagogical underpinnings of such an enterprise. Section two deals with the teaching of different dimensions of Muslim faith, community, and order. It focuses on four discrete topical courses, showing both how these courses might be taught and how they can be used to formulate larger issues within liberal arts curricula. Section three presents contemporary issues and challenges in the teaching of Islam as a religion. The essays there discuss both teaching about contemporary Islam and the considerations of looking at Islam as a religion from a modern and postmodern perspective.

A significant motivation for this work is to advance the integration of Islamic Studies into the general study of religion. Despite the role of Islamic materials in foundational studies of religion, few comparative or generic studies incorporate Islamic examples, and fewer still are written by scholars with expertise in Islamic Studies. Considering the rich resources available from Islamic contexts, it is remarkable that more theorists of ritual, canon, or myth do not emerge from within Islamic Studies. Perhaps other scholars of Islamic Studies will be inspired by the creative and practical aspects of the essays in this volume to imagine new ways of making Islamic materials relevant to the study of religion.

It is also hoped that the applied and reflective aspects of this book can benefit nonspecialists, who teach or are interested in incorporating Islamic Studies into their teaching of religion. The vitality of teaching and the continued growth of the discipline depend upon the careful but also creative work of scholars thinking not only about technical matters but also how specialized research is to be communicated with nonexperts. To what end is the study of religion? This book is meant as a heuristic device, an experimental and temporary step on the road to further developments. Our own ideas have evolved working with one another; new generations of scholars are emerging (and new graduate programs); and the general institutional support for Islamic Studies is improving. We aim to encourage others not to adopt our approaches but to consider for themselves how it is that their continued research and teaching can cultivate more interesting approaches and better understandings of the human activity we call religion.

NOTES

1. These numbers and those in the following paragraphs are derived from a careful, but admittedly not exhaustive, examination of the data compiled by several professional organizations associated with the study of religion and Islamic Studies. The American Academy of Religion (AAR) does not index their membership database by area of expertise, but current membership in the "Study of Islam" section of the AAR is roughly 50 people, many of whom are advanced graduate students. The Council of Societies for the Study of Religion (CSSR) lists roughly 1000 departments and programs in the study of religion, 43 of which offer courses specifically on Islam or concentrations in Islam. Of this 43, about half have full-time faculty members whose primary area of expertise is Islamic Studies. The National Center for Education Statistics does not index its database by field but includes roughly 900 institutions with departments or programs under the heading of "Philosophy and Religion."

The 2000 roster of members of the Middle East Studies Association (MESA) lists

59 names under the heading of "Religious Studies/Theology" and 30 names under the heading of "History of Religion." Some of these scholars listed here are not primarily working in Islamic Studies, and there are other scholars trained in the study of religion who may have selected another category as their primary field in their listing with MESA. In addition, to arrive at an overall number of scholars working on subjects related to Islam, one must take into account scholars in other disciplinary fields such as History, Anthropology, Comparative Literature, Political Science, and Area Studies.

2. For a negative evaluation of the relationship of Islam to the study of religion, a perspective which is still cited by many, see Charles Adams, "The History of Religions and the Study of Islam," in *The History of Religions: Essays on the Problem of Understanding*, ed. Joseph Kitagawa et al. (Chicago: University of Chicago Press, 1967), 177–193. This position is restated more strongly in Charles Adams, "The History of Religions and the Study of Islam," *American Council of Learned Societies Newsletter* 25.3–4 (1974): 1–10.

More recently, see the essays collected in *Approaches to Islam in Religious Studies*, ed. Richard Martin (Tucson: University of Arizona Press, 1985), which is limited by its dwelling on the issue of whether only Muslims can adequately understand Islam. Also see the essays in *Mapping Islamic Studies: Genealogy, Continuity and Change*, ed. Azim Nanji (New York: Mouton de Gruyter, 1997), most of which does not focus on the study of Islam in the study of religion, except for the overview by Jacques Waardenburg, "Islamic Studies and the History of Religions: An Evaluation," 181–219.

CONTENTS

Chapter Four
Islamicate Civilization: The View from Asia
BRUCE B. LAWRENCE

Part Two
DIMENSIONS OF MUSLIM FAITH, COMMUNITY, AND ORDER

Chapter Five
*The Essential Shari'ah: Teaching Islamic Law
in the Religious Studies Classroom*
JONATHAN E. BROCKOPP

Chapter Six
Disparity and Context: Teaching Quranic Studies in North America
JANE DAMMEN MCAULIFFE

Chapter Seven
*Between Orientalism and Fundamentalism:
Problematizing the Teaching of Sufism*
CARL W. ERNST

Chapter Eight
Engendering and Experience: Teaching a Course on Women in Islam
ZAYN KASSAM

Part Three
CONTEMPORARY ISSUES AND CHALLENGES IN TEACHING
ISLAM AS A RELIGION

Chapter Nine
The Wedding of Zein: Islam through a Modern Novel
MICHAEL A. SELLS

CONTRIBUTORS

CORINNE BLAKE is Associate Professor of History at Rowan University in
Glassboro, New Jersey. She teaches a series of courses on the Middle East
at Rowan, including Islamic Civilizations, Modern Middle East, Women in
Islam, and the Arab-Israeli Conflict, as well as World History Since 1500.
She received her Ph.D. in Near Eastern History from Princeton University
in 1991. Her dissertation focused on education and the Arab provinces in
the Ottoman Empire in the late nineteenth century. She has written several
conference papers and articles on pedagogical issues, and is currently
working on revising her dissertation for publication.

JONATHAN E. BROCKOPP is Associate Professor of Religion at Bard College. He received his Ph.D. from Yale University in Islamic Studies and has
continued his research in the Middle East with support from Fulbright, the
American Research Center in Egypt, and the Institute for Advanced Study
at the Hebrew University. He is currently co-chair of the Section for the
Study of Islam in the American Academy of Religion. His books include
Early Maliki Law (2000) and *Islamic Ethics of Life: Abortion, War and Euthanasia* (forthcoming). He is also co-author, with Jacob Neusner and
Tamara Sonn of *Judaism and Islam in Practice* (2000).

CARL W. ERNST is a specialist in Islamic Studies, with a focus on Iran and
South Asia. His research, based on the study of Arabic, Persian, and Urdu,
has been mainly devoted to the study of Sufism. He is also currently working on Islamic interpretations of Hinduism and questions of print culture
and communications technology in Islamic societies. His publications include *Teachings of Sufism* (1999); a translation of *The Unveiling of Secrets:*

Diary of a Sufi Master by Ruzbihan Baqli (1997); *The Shambhala Guide to Suf-*
ism (1997); *Ruzbihan Baqli: Mystical Experience and the Rhetoric of Sainthood*
in Persian Sufism (1996); *Eternal Garden: Mysticism, History, and Politics at a*
South Asian Sufi Center (1993); and *Words of Ecstasy in Sufism* (1985). He
studied comparative religion at Stanford University (A.B. 1973) and Harvard University (Ph.D. 1981), and has done research tours in India (1978–
79, 1981), Pakistan (1986, 2000), and Turkey (1991) and has also visited Iran
(1996, 1999). He has taught at Pomona College (1981–1992) and at the University of North Carolina at Chapel Hill (1992–), where he is now Zachary
Smith Professor of Religious Studies.

MARCIA K. HERMANSEN is Professor of Islamic Studies and Comparative
Religion at Loyola University in Chicago, and former Director of the Reli-
gion, Culture and Society program. She received her Ph.D. in Near Eastern Languages and Civilizations from the University of Chicago in 1982.
She has also taught at Queen's, McGill, and San Diego State University.
Professor Hermansen has lived and conducted research in Iran, South Asia,
and the Middle East. She served as co-chair of the Study of Islam Section,
American Academy of Religion (1994–2000). Her teaching includes
courses on Islam, World Religions, Women and Gender in Islam, and
Comparative Mysticism. Professor Hermansen's most recent publications
include *The Conclusive Argument from God (Shah Wali Allah of Delhi's Hujjat
Allah al-Baligha)* (1996), and articles in the fields of Islamic Mysticism and
Muslims in North America.

TAZIM R. KASSAM is Associate Professor of Islamic Studies and Director of
Graduate Studies in the Department of Religion at Syracuse University
and has also taught at Middlebury College and Colorado College. She received her Ph.D. at McGill University in the History of Religions and specialized in the Islamic tradition with a focus on South Asia. Her research
and teaching interests include gender, ritual, devotional literature, syn-
cretism, and the cultural heritage of Islam. Her book *Songs of Wisdom and
Circles of Dance* (1995) explores the origins and creative synthesis of Hindu-
Muslim ideas expressed in the song tradition of the Ismaili Muslims of the
Indian Subcontinent. She has co-chaired the Study of Islam section of the
American Academy of Religion, served as president of the AAR Rocky
Mountain–Great Plains Region, is a Lilly Teaching Scholar, and is on the
editorial board of the Journal of the American Academy of Religion. Her
awards include fellowships from the National Endowment for the Hu-
manities, the Social Science Research Council, and the Institute of Ismaili

Studies. She also pursues interests in Indian classical music, using learning technologies in the classroom, and community service.

ZAYN KASSAM is Associate Professor of Religious Studies at Pomona College, Claremont, California. A graduate of McGill University, Montreal, Canada, Professor Kassam has won a Wig Award for Distinguished Teaching at Pomona College and is currently co-chair of the Section for the Study of Islam in the American Academy of Religion. She has lectured widely on gender issues in the Muslim world, and recent publications in that area include "Politicizing Gender and Religion," in Joseph Runzo and Nancy M. Martin, eds., *Love, Sex and Gender in the World Religions,* and "Islamic Ethics and Gender Issues," in Runzo and Martin, eds., *Ethics and the World Religions.* She is a Lilly-Luce Teaching Scholar and was recently awarded a National Endowment for the Humanities FOCUS Grant for a series of faculty workshops entitled "Engaging Islam."

BRUCE B. LAWRENCE is both an Islamicist and a comparativist. He earned his Ph.D. at Yale University in History of Religions. He has taught at Duke University since 1971, and at present is the Nancy & Jeffery Marcus Humanities Professor of Religion, as well as Chair of the Department of Religion. His early books explored the intellectual and social history of Asian Muslims. *Shahrastani on the Indian Religions* (1976) was followed by *Notes from a Distant Flute* (1978), *The Rose and the Rock* (1979), and *Ibn Khaldun and Islamic Ideology* (1984). Since the mid-80s, he has been especially concerned with the interplay between religion and ideology. The test case of fundamentalism became the topic of his award-winning monograph, *Defenders of God: The Fundamentalist Revolt Against the Modern Age* (1989/1995). A parallel but narrower enquiry informed his latest monograph, *Shattering the Myth: Islam beyond Violence* (1998/2000), while his next two monographs will once again tackle broader theoretical issues. *Go, God, Go: Feisty Religion in the Global Century* (forthcoming) looks at the complex interaction of ideology, theology, and spiritual practices in multiple contexts throughout the twentieth century, while *New Faiths/Old Fears* concerns Asian religions in America, especially since 1965. He has written a trade book introducing the new twists of religion on the Internet: *The Complete Idiot's Guide to Religions Online* (2000).

KEITH LEWINSTEIN is Assistant Professor in the Departments of Religion and History at Smith College, where he teaches courses on a variety of aspects of the Islamic religious tradition and Middle Eastern history. In 2002, he became a Visiting Scholar at the Center for Middle East Studies at Harvard University. He received his Ph.D. in Near Eastern Studies from Princeton in 1989, and taught at Brown University and Wellesley College before coming to Smith. He has since been the recipient of Fulbright, Charlotte Newcombe, and National Endowment for the Humanities fellowships. He publishes largely in the area of early Islamic sectarianism and Islamic law and is currently preparing *Heresy and Dissent in Early Islam* for Cambridge University Press.

JANE DAMMEN McAULIFFE is Dean of the College and Professor of History and of Arabic at Georgetown University. Previously, she was Chair of the Department for the Study of Religion, as well as Professor of Islamic Studies in the Department of Near and Middle Eastern Civilizations, at the University of Toronto (1992–2000) and Associate Professor of Islamic Studies at Emory University (1986–1992). Her work has been supported by fellowships from the National Endowment for the Humanities, the Rockefeller Foundation, and the Guggenheim Foundation. Her publications include *Qur'anic Christians: An Analysis of Classical and Modern Exegesis* (1991) and *Abbasid Authority Affirmed* (1995). Presently, she is general editor of the multivolume *Encyclopaedia of the Qur'an* (2000–).

A. KEVIN REINHART is Associate Professor at Dartmouth College, Hanover, New Hampshire. His Ph.D. (1986) is from Harvard University, Committee on the Study of Religion. His primary field of research is Islamic law and legal theory. He is finishing a book entitled *Vernacular Islam: Diversity and Unity in a Cosmopolitan Tradition* and teaches courses in Islamics, Comparative Religion, and Method in the Study of Religion. His first book was *Before Revelation: The Boundaries of Muslim Moral Knowledge* (1995). Other publications include articles on Islamic ethics, late Ottoman religion, Muftis and Qadis as religious interpreters, and analyses of Islamic purity laws.

MICHAEL A. SELLS is Emily Judson Baugh and John Marshall Gest Professor of Comparative Religions and Professor of Religion at Haverford College in Pennsylvania. He received his Ph.D. in Comparative Literature from the University of Chicago in 1982 and was a Mellon postdoctoral fellow at Stanford University before coming to Haverford in 1984. Professor Sells's books include *Desert Tracings: Six Classic Arabian Odes* (1989); *Mystical Languages of Unsaying* (1994); *Early Islamic Mysticism* (1999); *The Bridge Betrayed: Religion and Genocide in Bosnia* (1996); *Approaching the Qur'an: the Early Revelations* (1999); *Stations of Desire: Love Elegies from Ibn 'Arabi and*

New Poems (2000); and *The Cambridge History of Arabic Literature,* al-Andalus volume (2000), for which he is co-editor and contributor.

BRANNON M. WHEELER is Associate Professor of Islamic Studies and Chair of Comparative Religion at the University of Washington in Seattle, where he is also Coordinator of the Comparative Islamic Studies program. He received his Ph.D. in Near Eastern Languages and Civilizations from the University of Chicago in 1993. He has also taught at Macalester College, Earlham College, Vanderbilt University, and Pennsylvania State University; was a Visiting Scholar at the College of Shariʿah and Islamic Studies at Kuwait University; and was the Islamicist-in-Residence at the American Research Center in Egypt. His teaching includes courses on Islam and the Quran, Western religions, theories of religion, and text courses in Arabic, Hebrew, and Syriac. Professor Wheeler's books include *Moses in the Quran and Islamic Exegesis* (2002), *Prophets in the Quran: An Introduction to the Quran and Muslim Exegesis* (2002), and *Applying the Canon in Islam: Authorization and Maintenance of Interpretive Reasoning in Ḥanafī Scholarship* (1996).

NOTE ON CONVENTIONS
AND TRANSLITERATIONS

Many of the essays mention and discuss technical terms in Arabic, Persian, or other related languages which may not be familiar to nonspecialists. Indeed, this unfamiliarity with terms that are central to Islamic traditions is one of the issues addressed by several of the contributors to this volume. By convention, specialists regularly use full diacritical marks for the transliteration of these foreign terms, but given the wider readership of this volume, we have attempted to keep the use of diacriticals to a minimum. Some of the contributions retain more untranslated terms, in part, to problematize the pedagogic issues they raise. In most cases, foreign terminology is translated or explained by the context of its usage, but in some cases, nonstandard transliteration is used for colloquial Arabic expressions. At other times, foreign terms are provided in square brackets to indicate the original word to which is being referred. Commonly used foreign terms (e.g., Quran, Sunnah, Shari'ah, Sufi) are not italicized nor transliterated with diacritical marks, except in certain cases.

Part One

THEORETICAL AND PEDAGOGICAL
FRAMES FOR PRESENTING ISLAM IN THE
RELIGIOUS STUDIES CLASSROOM

CHAPTER ONE

What Can't Be Left Out?
The Essentials of Teaching Islam as a Religion

BRANNON M. WHEELER

OVER THE PAST TEN YEARS OR SO, I have struggled with issues of how to conceptualize and teach Islam, especially "the introductory course" within the context of the academic study of religion and the larger context of a liberal arts curriculum. My concerns have ranged from having too much material to cover in a single semester or quarter, to not having adequate textbooks or English translations of certain key texts. But my overriding concern has been, and continues to be, how to integrate teaching about Islam into the liberal arts curriculum through the study of religion. My interest in combining Islamic Studies and the study of religion is as a means to further this integration of Islam and the liberal arts.

It is my contention that Islam is taught as a religion only insofar as Islamic materials are used to address issues of theoretical concern within the study of religion. This does not mean, however, that Islam is used to reinforce unyielding and inappropriate theoretical stereotypes. The history of the relationship between Islamic Studies and the study of religion is too often cast in terms of competing methodologies and incompatible subject matter. By "theory" I mean simply "explanation" with the concomitant understanding that to teach Islam as a religion means using explanations developed in the study of religion to contribute to our understanding of Islam. In the long run, the implication is that our understanding of Islam will be influenced by theories developed to explain other things identified as "religious," and the theories of what is "religious" will be affected by the Islamic materials we are attempting to understand.

In what follows, I provide some examples of how I have tried to integrate

Islam and the study of religion in some of my introductory courses. These experiences are drawn from a variety of contexts. I have taught the "Introduction to Islam" course three different ways at four different institutions. This variety is, in part, due to my continuing attempts to experiment with different approaches. It is also due to the different circumstances in which I taught the courses, ranging from a small class of five students to over 100 students, from small liberal arts colleges to large universities, from students with no background in Islam, to large classes where more than 75 percent of the students come from Muslim backgrounds. Because of this, it is important to stress that, although I have tried to choose examples which worked well in my particular circumstances, similar approaches might not work well in other settings. What does remain consistent, though, is my attempt to combine Islamic materials and the study of religion in a way that contributes to the students' development within the context of a liberal arts education.

The Prophet and Prophethood

One of my main criteria for determining the content of the course is the availability and accessibility of material to undergraduate students. Unfortunately, many useful original texts are untranslated, and those that are translated are often out of print or the translation is poor. This has led me to rely on a combination of photocopies and my own translations. More important, students' reading assignments should be pertinent to the larger pedagogical goals of the course, not just padded with a lot of information that might be thought necessary background knowledge. This means that, as I have taught the course, I have shortened the length and the number of reading materials, but at the same time, raised my expectations for the amount of time students spend with those assignments. My goal is to have students spend more time on less pages, not memorizing a lot of information but rather thinking through some of the issues raised by the reading, especially as it pertains to what we are doing as a class over the length of the course.

Original and secondary literature on the Prophet Muhammad and prophethood in general is voluminous. There are sound translations of many key texts such as Tabari's history and Ibn Ishaq's biography,[1] and a huge number of secondary studies on the history and significance of the Prophet Muhammad are available. Likewise, a number of Sufi texts and studies dealing with prophets and prophethood can be found. Excerpts from the Quran and the Bible are also readily available, although caution is to be exercised with some available translations. Students are usually familiar with the stories of the biblical prophets, especially figures like Moses, Jesus, and Abraham, although sometimes from movies, television, or Sunday School rather than first-hand experience with the Bible or Quran.

From my perspective as teacher, getting students to articulate issues and argue through various explanations, the stories surrounding the Prophet Muhammad, his relation to earlier prophets, and the concept of prophethood present pedagogically useful theoretical problems. For example, given the diversity of accounts about the life of Muhammad, students are easily struck by a question about the historicity of Muhammad. Did Muhammad "really exist" and if he did, was he a prophet or did he do the things he is reported to have done? The discussion of whether Muhammad "really existed" can be unpacked to disclose some different sorts of issues. The reaction of Muslim students, who are often hesitant or defensive about even asking such questions, also serves to stimulate a discussion about the difference between "faith" or "belief" and "history." Students might discuss this along the lines followed by Wilfred Cantwell Smith[2] or consider the difference between an observer and participant as defined in Victor Turner's work.[3]

These historiographical and epistemological questions can be particularly fruitful in introducing issues and the sort of comparative thinking pertinent throughout the rest of the course. On the one hand, I might ask students to compare the historicity of and belief in the existence of Muhammad to the existence of Jesus, Moses, or even George Washington. What different sorts of evidence are available in these cases, how do we determine the historical or religious value of such evidence, and to what ends? Current debates over the use of archaeology to "prove" or "disprove" the events described in the Bible can also be a useful point of discussion. On the other hand, we might think about making a distinction separating "history" from the "past" along the lines suggested by Plumb or Collingwood.[4] When we talk about "history" are we talking about "what really happened" or someone or some people's accounts of what happened? In both cases, I encourage students to consider that evidence can be interpreted in different ways, and that the interpretations given to evidence are usually meant to support the agenda of the interpreter. In the past, I have asked students to make short lists of reasons supporting the contention that Muhammad is a prophet, taken from the Quran or the biography of Ibn Ishaq.

Thinking about Muhammad and his prophethood also encourages students to think in generic terms. For example, I have asked students to read several selections from the Quran or Tabari on earlier prophets such as Moses or Salih, and then asked them to compare this with the stories of Muhammad's life. The contention made, in many sources, is that Muhammad's prophethood and that of other prophets are modeled after one another, or that all prophets are thought to do basically the same things. As a class, then, we might consider how the stories of Muhammad make him out to be a "hero" figure. Can the stories of the prophets and of Muhammad be compared with the hero and other mythic archetypes? Drawing on the work of Eliade and Campbell, I might ask the students to identify episodes from the life of Muhammad that correspond to the stages of the hero's quest.[5] We could also discuss, using models developed by Weber and Wach, how the life of Muhammad compares with the sociological position of other "founders" of religions and "holy men." Students could discuss some of the comparative proposals made by Geo Widengren concerning the ancient Near Eastern model of the "apostle of God" and the "heavenly book."[6] In all these cases, by being presented with this diverse comparative material, students learn how to ask questions and begin to perceive how asking certain questions and looking in certain places for answers affects the sorts of explanations produced.

Canon and Law

Just as with the concept of prophecy, there is a lot of common ground between concepts of canon and law in Islam and theoretical discussions in the study of religion. Biblical Studies has a long tradition of research into questions of canon formation and exegesis. There are numerous specialized subdivisions in Jewish studies, and more particularly Rabbinic studies, which focus on issues of exegesis, the masoretic text, and the derivation of law from a canonical corpus. More recently, scholars from diverse fields, but including many in Hindu and Buddhist studies, have begun to examine the concept of canon and its relationship to "commentary" and exegesis more broadly defined.

Unfortunately, the materials available to students about the Islamic canon and law are few and are often inaccessible, even when available in translation, because of uneven standards in translation or because of mere bulk. For example, several of the best known collections of prophetic hadith, including the Sahih of al-Bukhari and the Sahih of Muslim, have been published in English translation and are even available on the Internet. The translation, however, is not up to academic standards, nor are there any notes or commentary to help the introductory students. Simple terms such as "zakat" or "hajj" are often left untranslated and unexplained. There are also some later legal compendia translated, but in most cases the publisher is obscure and/or the price is prohibitive. The secondary literature also, especially in the fields of hadith criticism and law, is usually far too technical for beginning students. This means that many of the readings come from my own translation of certain texts, and that the bulk of the explanation is done as a class rather than in background reading. It is also important to keep in mind that the acquisition of too much background and technical information might hinder the students' focus on identifying and thinking through problems.

Looking at canon and its exegesis is appropriate after having dealt with prophethood and issues of interpretation. The Islamic material allows students to focus on the problems associated with deriving "law" through the interpretation of a canonical corpus. Recent scholarship, such as that of Laurie Patton and Paul Griffiths, has shown that this is a general problem affecting any number of traditions in which a relatively fixed canon is interpreted to apply to everyday life.[7] One exercise I have used before is to have students write a definition of how to pray using only the Quran, and then the long section in Bukhari on prayer. With the Quran, students find there is not enough information to write a detailed definition, but with Bukhari there is too much information, much of which might appear contradictory. Another assignment involves having the students read a series of verses in the Quran which have traditionally been taken to refer to the limiting or prohibition of wine. In class, we then read some of the conflicting opinions of the classical legal scholars about the prohibition of alcohol, and we discuss the use of concepts and methods such as deductive reasoning [qiyās], abrogation [naskh], and what might be called "juristic convenience" [istiḥsān]. Students are encouraged to think about these Islamic methods of interpretation as examples of how some scholars in one religious tradition have tried to solve the problems inherent in the exegesis of a canon.

The discussion of exegesis also raises the issue of comparing Islamic exegesis and its conception of canon to what is found in other religious traditions such as Judaism or Buddhism. Having already studied some of the stories of prophets found in common in the Bible and in the Quran, students can think about the criteria that make one set of stories a canon and another just a collection of stories. If the Bible and Quran contain some of the same stories, if both are thought to be revealed by God, then why is only the Quran but not the Bible used by Muslim scholars to derive law? Students can read some of the discussion in hadith and law collections about the so-called stoning verses or the verses in the Quran which refer to the "old" laws followed by the Jews and Christians. Using the life of Muhammad and his Sunnah to interpret the Quran can also be compared to the notion of the "New" and "Old" Testaments in Christianity, the Oral and Written Torah in Judaism, or the "three baskets" in Buddhism. How is it that Islam, both like and unlike these other traditions, maintains its link to an ideal past and a received text but continues to address problems in a changing world? Such an issue might involve the discussion of Edward Shils' work on tradition or Thomas Kuhn and Stephen Toulmin's work on changing paradigms.[8]

Having the students discuss the concept of "canon" itself is also of value

in helping to explain the Islamic use of the Quran and the Sunnah in the derivation of law. What is the difference between a "revealed" or "sacred" text
and a "canonical" text, and how do Muslims conceptualize these things? On
the one hand, we might discuss example of how the term "Quran" can sometimes refer to the recitation of verses but not to the physical presence of the
"book" itself. Some of the comparative material from William Graham and
W. C. Smith on sacred texts can be introduced to help understand the Islamic
case.[9] On the other hand, students might consider the use of the "Quran" as
a ritual object, the handling of which is prescribed in specific ways such as the
prohibition of contact with it by anyone not in a state of ritual purity. This
might allow for comparisons with Durkheim's definition of sacred and profane or W. R. Smith's use of the term "holy."[10] Working through the Islamic
material can facilitate students' understanding of such key concepts in the
general study of religion. More generally, by thinking in comparative terms,
students learn how unfamiliar concepts can be understood from theories developed to explain other cases.

Ritual

Studies of ritual have often made reference to Islamic practices, although until
recently, there were few theoretical works which drew heavily upon Islamic
materials. Fortunately, there are many different types of materials available
for the study of Islamic rituals, including ethnographic descriptions, translations of classical legal texts, pilgrimage handbooks, and books or movies with
pictures of rituals and the sites at which they are performed. In most areas of
the United States and Canada today, it is also possible to have the students visit
a nearby mosque during Friday prayers or, depending on the timing, during
Ramadan or other holidays celebrated locally.

Students, both Muslim and non-Muslim, are often comfortable with the
idea of religion as being ritual and are quick to make comparisons among the
outward appearances of Islamic and non-Islamic practices. These first impressions of students can be developed, and the students encouraged to analyze practices similar to how they have learned to analyze texts. For example,
we might discuss Geo Widengren's ideas about the evolution of Islamic practices from the social order of the ancient Near East, or I might have students
read one or two of Arent Jan Wensinck's essays on the comparison of seasonal
festivals in the religions of the Near East.[11] This encourages students to begin
to conceptualize a continuity among these different ritual practices, and they
can evaluate the efficacy of explaining similarities in terms of a shared historical past or common regional roots. It can be pointed out to students that such
explanations are in sharp contrast to ones discussed earlier, from Durkheim

or Eliade, where functional, structural, or other nonhistorical ties are postulated. Students may also be struck by the analytical rigor and the sheer number of languages needed to make detailed historical and philological comparisons among these religious traditions and practices. We might discuss that some scholars, like Ugo Bianchi or Kurt Rudolf, argue for the necessity of grounding such explanations in historical and linguistic detail.[12]

Another of my goals is to expose students to different sorts of Islamic practices, including the variety inherent in the so-called pillars of Islam and the sort of variety found in the practice of any given type of ritual. For example, students might focus on three different examples of pilgrimage in Islam: the pilgrimage to Mecca, visits to saints shrines such as the pilgrimage to the "seven men" of Marrakech, and Islamic pilgrimage in Mamluk Jerusalem. All of these examples can be illustrated both by texts, in which the routes and the significance of the practice is explained, and by pictures of the sites and of people performing the pilgrimage. In the case of the pilgrimage to Mecca, I like to show students video selections from Saudi television on the Hajj or on the nightly services during Ramadan when many perform the 'Umrah. The comparison of these different practices allows students to identify certain generic aspects of Islamic pilgrimage while also noting cultural, geographical, or historical reasons for differences. By thinking about other examples of pilgrimage with which the students are familiar such as the Canterbury Tales, or discussing "tourism" as pilgrimage, students can induce from the Islamic examples a more general understanding of what is meant by pilgrimage or ritual.

It is also useful that students perceive the link between certain ritual practices and the social structure in which they are performed. For example, we might discuss how prayer, fasting, and the pilgrimage to Mecca all seem to require or create a certain uniformity or equality among those practicing these rituals. Is a distinction made between Muslims who do and do not pray regularly or fast during Ramadan? Students could read selections from Loeffler's interviews with Muslims in an Iranian village and consider that many Muslims do not pray five times a day yet still think themselves to be Muslims.[13] What sort of social authority is bestowed on Muslims who complete the pilgrimage to Mecca, or the religious scholars who are in charge of explaining which rituals are required and how they are to be performed? Students might also consider the case of the "Great Sacrifice" in Morocco, and how the practice of this ritual is said, by scholars such as Combs-Schilling and Abdellah Hammoudi, to represent and reinforce a certain social order.[14] These sorts of examples allow students to question how ritual is used to define the social boundaries of Islam, in what ways ritual is utopian in its depiction of the ideal society, and in what ways it is instrumental in shaping the day-to-day lives and identities of Muslims.

Given enough time, it would be possible to dwell longer on the implications of using Islamic examples to theorize about ritual in general. Students could read short theoretical selections from Ronald Grimes or Catherine Bell on ritual and social structure, comparing the more general theories of ritual in these works with Islamic examples.[15] With the recent work on Islamic "sacrifice," students could also use Islamic examples to evaluate other well-known theories of sacrifice such as those associated with Freud, Rene Girard, or Evans-Pritchard's work on the Nuer.[16] The goal of such exercises is to have the students think of theory in terms of its ability to explain a given set of facts or material taken from an Islamic context, and to think of how their understanding of the Islamic materials affects their view of the more general theorists. Closer investigation of the relationship of these theories to some of the Islamic examples allows students to test "ritual" as what has become a privileged category in the study of religion.

The examination of Islamic ritual practices also provides the opportunity for students to synthesize materials learned from other parts of the course. For example, we could discuss how the pilgrimage to Mecca is linked with the stories of the prophets Adam, Abraham, and Muhammad in the Quran and its exegesis. We could also look at the ideas of Henri Corbin or Arthur Christensen concerning the links between certain rituals and Iranian stories of the "first man" or other mystical figures.[17] Reading through these stories and ideas in light of ritual practices encourages students to make connections between disparate pieces of knowledge. Students can begin to think in terms of "Islam" as a concept encompassing these various aspects, pulled together by the students' own imaginative explanations of different materials. At this stage of the course, it is important that students start to connect parts of the course in larger comparative terms, and that they practice developing the conceptual skills necessary for synthetic thinking.

Society and Culture

Using society and culture as heuristic categories is somewhat unlike the others because they are not necessarily associated only or primarily with the study of religion. Students are sometimes confused by the regular use of both "society" and "culture" as explanations of religion, and the understanding of religion as a subset or type of society or culture. I include this section in my course because it allows students to broaden their view of Islam, while at the same time giving them reason to question simple characterizations of Islam. During the past two decades or so, a large number of ethnographic studies have appeared, focusing on specific Islamic societies or practices in diverse areas. This is supplemented by the rapid growth of Islam in U.S. society and the prominence of Islam in news media and popular culture. Drawing even half a dozen examples, from Java, Yemen, West Africa, North America, Turkey, or Europe is relatively easy given the availability of resources.

It is important that students address these issues not at the beginning but at the end of the course.. From the experience of having tried it before, I found that starting the course by confronting students with the diversity of Islam was too difficult. Students are usually not prepared to make the conceptual jump from ignorance to a pluralistic definition of Islam, nor are students expecting this sort of discovery. At a later point in the course, however, students can take advantage of a more open-ended perspective, to consider that there might be competing views of what constitutes "orthodox" Islam, or of historically and culturally different ways of defining what it means to be Muslim. Students are presented with a number of "case-studies" as examples of some of the significant differences in Islam today. Coming later in the course, these issues also allow students to stress the connections between concepts and historical aspects of Islam studied earlier and the kinds of Islam found in "practice" in various places throughout the world. Students can see how various trends or trajectories are continued, incorporated, or modified in diverse contemporary Islamic settings.

One distinct advantage of having the students look at a number of diverse cases of Islam is making students think about Islam for themselves. Students might read Geertz's observations on Islam in Morocco and Indonesia, or Gilsenan's descriptions of Islam in Lebanon and North Africa, to see how other observers have tried to identify different expressions of Islam.[18] By reading these observations, students learn how certain "symbols" are recognized and interpreted. The comparison of different cases shows students that what are recognized as symbols, and how these things are interpreted, depends on many things. How do the "local" interpretations of these symbols compare to the interpretations of the nonlocal or nonindigenous observer? What role does the outside observer play in determining which symbols are most significant and what these symbols mean? These sorts of questions allow students to get at the heart of the issues central to thinking about interpretation, and the process of synthesizing examples taken from different contexts and from different perspectives.

By allowing students to question and think about what Islam might be in different contexts, a case-studies approach also raises a number of important issues concerning the relationship of religion to society and culture. Is it possible to discuss Islam apart from politics or economics? Students might read from Leonardo Villalón, Edward Reeves, or Mark Woodward about the interconnections between Sufism and political authority in different contexts.[19] There are a number of recent ethnographic studies, such as those of Messick,

Antoun and Gaffney, of how the "text" and varying Islamic understandings of texts are integral to an understanding of authority and social structure.[20]

Another effective means of getting students to consider Islam from different perspectives is through novels and travelogues. Novels allow students to see Islam through the eyes of someone participating in the local culture, and because students tend to have the impression that the "indigenous Muslim" is a more "authentic" representation of Islam, students are often more receptive of distinctions and criticisms made in novels.[21] Travelogues can be used in a variety of ways. The writings of Muslim travelers, such as Ibn Battutah, can give students some of the same insights that can be drawn from novels. Non-Muslim travelers are often more analogous to ethnographers but easier to read and sometimes more observant of small but important details which are outside of more formal ethnographic writing.[22]

Examining these sorts of cases, students can question whether or not, or how, religion is to be distinguished from other examples of culture. If there is no neat distinction separating religion and culture, then how can Islam be understood "only" as a religion? Such theoretically difficult cases demonstrate to students that explanation is not just about logical consistency nor does it always fit within disciplinary boundaries. The complexity of the issues, how to interpret certain aspects of Islam, and how to generalize from that to a realistic definition of Islam, are instructive of the difficulties involved in identifying and resolving explanatory problems.

Another advantage of this case-studies approach is that is allows students to recognize that Islam is not a monolithic thing. By looking at how Islam is "lived" in a variety of times and places, students are confronted with the fact that "Islam" as a concept is malleable. At this point, it might be useful for students to peruse the table of contents from some of the more widely distributed introductory textbooks on Islam. Students can then compare the more compartmentalized picture of Islam presented there with some of the examples found in our ethnographic accounts, or the diversity we found in looking at ritual or canon. By introducing this variegated material to students, this course helps students to understand that any attempt to reduce Islam to a particular time period, text, school of thought, or the practices of a particular village would be to miss the opportunity to see how "Islam" is variously conceptualized and used by people in different circumstances. The conceptualization of Islam, from these difference perspectives, is important as an example of more general conceptual thinking.

Stressing the malleability of Islam, and the complexity of explanation, is important because, on the one hand, it gives students a fuller and more realistic image of what Islam has been and continues to be. Islam is not a strange religion from a time long ago in a land on the other side of the earth. Instead,

Islam means many of the same things to Muslims in Iran or France as certain cultural norms mean to students in the United States. On the other hand, struggling with such concepts equips students to extract and understand from Islamic materials, or from examples taken from the study of other religions or disciplines, what they deem to be significant and to articulate why they deem it to be so. Thinking along these lines compels students to consider the variegated character of their own cultural norms, to reflect on their own daily use of culture, and their perception of how it informs their lives.

Teaching Islam in a Liberal Arts Curriculum

By dividing the material in my course into these and similar "themes" or "issues," I have been able to introduce students to Islam and the study of religion, one through the other and vice-versa. I am not always satisfied, however, that my attempts strike the right balance between the specific facts of Islam and the general study of religion. This is especially a problem with students who have come to expect a certain "Protestant" approach to the study of religion or Muslim students who expect my course to include certain facts or subjects that are supposed to be "standard" for any course in Islam. This is outside of considerations of interpretation. In my experience, many students, both Muslim and non-Muslim alike, are hesitant to accept explanations of Islamic rituals or beliefs that draw heavily on comparisons with non-Islamic cultures, or are explicitly anthropological and sociological in character, so I can find myself wrangling with students over the approach or the material per se but not the intersection between the two.

This latter reason for hesitation among students deserves more comment because, despite the increasing integration of varied approaches into the study of religion and the rapid development of these approaches, most students, especially those in an introductory course or those for whom the intro to Islam course is the only course in "religion" they plan on taking, are at a relatively extreme disadvantage when studying religion. Although most other college-level subjects are studied by students for years before coming to college, religion, especially as "religion," is not. This is compounded by the presumption of many students that the study of religion is something like "advanced Sunday school," that all religion professors are ministers or at least devout adherents to the religions they teach. If this presumption and the fear of teaching "religion" in public schools were not so strong, students might feel more comfortable approaching religion courses with the skills and insights they had gained previously in other history and social studies courses.

My introduction to Islam course is not primarily a matter of teaching students a certain corpus of facts, whether these facts consist of the widespread

"standard" definitions of Islam found repeated in most textbooks and classrooms, some updated and modified version of these definitions, or a view influenced by my own particular experiences. To make the content of my
course dependent upon my objective in teaching the course is to make the
content justified not from a historical or factual but rather from a pedagogical perspective. This means that I want to know first not what I am teaching
but why: not what facts I need to impart but what skills I am helping students
develop as a part of their liberal arts education. To teach Islam as a religion is
to use Islamic materials to illustrate for students the general study of religion,
in so far as the study of religion serves to develop those skills valued and most
closely associated with a liberal arts education.

From this perspective it would seem that no "fact" is essential, nothing cannot be left out unless it is shown to be crucial in the more general educational
development of students. In this respect, I have been influenced by the pedagogical approaches of my own teachers, both as an undergraduate and a
graduate student. As an undergraduate, I went to a small liberal arts college,
where learning was an activity that the teacher facilitated, but the teacher did
not "teach" in the sense of giving us a certain body of knowledge which we
were expected to memorize and later regurgitate. As one of my undergraduate advisors put it, a student should be able, when presented with options "A"
and "B," to argue for option "C." In graduate school, this same attitude prevailed. Even in language courses, I remember being asked to think about the
possibilities of what a particular phrase might mean, not reproved for not hitting on the same translation as the instructor.

Most of my experience is well characterized in a short article called "Less
Is Better" by Jonathan Z. Smith with whom I studied at the University of
Chicago. The point of clarity in the article is the assertion that everything presented to the student is an "e.g.," an example of something else. The trick is
not in picking the examples which someone else has or has not picked, which
others might argue are essential knowledge. Rather, the point of an example
is that it exemplifies something else. Therefore, the art of picking and using
examples, which is basically the primary expertise of the teacher, is the ability
to choose things that best "exemplify" for students what it is one is attempting to teach them. The examples themselves are not the point of the class, but
are rather a means for students to learn something beyond and more
significant than the examples themselves. J. Z. Smith is clear about this in his
writing on the task of the historian of religion. He states that the primary expertise of the historian of religion is not knowing a certain body of facts, nor
knowing a certain field of theory, but of being able to show how one relates
to the other. How can one better understand, and explain to others, the "Hajj"

after reading Durkheim or Catherine Bell? Or how does reading about Islamic purity laws affect our view of Durkheim and Freud?

From these experiences, I have come to see my approach to the teaching of Islam as analogous to the teaching of any other discipline in the liberal arts or in the sciences. For example, in the teaching of chemistry, certain experiments are used to exemplify certain general principles of chemistry. In an introductory language course, one does not begin by memorizing a dictionary, but rather certain words and phrases are presented so that students can learn the general rules of grammar and usage of that language. Similarly, when I teach Islam, it is as an example of "religion." Specific facts are presented to students in order that they might be able to conceptualize some more general characteristics of what is generically understood to be "religion."

This does not mean that I am naive about the great diversity and disagreement within the study of religion over even fundamental questions, such as are generally more settled, or at least appear to be, in fields like linguistics and chemistry. Most students of religion are familiar with debates over issues as basic as whether or not "religion" exists and whether the study of it is to be distinguished from the study of society, culture, and history. The study of religion, despite many interesting attempts, has no table of elements, nor is there general agreement on the usefulness of abstract mathematical formulas to describe things like pilgrimage or canon.

Yet there is a difference between teaching about certain facts of Islam for their own sake and using these same facts to exemplify certain problems, categories, or concepts current in at least some or most studies of religion. To justify the use of certain facts in terms of their usefulness as examples of "religion" does not mean that we should pick "obscure" aspects of Islam only because they fit well into certain categories in the study of religion. The requirement of such a justification does mean that no given aspect of Islam can simply be assumed to be an essential part of any course. Is it necessary to teach about Islamic purity laws because they are supposed to be an obligation every Muslim practices, or are Islamic purity laws useful as a peculiar example of the more general notion of "purification"? The knowledge of such specific, Islamic facts is not presented to students, nor justified in my own mind, as essential to accomplishing my objectives in teaching about Islam. The knowledge of such things is presented to students, explicitly, as a means to learn something more general about religion and the ways in which it might be analyzed and understood.

It is my belief that, despite the quality or range of specific facts I might present to students, without acquiring the skills to distinguish and evaluate these facts (using, although not limited to, approaches developed and used in the study of religion), students cannot conceptualize and think about Islam as a "religion." Without the development of analytical skills, at best, students can only memorize the definitions of Islam presented to them. For this reason, I am hesitant to justify my own teaching of Islam on the basis of observations such as the growing number of Muslims in the United States or the importance of Islam historically and in contemporary world politics. To say that I am teaching Islam because there is a growing number of Muslims in the United States would imply that if there were less Muslims then it would not be as important to teach about Islam. If my justification, however, is based on the usefulness I can show the Islamic materials to have for the general study of religion, and the justification for the study of religion is based on its contribution to the objectives of a liberal arts education, then my teaching about Islam is an integral part of a liberal arts education.

Conclusions

If Islam is to be taught as an example of religion, and religion is to be a discipline within the liberal arts, then there are no Islamic facts or theories of religion that cannot be left out of an introductory course. What must be included, however, is that which is normally left out of such courses: attention to the skills students should be acquiring and refining in the context of a liberal arts education, including but not limited to the ability to read carefully, think critically, and argue effectively.

NOTES

1. Abū Jaʿfar Muḥammad b. Jarīr al-Ṭabarī (839–923) wrote one of the largest extant and earliest commentaries on the Quran, and an extensive history beginning with Creation, through the time of the Prophet Muhammad, up until his own death. For a first-rate translation of the history, see the (39 eventually) volumes in the series, *The History of al-Ṭabarī,* ed. Ehsan Yarshater (Albany: State University of New York Press). Although not all the volumes have been published, those on the life of the Prophet Muhammad have been. Ibn Ishaq's biography of the Prophet Muhammad, as extant in the recension of Ibn Hisham, has been available in a scholarly English translation for some time, though it is not always in print. See A. Guillaume, trans., *The Life of Muhammad: A Translation of Ibn Ishaq's Sirat Rasul Allah* (1955; reprint, Karachi: Oxford University Press, 1967). For the earlier, nonextant portion of this biography, covering the prophets leading up to Muhammad, see Gordon Darnell Newby, *The Making of the Last Prophet: A Reconstruction of the Earliest Biography of Muhammad* (Columbia: University of South Carolina Press, 1989).

2. Although (or perhaps because) I find questionable the theoretical value of some

of his positions, Wilfred Cantwell Smith's distinctions between "belief" and "history" is useful as a means to compare how one's conviction concerning the existence and meaning of certain historical events relates to the types of evidence or lack thereof for that existence and meaning. I have been most impressed by W. C. Smith, *Belief and History* (Charlottesville: University Press of Virginia, 1977) and W. C. Smith, *The Meaning and End of Religion: A New Approach to the Religious Traditions of Mankind* (New York: Macmillan, 1963). A helpful, but somewhat differently focused Christian analogy can be found in Karl Löwith, *Meaning in History* (Chicago: University of Chicago Press, 1949).

3. I have found it particularly useful to borrow and adapt Victor Turner's analogy between the observer/participant in field work and the audience/actor in theatre. Turner argues that the observer, like the audience, has a wider and better overall perspective of the ritual or drama than the participant or actor who is in the midst of the action and may only interact with other participants at selected times throughout the production. This perspective is found in Victor Turner, *The Ritual Process: Structure and Anti-Structure* (New York: Aldine, 1969) and V. Turner, *The Forest of Symbols: Some Aspects of Ndembu Ritual* (Ithaca: Cornell University Press, 1967). Some helpful insights into this idea in Turner's work can be found in Bobby C. Alexander, *Victor Turner Revisited: Ritual as Social Change* (Atlanta: Scholars Press, 1991).

4. Without moving into more sophisticated treatments of historiography, I challenge students to consider the difference between "what actually happened" (if such a thing even exists) and how what happened is experienced and related to others. This simple distinction is made by J. H. Plumb, *The Death of the Past* (Boston, 1971), but a more extended contemplation of historical experience is found in R. G. Collingwood, *The Idea of History* (Oxford: Clarendon Press, 1946).

5. Most useful in their broad outlines are Joseph Campbell, *The Hero with a Thousand Faces*, 2d ed. (Princeton: Princeton University Press, 1968) and Mircea Eliade, *The Myth of the Eternal Return* (Princeton: Princeton University Press, 1954). By stressing Campbell's macrocategories of hero mythology, students can begin to universalize the Muslim notion of Muhammad. Eliade allows for this in more historically defined and ritually specific forms which can be useful to convey to students in basic outline.

6. Although it is not well known and not readily accessible, Geo Widengren's six-volume "King and Savior Series" is an excellent source of historical insights stimulating many comparative analyses. For the last volume of the series that focuses most directly on the prophet Muhammad, see Geo Widengren, *Muhammad, the Apostle of God, and His Ascension* (Uppsala: Uppsala Universitets Årsskrift, 1955:1).

7. See the rich theoretical sophistication found in Paul J. Griffiths, *Religious Reading: The Place of Reading in the Practice of Religion* (Oxford: Oxford University Press, 1999). Laurie Patton has collected a number of essays dealing with the issue of canon and its interpretation in her edited volume *Authority, Anxiety, and Canon: Essays in Vedic Inter-*

pretation (Delhi: Sri Satguru Publications, 1995). Another collection to be consulted is Jeffrey Timm, ed., *Text in Context: Traditional Hermeneutics in South Asia* (Albany: State University of New York Press, 1991).

8. The general idea of "paradigms," including how traditions are established and maintained, can be a useful model for characterizing the tension between the precedent of a received text and the novelty of changing circumstances. Paradigm changes are stressed in Thomas Kuhn, *The Structure of Scientific Revolutions*, 2d ed. (Chicago: University of Chicago Press, 1970). Somewhat more apt for the issue of canon and law are attempts to explain continuity such as Edward Shils, *Tradition* (Chicago: University of Chicago Press, 1981) and Stephen Toulmin, *Human Understanding*, vol. 1 (Princeton: Princeton University Press, 1972).

9. The comparative and insightful treatment of Islamic examples in W. C. Smith, *What Is Scripture?* (Minneapolis: Fortress Press, 1993) shows the broad range of possibilities in the categorizing and understanding of "canon" both within and outside of the category of text. The more focused but broadly comparative studies of William Graham allow for a range of examples with which to emphasize the oral aspect of the Quran. See William Graham, *Beyond the Written Word: Oral Aspects of Scripture in the History of Religion* (Cambridge: Cambridge University Press, 1987) and his more narrowly defined "Qur'an as Spoken Word: An Islamic Contribution to the Understanding of Scripture," in *Approaches to Islam in Religious Studies*, ed. Richard C. Martin (Tucson: University of Arizona Press, 1985), 23–40.

10. In some cases (given smaller class size or more upper-division students), I have had students read and comment on selections from Durkheim's *Elementary Forms of the Religious Life* and William Robertson Smith's "Holy Places in their Relation to Man," in his *Lectures on the Religion of the Semites*. The relationship of Islamic examples to these theories is particularly fruitful, and as such, this exercise can help to show how Islamic materials can be used to modify and generate more generic theoretical concepts in the study of religion.

11. Geo Widengren's ideas about the morphology of rituals can be seen most clearly in his *Religionsphänomenologie* (Berlin: Walter de Gruyter, 1969), though similar theoretical concepts underly his account in the "King and Savior Series." Among Arent Jan Wensinck's more accessible works are his "Arabic New-Year and the Feast of Tabernacles," *Verhandelingen der Koninklijke Akademie van Wetenschappen te Amsterdam. Afdeeling Letterkunde*, n.r. 25.2 (1924) and his "The Ideas of the Western Semites Concerning the Navel of the Earth," *Verhandelingen der Koninklijke Akademie van Wetenschappen te Amsterdam. Afdeeling Letterkunde*, n.r. 17.1 (1916). Somewhat longer but also illustrative of Wensinck's approach is his "Some Semitic Rites of Mourning and Religion: Studies on the Origin and Mutual Relation," *Verhandelingen der Koninklijke Akademie van Wetenschappen te Amsterdam. Afdeeling Letterkunde*, n.r. 18.1 (1917).

12. The most systematic statement of Ugo Bianchi's position can be found in his *The History of Religions* (Leiden: E. J. Brill, 1975). Bianchi's preference for a philologi-

cally and historically based phenomenology comes out most clearly in the conclusion (pp. 201–220). Kurt Rudolf more directly champions a philological approach in his *Historical Fundamentals and the Study of Religions* (New York: Macmillan, 1985) and his "The Foundations of the History of Religions and its Future Task," in *The History of Religions: Retrospect and Prospect*, ed. Joseph Kitagawa (New York: Macmillan, 1985), 53–72.

13. See Reinhold Loeffler, *Islam in Practice: Religious Beliefs in a Persian Village* (Albany: State University of New York Press, 1988). The bulk of this book consists of translations of interviews, representing the various voices of Muslims, how individuals interact differently with more widely recognized religious norms and legal precepts.

14. See M. E. Combs-Schilling, *Sacred Performances: Islam, Sexuality, and Sacrifice* (New York: Columbia University Press, 1989) and Abdellah Hammoudi, *The Victim and Its Masks: An Essay on Sacrifice and Masquerade in the Maghreb*, trans. Paula Wissing (Chicago: University of Chicago Press, 1993). With smaller classes, I have had students read and compare both of these books in an attempt to contrast Combs-Schilling's larger Moroccan-wide context of the celebration of the Prophet's Birthday and the Wedding Ceremony with Hammoudi's more limited focus on the performance of the Masquerade in juxtaposition to the Sacrifice among the Ait Mizane. For larger classes, discussion of all four of these rituals and their connection with the perpetuation of certain social structures allows for an effective presentation of a "functionalist" or "structuralist" perspective on ritual.

15. Of the many publications of Ronald Grimes, I find his *Ritual Criticism: Case Studies in its Practice, Essays on Its Theory* (Columbia: University of South Carolina Press, 1990) to provide instructive examples for raising comparative issues. Catherine Bell, *Ritual Theory, Ritual Practice* (Oxford: Oxford University Press, 1992), especially part III "Ritual and Power," provides a useful synthesis of recent theories of ritual and action, though students sometimes find it rough going without a solid grounding in the original theorists Bell cites.

16. Succeeding generations of students seem to be less and less familiar with Freud's description of the "Totem Meal" and its relation to the origins of religion. With more advanced students, I have found it useful to assign parts 4–7 of Freud's "The Return of Totemism in Childhood" (from Robertson Smith to the end of the book) in his *Totem and Taboo*, trans. James Strachey (New York: W. W. Norton, 1950), 132–161. Rene Girard, *Violence and the Sacred*, trans. Patrick Gregory (Baltimore: Johns Hopkins University Press, 1977) is a thickly theoretical work which has found wide application in a number of different disciplines, though the close connection between "Islam" and "violence" in many students' minds makes for lively discussion and consideration of a quasi-catharsis view of Islamic rituals. Examples of Islamic definitions of "pure/impure" and "sacred/profane" (taken from Bukhari or a standard *fiqh* manual on ritual purity) can be used by students to refute effectively some of Girard's theoretical assumptions. E. E. Evans-Pritchard's *Nuer Religion* (Oxford: Oxford University Press, 1956) is a model of how one can interpret almost any ritual or cult within an

"Old Testament" framework. Such a critique of Evans-Pritchard can be found in Luc de Heusch, *Sacrifice in Africa: A Structuralist Approach,* trans. Linda O'Brien and Alice Morton (Bloomington: Indiana University Press, 1985), especially 1–25.

17. See Arthur Christensen, *Les types du premier homme et du premier roi dans l'histoire légendaire des Iraniens* (Archives d'Études Orientales 14. Leiden: E. J. Brill, 1943) which can be expanded even further afield with Georges Dumézil, *The Destiny of a King,* trans. Alf Hiltebeitel (Chicago: University of Chicago Press, 1973). Of Henri Corbin's many publications, I find his *The Man of Light in Iranian Sufism,* trans. Nancy Pearson (London, 1978) most helpful.

18. See Clifford Geertz, *Islam Observed: Religious Development in Morocco and Indonesia* (Chicago: University of Chicago Press, 1968). Although this work is severely outdated (especially for Indonesia) and has raised a number of serious theoretical objections among scholars of religion and Islam, I find his model focusing on the recognition and application of a limited range of "Islamic" symbols (esp. as laid out in chapter 4) to provide students with an analytically effective approach to the diversity of Islamic identities. Michael Gilsenan, *Recognizing Islam: Religion and Society in the Modern Arab World* (New York: Pantheon Books, 1982) remains one of my top recommendations for a one-book introduction to Islam, with the caveat that his focus remains that of the modern Middle East. Some of the same issues are dealt with in a broader geographical setting in Dale Eickelman and James Piscatori, *Muslim Politics* (Princeton: Princeton University Press, 1996).

19. Leonardo A. Villalón, *Islamic Society and State Power in Senegal: Disciples and Citizens in Fatick* (Cambridge: Cambridge University Press, 1995) gives a sound overview of Sufism and political authority in West Africa. Edward B. Reeves, *The Hidden Government: Ritual, Clientelism and Legitimation in Northern Egypt* (Salt Lake City: University of Utah Press, 1990) is a theoretically rich analysis of the important but often ignored annual Sufi rituals in Tanta. Mark R. Woodward, *Islam in Java: Normative Piety and Mysticism in the Sultanate of Yogyakarta* (Tucson: University of Arizona Press, 1989) contains much useful information on Islam in Java, but particularly helpful as an example is his suggestive analysis of the Yogyakarta Kraton (palace) as a symbol of the mystical path of Sufism.

20. Brinkley Messick, *The Calligraphic State: Textual Domination and History in a Muslim Society* (Berkeley: University of California Press, 1993) is a book I have used in many different classes. For the introductory course, I have found his description of the "text" in the "Shariah Society" to exemplify for students a certain "traditional" model of an Islamic society, one in which students can recognize some of the classical patterns and statuses and see how these are adopted and adapted to contemporary and changing circumstances. Richard T. Antoun, *Muslim Preacher in the Modern World: A Jordanian Case Study in Comparative Perspective* (Princeton: Princeton University Press, 1989) and Patrick Gaffney, *The Prophet's Pulpit: Islamic Preaching in Contemporary Egypt* (Berkeley: University of California Press, 1994) both provide fascinating examples of

how certain "core" or "canonical" texts and ideas are modified and transmitted on a popular level. Antoun works effectively with the notion of the "Culture Broker" which seems to fit well with students' understanding of the more general approaches of Geertz and Gilsenan.

21. In the past, I have used a number of novels. Generally, in large classes, I order four different novels, divide the students into four groups, and have each group read one novel. I try to ensure that each of the student study groups (formed at the beginning of the class) have representatives for each of the four novels. Among those I have used are Tayeb Salih, *Season of Migration to the North*, Salman Rushdie, *Midnight's Children* and his *Shame*, Fatima Mernissi, *Dreams of Trespass: Tales of a Harem Girlhood*, Naguib Mahfouz, *Palace Walk* and (although not strictly a novel) Elizabeth Warnock Fernea, *Guests of the Sheik: An Ethnography of an Iraqi Village*.

22. In the past I have used Eric Hansen, *Motoring with Mohammed: Journeys to Yemen and the Red Sea* (New York: Vintage, 1991) and Tony Horwitz, *Baghdad without a Map, and Other Misadventures in Arabia* (New York: Plume, 1992). The Horwitz book is badly out of date since the Gulf War, but often still allows students to see, in contrast, some of the biases of Western reporting. Hansen's account is not only highly entertaining but also remains one of the best introductions to Yemeni culture which, for students, presents a good case-study of a particular local context for Islam. Other useful accounts include Nicholas Clapp, *The Road to Ubar* (Boston: Houghton Mifflin, 1998), and his *Sheba* (Boston: Houghton Mifflin, 2001). Recently reprinted are Freya Stark's *The Southern Gates of Arabia* (New York: Modern Library, 2001) and *The Valleys of the Assassins* (New York: Modern Library, 2001).

CHAPTER TWO

On the "Introduction to Islam"

A. KEVIN REINHART

W HAT GOES INTO AN "INTRODUCTORY" COURSE? To a large
extent the truisms of the culture, the discipline, and the field are
catalyzed by the biography of the instructor. And so the introductory course, at least at first, is constructed reactively as much as "proac-
tively." There is first the Oedipal stage in an instructor's career (where every
lecture is a critique of every book read, every mistaken idea inflicted on the
instructor in the course of his/her education). Next comes the market-driven,
student pulse-taking phase (in which he[1] figures out what, besides the finest
graduate school nuances of disciplinary history, might interest undergraduates). Thereafter, an instructor may have the good fortune to be able to re-
think that introductory course. In the process, it is likely to be problems he has
found in teaching Islam that shape his notion of how Islam ought to be
taught. So the third phase of course-construction is marked by engagement
with the field, with student interest, and the experienced problems of teaching an introductory course. It is important, in this third phase, to have not
merely reactions but also goals that inform the course's shape and content.

What follows (somewhat idealized)[2] is my current attempt to teach the
"Introduction to Islam." The course is, more or less, chronologically organized (for reasons explained below) and is "back-loaded," that is, modernity is
given a chronologically proportionate amount of coverage. The result is
something of a "heritage" course.[3] After teaching the introductory course for
a few years, I have shaped Religion 8, "An Introduction to Islam," around two
critiques and three desiderata. Before sketching out the course itself, I would
like to lay out briefly these metaconcerns. The two critiques are, first, of the

media and cultural truisms about Muslims and Islam, and second, of students' natural tendencies to essentialize religion and exotic cultures. The desiderata are to provide an easily grasped narrative, to convey the moral seriousness of Islam (and of religion), and to leave students with an appreciation of the religious achievements of Muslims and their religious history.

Metaconcerns

CRITIQUE

The Media Heritage

Teaching Islam poses special problems, but these problems are not problems of ignorance, as with for example, African Religion, or problems of pop vulgarization, as is frequently the case with Hinduism, or with zealous identification, as with teaching the Bible or New Testament.[4] What we are confronted with instead are problems with "pseudo-knowledge."

All students who walk into an Islam class, though they profess ignorance, still "know" something about Islam—if only from the news. Every Islamicist is aware that, whether it is in *The New York Daily News* or on National Public Radio, it is the negative, the violent, the ignorant that characterize the images and voices presented in the media as Muslim. Garbled or dated history, plotted summaries of creed and practices—all these are framed by distaste, dislike, or outrage. Yet in the end, this is less a problem of fact than a problem of affect: students arrive with a constellation of terms, mostly negative, that cluster around the notion of Islam, so that words like "terrorist" come naturally and unreflectively when they answer an exam question about, say, the Kharijis. The classroom goal is not to ban such terms (there *are* Muslim terrorists) but to bring students to reflect on how they come to analyze with these particular categories.

Almost always, it emerges in discussion that these reflexive categories of analysis are media terms, alongside words like "moderate" versus "radical," "violence," "fanatic," and the like. It usually suffices to point this fact out and demonstrate it with clippings, excerpts from popular novels, and video clips. Students want to be savvy media critics, as one of the panelists at the 1995 MESA workshop on "Teaching the Introduction to Islam," where this paper was first given, pointed out, and it is our job to help them become so.

Essentialism

To my surprise, I have found the media-stereotype problem less profound and less difficult to change than some larger epistemological errors that may be peculiar to the study of religion and particularly afflict the study of Islam.

A cursory survey of other college and university religion department course offerings confirms my impression that a course called "Introduction to Christianity" is very rare, while "Introduction to Buddhism, Islam, Judaism" is much more common. We know so much about Christianity that "Introduction to Christianity" would seem impossibly wide in scope, if not downright offensive. Course titles in that field are more likely to be "Early Christianity" or "Medieval Christianity." When teaching about Islam (and other non-Christian traditions), however, there is a tendency to smudge the particularities and varieties of the tradition, and, of course, when covering a 1,400-year tradition that stretches from the Philippines to Philadelphia, it is tempting to essentialize. This is equally a problem for the instructor who knows too much, as well as for the instructor who knows too little.

Students too, once they are convinced how little *they* know, also want to essentialize. "What is Islam's position on abortion?" they ask. My stock mantra in reply is *"which Muslims and when?"* It is crucial to insist that it is Muslims who are agents and to avoid the hypostatization of something called "Islam" into an agent that acts, thinks, or believes. Islam does not think, require, or hold positions; Muslims do. Similarly, for the instructor, it is important also to choose representative examples, without representing them as exhaustive of the Islamic possibilities. There are, I find, two kinds of essentialism toward which students and instructors are drawn—phenomenal and historical/geographical.

PHENOMENAL ESSENTIALISM Phenomenal essentialism is the assumption that there is some intrinsic form of Islam that transcends time and place; an essence of Islam. This is a mistake characteristic of both Muslim and non-Muslim students—Muslims, because they are committed to the idea of a transcendent truth to which they adhere, and non-Muslims because they assume the stability of that which is labeled by the word "Islam," just as Judaism, slavery, or democracy are also understood to be stable essences represented by the word.

To subvert this metaphysical approach I make Hodgson's terminology from his prolegomena to *The Venture of Islam*[5] standard for the course. The differences underlying his distinctions between Islam and Islamdom, Islamic and Islamicate are so commonsensical and so taken-for-granted in other fields of academic study that *not* to use them is a kind of intellectual sloth that requires justification by those who would choose not to take pains to speak precisely. No one would say, "with Clive's victory in the Battle of Plassey, Christianity controlled all of India." Yet it is commonplace to say that "after the battle of Yarmouk, Islam was victorious throughout the Middle

East." Bulliet and many others have shown, of course, that it was not "Islam" that was victorious but the Arab armies; and centuries were to pass before "Islam" was the dominant religion of the Middle East or anywhere else besides Arabia.[6] Similarly, the difference in usage and implication is obvious between, on the one hand, "the decline of Christianity in Europe" or "the decline of Judaism in Cochin," and, on the other, "the decline of Islam in the eighteenth century." The former clearly suggest a loss of allegiance or a decline in population, while the latter implies a loss of military or political power.

A course on "Islam" must clarify its object of study—the Religion of Islam—to inoculate its students against the conceptual drowsiness of many who teach and write about Islam and Islamdom, and who conflate religion and state, religion and power, or religion and identity.

HISTORICAL AND GEOGRAPHICAL ESSENTIALISM Historical essentialism is the belief that some *period* of Islam is quintessential, that the *real* Islam is to be seen in the middle ʿAbbasid period, for example, or in the Damascus circles of Ibn Taymiyyah, or in the community of Muhammad, and versions of Islam outside those are irrelevant, decadent, or merely marginal. Geographical essentialism is the assertion that Islam's true home is the Arab world, or that Muslims in the Middle East are archetypal Muslims and Muslims in India are syncretists, inauthentic, or novice Muslims.

A clear instance of this essentialism is found when a course on Islam stops at 1258 and then segues into "the Western Impact" in the nineteenth century. Surely, the implication is that Muslims who lived after 1258 or outside the ʿAbbasid world are marginal to our concern. To the contrary, I would suggest that the Islam of the Middle Periods is more crucial to understanding most varieties of Islam than is the state-centered Islam of 750–1258.[7] A similar mistake is teaching Shiʿism as if what distinguishes Shiʿism from Sunnism is a dispute over the caliphate between 632–661. Shiʿism may have begun in this dispute, but the political struggle was never all that was at issue. To focus on these events is to make the Shiʿah seem like losers when they might just as easily be presented as tenacious survivors. In any case, Shiʿism, like Sunnism, has a history and to slight that history is to deform the history of Islam.[8]

An introduction to Islam must leave students with an appreciation for various forms of Islam, in various times and places, while giving them the means to see how all of these can usefully be identified by the term "Islam." It takes work, particularly to get across the idea that Arabs are not normative Muslims, and that works in Arabic are not the only important Islamic scholarship.

DESIDERATA

Narrative

Shifting from the negative to the positive part of the course design, I can now discuss what I hope to convey and the means by which I hope to convey it. The course must be carried, I think, by some kind of narrative, and in the effort to de-essentialize the teaching of Islam, I have found a historical narrative to work best.

A story is something we try to create from the jumbled stimuli of our own lives, and it seems that we are hard-wired to look for narrative sequence. A good narrative keeps students coming to class and helps them keep track of change and variation. As importantly, narrative subverts essentialism, since it shows transformation and development, without valuing one period over another. A narrative can reflect the repeated reconceptualization of ideas, practices, and meanings, so that students grasp that the term "Islam" meant differently in different times, places, and contexts. A chronological narrative, properly done, also subverts the idea that the early period was dynamic, the middle period sclerotic, and the latest period merely reactive. This course then is a roughly chronological story of the elaboration, adaptation, and change of "Islam" by Muslims.

Moral Seriousness

The second task of the course, a particular concern of the historian of religion, is to convey the seriousness of the enterprise. This "Islam stuff" is about the practitioners' eternal destiny, and I am convinced that important figures in the history of Islam took that very seriously. A course that merely presents changes in dogmas or practices without reference to the weightiness of Islam's consequences for Muslims leaves students adrift in a Sargasso of facts with no sense of why Muslims undertook the voyage.

In general, moral seriousness is a hard thing for our students to grasp, particularly since most of them are only faintly religious, and ironic distance is the fashionable stance of our times. Moreover, the academy often encourages them to see religious life merely as a mask for some other "more fundamental" force—control, domination, or profit. They also see religious life as a species of consumer choice, like the choice of a career or even which sports team to support. Becoming a Sufi is not a "lifestyle decision," like wearing plaid shirts and buying a four-wheel drive vehicle, and undertaking to live according to the Shari'ah is not just a matter of reading the user's manual. These are life-altering commitments more serious even than deciding between investment banking and law school.

Sometimes, in these conservative times, analogies to the language of nationalism, ethnicity, and patriotism work to explain the communal commitment of Muslims. One must be clear that these are analogies, but such comparisons help students to understand emotion and identification.

Appreciation

Fnally, and perhaps more controversial, I think an introductory course on Islam should leave students with an appreciation, and ideally, a positive feeling about Islam. To convey what it is that has appealed to the believer is a goal taken for granted in the introduction to Judaism,[9] Chinese religion, or Buddhism, but that same appreciation is seen by some as pandering, in an Islam course.

So, for the ever-troubling "woman-problem" (see below), it is important to locate structures of Islamic anthropology and point out that historically, these have depicted men and women as located in different and hierarchically arranged domains. One should also point out that many Muslim women and men find this anthropology, in fact, to be un-Islamic and an artifact of the gender of the medievals who developed Islam's law. When essentialism is avoided, the ethical failures or evil acts of Muslims are seen no more to indict Islam than Jim Jones or the St. Bartholomew's Day massacre indict Christianity. Islam has been an immensely successful missionary religion. It seems to me that an introductory course fails if it does not convey what has drawn millions to the faith.

The Course Structure

All of the foregoing is an attempt to articulate, after the fact, sensations and perceptions that have resulted in the course described below. This course was not designed from the top down, but over time it evolved, in dialogue as it were, between students' questions and the instructor's agenda.

The course as it exists now is an argument that Islamic religious history is a repeated encounter by Muslims with the Quran, the Quran-bearer, the ritual practice of the community, and a tradition of socio-moral dissent. In a series of elaborations arising from these encounters, the range of practice and belief we call "Islam" has emerged. In addition, there is a prologue to the course, and there are various points at which certain technical problems in the study of Islam are addressed.

THE HISTORY OF THE STUDY OF ISLAM

"Orientalism"

The first course topic is a discussion of what is called in shorthand, "Orientalism." This lecture and discussion is conceived of less as conveying information than of inoculating against pseudo-information. Here I lay out a brief history of the study of Islam, and, drawing on Norman Daniel[10] and Jean-Jacques Waardenburg,[11] some of the misinformation characteristic of the field is shown to be reflected in various contemporary journalistic and popular accounts. For a few years we read and discussed the famous *New York Review of Books* debate between Bernard Lewis and Edward Said.[12] We've also read Said's later reflection on "Orientalism"[13] and Grafflin's shrewd article in the *Bulletin of Concerned Asian Scholars.*[14]

More effective than these rather detailed slanging matches have been accounts from *Newsweek* that embody the tropes I discuss, nineteenth-century Orientalist paintings and popular culture novels—especially Leon Uris's vile *Haj* and Jonathan Kellerman's startlingly racist *Butcher's Theater.*[15] It is through popular media that the clichés are perpetuated and ingested, and students are most attentive when the medium is something with which they are familiar. For that reason, I'm beginning a videotape anthology of "greatest anti-Arab/anti-Muslim scenes from the cinema." Fifteen minutes of Chuck Norris and Arnold Schwarzenegger killing "towel-heads" while they run around yelling "Allahu Akbar," and Omar Sharif (as an Arab) being told by blonde Peter O'Toole (as Lawrence), "The Arabs are a silly people," may be more effective still.

The difficulty, of course, is that many of our students are primed either to see "Orientalism" as yet another in the catalog of Western sins or as whiney, liberal, West-bashing. So it is important to move from Orientalism to a discussion of the cultural construction of others. We usually end the discussion with a bit from Mawdudi's *Purdah,*[16] where he offers stereotypes of America—our sexual excesses and other peculiar customs. The final point, usually drawing from Usāmah,[17] is to discuss the difference between the construction of others from positions of power and positions of less power.

Though the topic comes up again in the course from time to time, I have been quite surprised at the extent to which students "get it" and bring to the class clippings that demonstrate other weird journalistic takes on Islamdom.

THE MATRIX

After this brief theoretical flirtation, we come to what is the heart of the course—both methodologically and organizationally—the section entitled "the matrix of Islam." The argument of the course is that Muslims have encountered the elements of the matrix—Quran, Prophet, Ritual, Dissent—over and again throughout Islamic history. While variables like social organization, class, and economy have shaped what Muslims have made of these crucial elements, these four remain the building blocks of any given Islam at any time in any place. These encounters and reencounters form the narrative of the course, which is, in short, that Muslims have "thickened" their understanding of Islam and of the contents and implications of Quran until the modern era, when they have deliberately "thinned" out the compound of things Islamic.[18]

Quran

The first element of the matrix is the Quran. As much as possible I try to focus on the "unmediated" Quran, as found in some of Michael Sells's work[19] and that of Angelika Neuwirth.[20] The Quran is sound and rhythm, as well as a content that can be summed up as, among other things, a Muhammadian dialog with Arab mores, and with Christian and Jewish "mistakes." We read from Arberry's translation,[21] which, despite his misguided use of the Flügel numbering system, remains the most successful attempt to capture the oral qualities and resonances of the Quran. Our approach is to make sense of the Quranic content and show it presenting a cosmology, an anthropology, a soteriology, and a *Heilsgeschichte*. It is also very important to make sense of the Quranic style, and to this end I use Norman O. Brown's brilliant article[22] (with Angelika Neuwirth's on reserve) to take apart a "typical" surah.

Quran-Bearer: Muhammad

As with the Quran, our goal in these lectures is to capture something of the unmediated Muhammad. I try and reconstruct him and his role from Quranic citations, and point out that in contemporary seventh-century documents, such as the Aphrodito papyri, he is not mentioned—suggesting that his importance to Muslims as a source of knowledge grew over time. I point out the late date of Ibn Hishām and even Ibn al-Kalbī's hagiography.[23] And it is here where the (in my view largely untenable) views of Crone,[24] Wansbrough,[25] etc., are discussed. Peters's article on the quest for the historical Muhammad[26] is particularly to the point here, but it has to be counterbalanced with works like those of Watt, Serjeant, and Chabbi.[27] I try also to call attention to Muhammad's theoretical dispensability: There is, in Muslim understanding, Islam without Muhammad, and in early understandings it appears his role was as a vehicle for the miraculous, rather than as a miraculous being himself. This point will provide a contrast for the later discussions of Muhammad.

Ritual

A few ritual *prohibitions,* but more important, the ritual *obligations* of Islam are discussed. The thrust of these lectures is that ritual shapes (Islamic) time and space and creates, in the quotidian, a pattern of sacramental moments. I also discuss ritual as a structuring of community and review the (rather slender) Quranic ritual stipulations, which nonetheless adumbrate all the rituals understood today by Muslims to be central to Islam.

A lecture also describes "popular" religion and the soft margins of religious identity. It argues that "lived" Islam is always a mix of the "universal" or "standard" Islam and "vernacular" Islam.[28] Various films show nonofficial but nonetheless, efficacious religious behaviors that are, for their practitioners, part of Islam as well.[29]

Dissent: Socio-Moral Criticism: "Commending the good and forbidding the reprehensible"

The last of the matrix elements is the notion of socio-moral criticism.[30] This has, of course, been part of Islam from its very beginning; the Quran is full of critiques of contemporary practice, as well as of general moral injunctions. It is argued that the 'Alid revolts and resistance to them were, in part at least, driven by socio-moral concerns. Here the main reading is Shaykh al-Mufīd's account of "the Commander of the Faithful" and of "the Passion of al-Ḥusayn."[31]

I also discuss the Kharijis as critics of urbane Arab norms and moral laxity, as well as resisters of irreligious, dynastic claims to the caliphate. Here Watt's distinction between charismatic community and charismatic leader provides a useful starting point for contrasting the 'Alid with other Islamic orientations.[32]

FIRST ELABORATION: MIDDLE PERIOD (650 – 850 C.E.)

This unit establishes the dynamism of Islam. Each lecture's reading includes Quranic passages and hadith cited by those engaged in the enterprises I describe.

The introductory lecture for this unit attacks two problems: the first is, what does it mean to say "religions evolve"? This is particularly important not only for Muslims in the class but also for all the religiously identifying students, who may feel either threatened by the notion that religions change or feel that situating these changes in society and culture compromises the "truth" of Islam. The second problem is what we mean by "influence." Here I discuss romantic roots of the idea of "originality," as the correlate of "sincerity," and try to situate Islam in its Near Eastern environment.[33]

The Commentarial Sciences: Defining 'ilm

For this section, our "hook" is the development of the notion that Islam has five (or six) pillars. In the course of discussing the various versions of this cliché of Islamic studies (and of Muslim apologetics), I introduce them to the development of commentarial literature on the Quran and to hadith.

QURANIC COMMENTARY This lecture points out problems in the redaction and transcription of Quran. The development of lexicography and grammar as Muslim sciences; different commentarial strategies; something of the history of Revelation-supplements (the *qāṣṣ* literature [religiously edifying stories] for example) are all described. The Wansbrough and Burton[34] perspectives on the Quran's redaction are examined.

BIOGRAPHY, SUNNAH, AND HADITH Similarly, the development of Sunnah and hadith literature are sketched in this unit. The debate on "authenticity" among Goldziher, Abbot, Sezgin, and most recently Juynboll, Calder, and Motzki[35] is examined. I also trace the development of biography as a Muslim science, in the service of history and of hadith. Finally, as a case study, I offer a dissection of an *isnād/matn* [headnote/text] complex, taken from Juynboll.[36]

PIETISM [WAR] AND RIGOR [ZUHD] This lecture is presented as an iteration of the tradition of socio-moral dissent. Our focus here is on al-Ḥasan al-Baṣrī as a crucial figure in the early development of what became theology, fiqh, and Sufism, all *avant la lettre*. The controversy over the building of Wāsiṭ, the image of Abū Dharr, rebellions of the 'Abbasids and others, and the disengagement of the new class of religious quasi professionals from the 'Abbasids, are discussed.[37]

SECOND ELABORATION: MATURE PERIOD (850 – 1500)

Shari'ah and Fiqh: The Institutionalization of 'ilm

This unit presents the development of fiqh, then the later development of *uṣūl al-fiqh*, and the concept of Shari'ah. I make general points about the three categories of "applied fiqh" [furū']: "acts of bondsmanship" ['ibādāt] (i.e., ritual), "social relations" [mu'āmalāt], and "criminal law" [ḥudūd]. The focus of the lectures, however, is on the hermeneutics by which hadith and Quran are extracted so they can be brought to bear on novel problems. This lecture is oriented first to understanding how the fiqh process resolves certain important religious problems—the limitations of revelation, the need for an ongoing revelation, the desire to mythologize religious history, etc. Second, I show how fiqh solves practical problems, not just ideological ones. (This lecture is the background for the assignment described below.)[38]

THE ATOMS OF SCRIPTURE To understand the hermeneutic dominant in Islam requires further discussion of the commentarial tradition, particularly the approach that decontextualizes the Quran and Sunnah in order to extend its scope. Once the Quran is seen as a collection of particularities—devoid of historical or textual context—rather than general notions, the way is open to extend Quranic command to the minutia of the increasingly novel life of Muslims. This hermeneutic move allows a normative Islamic practice to expand with Islamdom through time and across a wide variety of cultures—in the period covered in this part of the course—to Iran, North Africa, and Central Asia.

THE MADRASAH   The institution that perpetuated 'ilm and its particular hermeneutic was the *madrasah*. The madrasah is best explained by its contrasts to the educational theory students all take for granted—of exams, fixed class durations, and written assignments. I emphasize the importance of the madrasah as a transmitter and shaper of culture and present it as a (theoretically) disinterested institution, whose graduates could broker between the government and the laity, could confer legitimacy, and who tried scrupulously—again, in theory—to maintain a distance from that powers-that-were. Here is where the importance of the religious endowment [waqf] is discussed.

Shi'ism: Drama and Certainty

These lectures cover Shi'ism roughly from Ja'far al-Ṣādiq to al-Shahīd al-Awwal (Shamsaddīn Muhammad al-ʿĀmilī d. 786/1384). The hagiography of the twelve Imams is presented with an emphasis on the occultation [ghaybah] of the twelfth Imam, and the adjustments to that fact that, in effect, created Islam's denominations.

Then, by contrast, I present the gnostic world of Isma'ilism: the thrust of the lecture is Isma'ilism's richness of vision, the aesthetic beauty of its metaphysics, and the exaltation of humans who are "in the know." Following al-Ghazālī,[39] I present Shi'ism and especially Isma'ilism as a response to the epistemological uncertainty that Sunnis were willing to live with, but that other Muslims seemingly found unbearable. I allude also to the subset of Isma'ili ideas that are shared with Sufism.

Taṣawwuf: The Institutionalization of Experiential Knowledge [ma'rifah]

Our discussion of Sufism [taṣawwuf] follows Massignon[40] in arguing the Islamic and particularly Quranic origins of Sufism. He shows that the distinction between the Shari'ah sciences and Sufism corresponds to different kinds of Quranic prose. This leads then to a discussion of the complementary and competing claims to knowledge ['ilm al-ma'rifah] of the jurist [faqīh] and the ascetic [faqīr]. After an overview, I discuss the history of formative Sufism. The thematic emphasis is on Sufism as a movement to recover and maintain immanence.

PERFECTED MAN: THE PROPHET AND SAINTS As a further link to Quran and Prophetic Islam, our focus when talking about saints is the Perfected Man as a reflex of the (later) understandings of the Prophet. Saints, then, are seen as reflections of the Prophet, and consequently, Sufi understanding of the Prophet changed more general attitudes toward Muhammad. Hadith as "I was, when Adam was between water and clay," a favorite of Sufis, led to an elevated role for the Prophet, as a Logos figure or demiurge.[41]

THE KHANAQAH This lecture, in addition to discussing the institution of the Sufi lodge [khānaqāh] and the Sufi order [tarīqah] with emphasis on the chain of transmission [silsilah], also presents Sufism as "the transparent membrane of Islam," the means by which Islam was affected by other traditions, and through which most post-Conquest Muslims were converted before the twentieth century.

THE RITUALS OF SUFISM The discussion of how Sufi ritual supplemented normative Islamic rituals begins by emphasizing the structural link between normative Islamic rituals such as prayer [ṣalāt] and Sufi devotional rituals and then to more extravagant practices.

Medieval Reformism

Reformism is defined as a move to respond to Muʿtazili and other technicalist thought, to resist particularly Sufi theosophy and Shiʿism, and to create a new mythology for Islam. It is important to emphasize that this reformism and indeed all kinds of scripturalisms are an outgrowth of the socio-moral dissent present in the Islamic matrix (they are in some sense heirs of the Kharijis). Yet despite their rhetorical claims, they are also temporally late and represent something new in Islamic history. Nonetheless, although the doctrines they presented were innovations, they managed to capture a certain rhetorical high ground that makes the reformists of the twelfth to fifteenth centuries the most likely premodern source to be read by contemporary Muslims.

THE HANBALIS The most articulate and long-lasting of these reformists were the followers of the Hanbali school. I discuss the history and legends of Aḥmad b. Ḥanbal, the inquisitorial Ibn al-Jawzī, and the brilliant polymath and scholar Ibn Taymiyyah. The reading is Ibn al-Jawzī's critique of Sufism (his text entitled *Talbīs Iblīs*)[42] and Ibn Taymiyyah's critique of syncretistic Islamic practice.[43] Students can see in these texts the theological emphasis on the transcendence of God that contrasts sharply with the immanentist emphasis of Sufism. Other scripturalist/primitivist movements in North Africa, Spain, and Arabia are noted here.

THIRD ELABORATION: MODERN ISLAM

The third reimagining of Islam took place from the seventeenth century onward and still continues. While it is true that these efforts to reimagine Islam have arisen in a milieu of change, particularly under European pressure, the emphasis in this course is on the initiative taken in response to internal Islamic developments, and continuity with the first and second elaborations of Islam.

Critiquing Muslims: Reformism

Here the discussion is of Muslims critiquing Muslims, as in the critique of various accommodationist practices by Meḥmed Birgevī, of Saint-veneration and Shiʿism by Muḥammad b. ʿAbdalwahhāb, various attempts at Shiʿi reform of the Akhbarīs, Shaykhīs, and Bābīs. And finally I discuss the critiques of Sufism by Sīrhindī and Shāhwālīallāh and various tendencies still usefully labeled neo-Sufism. This reformist impulse is carried on by ʿAlī Suavī in the Ottoman world, by Jamāladdīn al-Afghānī and Muḥammad ʿAbduh, al-Bannā, Mawdūdī, al-Quṭb, and various twentieth-century figures. Here the "reformers" come first, because it is our argument that beginning in the eighteenth century, it is the "reformers" of various sorts, who seized the initiative both socially and intellectually. It is they who define Islam for thoughtful Muslims.

Nationalism as Counter-Islam

This lecture is a discussion of anticolonial movements and Ottoman and other attempts to rebuild the (mostly military) power of Islamdom. Atatürk, Nasser, Bourguiba, and others are seen as successful nation-builders, but failures as culture-builders. Their campaign against, or to reform and subordinate, Islamic thought and practice is presented against the attempts of nationalists to decolonize or to fend off imperialist control.

Critiquing Islam: Modernism

The nineteenth century brought something new: the critique of Muslim practice on grounds not internal, but external, that is, the explicit comparison of Islam and Muslims to another culture, with that other culture serving as a model and standard. This tendency begins with Gasprinski, and Sayyid Aḥmad Khān, but of course continues through Wagdī, Fazlur Rahman, and now Arkoun and Saroosh. It is important for students to realize the range of Islamic opinion and that "fundamentalism" does not exhaust Islamic options in the fifteenth (Hijri) century. Fortunately, Kurzman's anthology provides a wide variety of interesting reading for students who think Islam means fundamentalism.[44]

Reappropriating the World: The Islamization of Finance/ Social Sciences/Natural Sciences

This area students find to be among the most engaging units in the course. The idea of reimagining, in Islamic terms, finance, insurance, management, the sciences, seems both quixotic and stimulating. It does raise for them questions about what, among the things they take for granted, are irresistible natural forces (the invisible hand, the market) and what are cultural constructs subject to change or improvement (ditto).

Making the World Islamic: Islamism

This is the obvious discussion of Islamism/fundamentalism in the late twentieth Christian century: Mawdūdī, Quṭb, and Khomeini. Here is where I discuss Islamism, Islamic politics, and militant action. The point is to focus on specificity, the difference between Iranian Islamism and other varieties, and to touch briefly on other places where such movements are important as a way of discussing the wider world of Islamdom—Indonesia, Malaysia, China, the Commonwealth of Independent States. The Rushdie affair can be a good way to widen the geographic focus, while pointing out the particularities of the politics involved in Britain, India, Pakistan, Iran, and Egypt.

Technical Problems

Finally, a word about the problems of teaching a subject far outside the students' ken and outside the majority of pedagogical resources available in most institutions.

CRAFT: LINES AND DOTS, ABU AND IBN

After more than ten years of undergraduate and graduate training in Islamic Studies, I was puzzled at the inability of students to master even the most important names and terms. Then I realized that every name starts with Abu or Ibn or ends in a "ī." Then there are all those dots, dashes, and raised "c's" (backward and forward). So now, in the first week, I have a day where I go over transliteration and names. I have found that by treating this as a language problem—as students are being taught Arabic "Ṣ," they become relatively comfortable with the transliteration and find it easier to recognize and remember names. A brief discussion of the root system of Arabic encourages them to look for meaningful patterns like ḥ-m-d and k-t-b. The presentation of the relation of Persian to Arabic means that they aren't troubled when in 'Aṭṭār's Tadhkirat al-Awliyā' they read of Ebrāhīm ebn Adham or Mohammad so-and-so. And best of all, in exam questions on Ibn Taymiyyah, they no longer refer to him familiarly as "Taymiyyah." The Islamic calendar is also discussed.

GEOGRAPHY: DISTRIBUTED MAPS

There are maps of the expansion of Islamdom on the course web site. Students are also given a map of Islamdom, and nearly every lecture is accompanied by a transparency map of Islamdom. Again, this is more orientation than anything else, but it seems to make a difference in their ability to follow references to Baghdad, Samarra, Delhi, and, say, Qūs.

VISUALIZING: VIDEOS, FILMS, THE CD

Via a web site, I offer links that allow students to follow up on questions that interest them, and to augment lectures with "trots" on, for example, Islamicate history. I also have a digitized video of a Dartmouth student performing ritual prayer [ṣalāt], with subtitles in English. (The television cliché of hundreds of Muslim rumps has become a threatening trope, but seeing "one of us" filmed from the front, they easily perceive the dignity of the ritual and its corporeal vocabulary.)

The students are also required to follow one or more discussion groups in USNET and to keep a journal of what they find. This is important to bring home the diversity of opinion among Muslims, the reality of Islam in the twenty-first (Christian) century, and the fact that there are lots of Muslims in the United States and Britain. They are encouraged to note the context of the discussant, for example, what university faculty, what country, the sex of the respondent, and other relevant tell-tales.

For popular Islam, various videos are effective, if framed by a discussion that locates it within Islamic practice. I have lately been using Wicket's "For Those Who Sail to Heaven," about the veneration (with roots in Pharaonic practice) of Sīdī Abu l-Haggāg. Elizabeth Fernea's *Saints and Spirits* also worked well. I have used various films about the pilgrimage to Mecca [ḥajj], including "Guest of God." None are very good. I need a good, straightforward ethnographic account of the Hajj (see below media list).

KEEPING THE CONNECTIONS

The biggest theoretical challenge is to keep in mind during the lectures that our point is the interconnectedness of all Islamic thought. Sufism is a kind of Quran-study, a kind of hadith, a kind of dissent, a kind of ritual. For each unit, in addition to the primary sources, there is a Quran reading that represents a Quranic text much-discussed by Sufis, legists, or reformers. Whenever possible, every lecture needs to refer to previous lectures, movements and ideas previously discussed, and anticipations of this point in earliest Islamic thought. Every unit has relevant hadith or Quran citations.

Assignments

In addition to the journals, which are graded check or check plus/minus, there are two or three quizzes and two assignments. The quizzes are 30 minutes of identification of terms and names. If the term refers to an event, or in the case of a person, a date accurate within 25 years must be provided. I really don't like giving such an exam (or grading it), but I find it essential to keep students wrestling with the difficult terminology and constructing for themselves a time-line and narrative. All terms are provided (undefined) on a handout at the beginning of the course.

THE TEXT STUDY

The first assignment is a careful reading of a text and an essay answering some question *solely from the text*. It is an assignment designed to counteract the solipsism of their English courses and to get them to recognize and avoid (where appropriate) isogesis. Rewrites are permitted and are often necessary, since most students have never done a close reading and explication of a text.

DO-IT-YOURSELF FIQH

Building on the skills they have developed in close reading, the second assignment is to write two legal rulings (fatwas) on problems presented to them. These are actual problems I have encountered in discussions with American Muslims and in reading the proceedings of the Egyptian *Lajnat al-Iftā'* and other sources. Using the Quran, the commentarial material available in Cooper, Ayoub, Wherry, and the Bayḍāwī[45] translation, together with the translated hadith collections, and the three fiqh works reliably available in English, students are to write a fatwa approving or disapproving some course of action, and justifying it in *takhrīj* fashion, by citation of appropriate sources. This turns out to be a very effective assignment. Model fatwas are available in Masud, Messick, and Powers.[46]

Conclusion

As I argued at the beginning of this chapter, every course is part critique. The critique of this class would be that it is overly ambitious, that it focuses too much on the "high tradition," and that it spends too much time on "marginal" groups like the Isma'ilis or Sufis-who-stick-skewers-through-their-cheeks. Fair enough. Ideally, an introductory course is a feeder into other courses in Islam, and so, perhaps, some of the more various aspects of Islam's practices and beliefs will seize their imaginations, and they will want to follow up on Sufism, or Reformism, or Islam in the United States. Some will read more widely as a result of the course, and some may want to visit Islamdom. My hope is that in that reading, or in those visits, students will not be astounded that such-and-such a thing is done by Muslims. They may have forgotten, but the "Intro to Islam" has been a success if, in those long-stored notebooks, they can find some anticipation of what they later find in reading or visiting Islamdom.

Media List

ISLAM IN GENERAL

The Five Pillars of Islam: Films for the Humanities & Sciences

ON THE PILGRIMAGE

The Guests of God: Meridian/BBC [available in the U.S. from Islamic Information Service, 434 South Vermont Ave., Los Angeles, CA 90020; (213) 383–9258 or (818) 764–6612]
Mecca the Forbidden City: IranFilm
The Hajj [videorecording]: A Journey of Faith / CNN; Cable News Network, ©1998
The Secret Mecca: Films for the Humanties

ON POPULAR ISLAM

For Those Who Sail to Heaven: First Run/Icarus Films
Saints and Spirits: Icarus Films
Al-Moulid: Arab Film Distribution

ON RITUAL PRAYER

Nasser Hiballah, on "Religion 8" Web site

ON SUFISM

Dervishes Lovers of God: Insight Media
I Am Sufi I Am Muslim: Films for the Humanities

ISLAM IN THE UNITED STATES

Islam in America [available from Lindsay Miller (617) 547–1733]

CONTEMPORARY ISLAM

Iran: A Righteous Republic?: Landmark Films
The Singing Shaykh [Shaykh al-Imām]: First Run/Icarus
The Islamic State [Hasan Turabi]: Films for the Humanties and Sciences

An Idealized Syllabus: Introduction to Islam

TOPIC	TITLE	READING (REQ., REC., FILM)
1.	Introduction to the Course	
2.	"Orientalism"; the "West" and the rest	Req: Current journalism (e.g., *The Economist*, "Are Islam and Democracy Compatible?"); Rec: Excerpts from Leon Uris, *The Haj*;[47] Mawdudi: Purdah (excerpts)[48] Video: "Muslims in Film" (personal)
3.	The Matrix: The Quran	Req: Readings from Arberry, *The Koran Interpreted*[49] Rec: Angelika Neuwirth: "Images and Metaphors"[50] Norman Brown, "The Apocalypse of Islam"[51]
4.	The Matrix: The Quran-bearer: Muhammad Amīn	Req: Readings from *The Sirah* of Ibn Hishām[52] Rec: F. E. Peters: "The Quest of the Historical Muḥammad"[53]
5.	The Matrix: Ritual	Ibn al-Naqīb, *Reliance of the Traveler*,[54] Sections I & J; Sections E & F
6.	The Matrix: "Vernacular Islam"	Video: "For Those Who Sail to Heaven"[55]
7.	The Matrix: Dissent: Commanding the Good and Forbidding the Reprehensible	Req: The Hadith of Ghadīr Kumm (Designation of 'Ali as Imam)[56] Shaykh al-Mufīd: "The Commander of the Faithful," and "The Passion of al-Ḥusayn (Excerpts)" Sermon of Abū Hamza al-Kharijī[57]
8.	First Elaboration: Scholarship; Quran-commentary	Readings from Ayoub, *The Qu'ran and Its Interpreters*.[58]
9.	First Elaboration: Sirah, Sunnah, and hadith	The 40 Traditions of al-Nawawī
10.	First Elaboration: Pietism and Rigor	Al-Ḥasan al-Baṣrī (so-called) "Epistle on Sufism"
11.	Second Elaboration: Shari'ah and fiqh	Reinhart, "Islamic Law as Islamic Ethics"[59] Ibn al-Naqīb, *Reliance of the Traveler*, Sections A–C Quran 4:1–44/45; 4:82/83 (legal sections); "al-Jarsīfī on the Ḥisbah"[60]
12.	Second Elaboration: Shi'ism: Drama and Certainty	Imāmī Creeds "The Twelfth Imam" *What Delivers From Error*: Sections 1–10[61]
13.	Second Elaboration: *Taṣawwuf*: Origins and History	*What Delivers From Error*: Sections 11–13 Quran 2:28/ 231; 7:171; 89:27 (little bits important for Sufis) Some Sufi biographies, including Rabī'ah (the woman who loved God), Ibrāhīm b. Adham (a sort of Islamic Buddha), Abū Yazīd al-Bisṭāmī (the ecstatic), and al-Ḥallāj[62]

TOPIC	TITLE	READING (REQ., REC., FILM)
14.	*Taṣawwuf:* Perfect Man and Saints	Suhrawardī "Stories"[63] Chittick/Ibn 'Arabī, "Summary of the Fuṣūṣ"[64]
15.	*Taṣawwuf:* the *khanaqah*	Ernst, "The Sufi Orders: Mastery, Discipleship, and Initiation" "The Names of God, Meditation, and Mystical Experience"[65]
16.	*Taṣawwuf:* Rituals	
17.	Second Elaboration: Medieval Reformism; the Ḥanbalīs	Req: Readings from *Talbīs Iblīs* of Ibn al-Jawzī;[66] G. Makdisi, "Hanbalite Islam"[67] "On the Virtues of Aḥmad b. Ḥanbal"[68]
18.	Third Elaboration: Muslim Reformism	Excerpts from "The Surest Path"[69]
19.	Third Elaboration: Nationalism as Counter-Islam	Shakib Arslan "Our Decline and Its Causes" Said Nursi "[Quran Commentary on Nationalism and Islam]"[70]
20.	Third Elaboration: Islamic Modernism	Readings from Sayyid Aḥmad Khan[71]
21.	Third Elaboration: Reappropriating the world; Islamicizing finance, management, and the sciences	Readings from the anthology *Islamic Law and Finance*[72]
22.	Third Elaboration: Islamism	Readings from Sayyid Quṭb[73]

Recommended readings as your interests take you, in M. G. S. Hodgson, *The Venture of Islam;* Ira M. Lapidus, *A History of Islamic Societies* (Cambridge: Cambridge University Press, 1988).

NOTES

1. Since the essay is about my course, this pronoun has been used throughout. For the same reason, the first person singular pronoun is all too present.

2. Dartmouth terms can vary in length, so that there are eight and a half weeks or 10 weeks. It is also possible to arrange a course from one meeting per week, to five.

3. A separate course, "Modern Islam," focuses more heavily on the period between the eighteenth century and the present.

4. Though the increasing number of Muslim students in our classrooms means that one can encounter Muslims whose zeal, and lack of self-consciousness and historical awareness, are a match for any Christian fundamentalist.

5. Marshall G. S. Hodgson, *The Venture of Islam,* 3 vols. (Chicago: University of Chicago Press, 1974), 1:3–69; especially pp. 56–60.

6. It is perhaps uncharitable to wonder if the blurring of categories is not encouraged by beleaguered scholars of things Islamic, Islamicate, and Middle Eastern so as to enhance a perceived range of their expertise. People with training in history and Near Eastern languages are regularly hired to teach in Religion departments, and pro-

gram offerings by religionists regularly must make do for offerings in History, Anthropology, and even Art History.

7. Both Hodgson, *Venture*, vol. 2, and Lapidus, *A History of Islamic Societies* (Cambridge: Cambridge University Press, 1988) cover this period in the depth it deserves. Both show how vibrant and creative Islamic religion was in this period.

8. Again, Hodgson's discussion of Shi'ism (passim) is very valuable here. See also sources cited below at note 31.

9. Imagine an Introduction to Judaism taught by a non-Jew that was designed as a critique of Judaism! Yet such courses are common in the teaching of Islam.

10. Norman Daniel, *Islam and the West: The Making of an Image* (Edinburgh: University Press, 1960); Norman Daniel, *Islam, Europe and Empire* (Edinburgh, Edinburgh University Press, 1966).

11. Jean Jacques Waardenburg, *L'Islam dans le miroir de l'Occident; comment quelques orientalistes occidentaux se sont penchés sur l'Islam et se sont formé une image de cette religion: I. Goldziher, C. Snouck Hurgronje, C. H. Becker, D. B. Macdonald, Louis Massignon*, [2.] ed. (Paris: Mouton, 1963).

12. Bernard Lewis, *New York Review of Books*, June 24, 1982; *New York Review of Books*, August 12, 1982.

13. Edward Said, "Orientalism Reconsidered," *Cultural Critique*, Fall 1985, pp. 89–107.

14. Dennis Grafflin, "Orientalism's Attack on *Orientalism*," *Bulletin of Concerned Asian Scholars* 15/3 (July/Aug 1983): 68–71.

15. Jonathan Kellerman, *The Butcher's Theater* (New York: Bantam Books, 1988). Leon Uris, *The Haj* (Garden City N.Y.: Doubleday, 1984).

16. S. Abul A'la Maududi, *Purdah and the Status of Woman in Islam*, trans. al-Ash'ari (sic) (Lahore: Islamic Publications, 1972 [1939]).

17. Usamah b. Munqidh (tr. Philip Khuri Hitti), *Usamah's memoirs entitled Kitab al-itibar* (Princeton: Princeton University Press, 1930).

18. This thinning out was adumbrated throughout Islamic history by populist figures like Aḥmad b. Ḥanbal, Ibn al-Jawzī, Ibn Taymiyyah, Ibn 'Abdalwahhāb, and consequently these are the figures in Islamic history seen as most relevant by contemporary Islamists.

19. Michael Sells, "Sound, Spirit, and Gender in Surat al-Qadr," *Journal of the American Oriental Society* 111 (Apr./June 1991): 239–59.

20. Angelika Neuwirth, "Images and Metaphors in the Introductory Sections of the Makkan suras," in *Approaches to the Qur'ān*, ed. G. R. Hawting and Abdul-Kader A. Shareef (London: Routledge, 1993), 3–36.

21. A. J. Arberry, trans., *The Koran Interpreted* (New York: Macmillan, 1955).

22. Norman O. Brown, "The Apocalypse of Islam," in *Apocalypse and/or Metamorphosis*, (Berkeley: University of California Press, 1991), 69–94.

23. Abd al-Malik Ibn Hisham, Muhammad Ibn Ishaq (tr. Alfred Guillaume), *The Life*

of Muhammad: A Translation [from Ibn Hisham's adaptation] of Ibn Ishaq's Sirat Rasul Allah (Karachi: Oxford University Press, 1967).

24. Patricia Crone and M. A. Cook, *Hagarism: The Making of the Islamic World* (Cambridge: Cambridge University Press, 1977).

25. John E. Wansbrough, *Quranic Studies: Sources and Methods of Scriptural Interpretation,* London Oriental Series, vol. 31 (Oxford: Oxford University Press, 1977) and John E. Wansbrough, *The Sectarian Milieu: Content and Composition of Islamic Salvation History,* London Oriental Series, vol. 34 (Oxford: Oxford University Press, 1978).

26. F. E. Peters, "The Quest of the Historical Muhammad," *International Journal of Middle East Studies* 23 (Aug. 1991): 291–315.

27. R. B. Serjeant, "The Sunnah Jami'ah pacts with the Yathrib Jews and the Tahrim of Yathrib: Analysis and Translation of the Documents Comprised in the so-called 'Constitution of Medina'," *Bulletin of the School of Oriental and African Studies* 41 (1978): 1–42.; W. Montgomery Watt, *Muhammad at Mecca* (Oxford: Clarendon Press, 1960), 192; W. Montgomery Watt, *Muhammad at Medina* (Oxford: Clarendon Press, 1966), 418; Jacqueline Chabbi, *Le seigneur des tribus: l'islam de Mahomet* (Paris: Noesis, 1997).

28. I am finishing a book, *Vernacular Islam: Diversity and Unity in a Cosmopolitan Tradition,* describing the interaction of the "vernacular" and the "standard" Islam. This lecture is a version of the theoretical argument in the book.

29. See below for media resources for teaching the practice of ritual prayer.

30. Readers should now note the very important work of Michael Cook, *Commanding Right and Forbidding Wrong in Islamic Thought* (Cambridge: Cambridge University Press, 2000).

31. Shaykh al-Mufīd [Muḥammad b. Muḥammad b. Nu'mān al-Baghdādī al-Karkhī (d. 413/1022)], *Kitāb al-Irshād; The Book of Guidance,* trans. I. K. A. Howard (Elmhurst, N.Y.: Tahrike Tarsile Qur'an, 1981), part I; and part II, chapter 2. See also Mahmoud Ayoub, *Redemptive Suffering in Islam: A Study of the Devotional Aspects of 'Ashura in Twelver Shi'ism* (The Hague: Mouton, 1978).

32. W. Montgomery Watt, *Islam and the Integration of Society* (Evanston: Northwestern University Press, 1961).

33. Norman Calder, *Studies in Early Muslim Jurisprudence* (Oxford: Clarendon Press, 1993), chapter 8, "The Origin of Norms," is good on this, especially pp. 198–201.

34. Wansbrough, *Quranic Studies;* John Burton, *The Collection of the Quran* (Cambridge: Cambridge University Press, 1977) .

35. Herbert Berg's book *The Development of Exegesis in Early Islam: The Authenticity of Muslim Literature from the Formative Period* (Richmond: Curzon, 2000) has as its introduction a first-rate summary of these disputes. This section is the standard reserve-reading. The controversy can be traced through the following: Ignaz Goldziher, *Muslim Studies* (Chicago: Aldine, 1967); Nabia Abbott, *Studies in Arabic Literary Papyri* (Chicago: University of Chicago Press, 1957), especially vol. 2; Fuat Sezgin, *Geschichte des arabischen Schrifttums* (Leiden: E.J. Brill, 1967), vol. 1, introduction to the section on

hadith; G. H. A. Juynboll, *Muslim Tradition: Studies in Chronology, Provenance, and Authorship of Early Hadith,* Cambridge studies in Islamic civilization (Cambridge: Cambridge University Press, 1983); G. H. A. Juynboll, *Studies on the Origins and Uses of Islamic Hadith* (Brookfield, Vt.: Variorum, 1996), vol. 1 (various pagings); Harald Motzki, "Quo vadis, ḥadīt-Forschung? Eine kritische Untersuchung von G. H. A. Juynboll: 'Nāfiʿ the mawlā of Ibn ʿUmar, and his position in Muslim ḥadīth Literature' [*Der Islam* (1993): 207–244]," *Der Islam* 73 (1996): 40–80; 193–231; Calder, *Studies.*

36. G. H. A. Juynboll, "Some *Isnād-*Analytical Methods Illustrated on the Basis of Several Woman-Demeaning Sayings from ḥadīth Literature," *al-Qantara; revista de estudios Árabes* 10/2 (1989): 343–384.

37. The survey section in Calder, *Studies,* is a useful read here. See especially chapter 7, "Literary Form and Social Context."

38. See "Do-It-Yourself Fiqh," p. 37, this volume.

39. Abu Hamid Muhammad Ghazali, *Freedom and Fulfillment: An Annotated Translation of al-Ghazali's al-Munqidh min al-dalal and Other Relevant Works of al-Ghazali,* tr. Richard Joseph McCarthy. (Boston: Twayne Publishers, 1980). See section on "taʿlīmism," pp. 81ff.

40. Louis Massignon (1883–1962), *Essay on the Origins of the Technical Language of Islamic Mysticism* (Notre Dame, Ind.: University of Notre Dame Press, 1997).

41. Annemarie Schimmel, *And Muhammad Is His Messenger: The Veneration of the Prophet in Islamic Piety* (Chapel Hill: University of North Carolina Press, 1985).

42. Ibn al-Jawzī, *Talbīs Iblīs* (not complete) (trans. as "The Devil's Delusion" by D. Margoliouth, M. Asad, et al.), *Islamic Culture* (each issue between 1935–1948).

43. Taqīaddīn Aḥmad Ibn Taymiyyah, *Ibn Taimīya's Struggle Against Popular Religion;* with an annnotated translation of his Kitāb iqtiḍā aṣ-ṣirāṭ al-mustaqīm mukhālafat aṣḥāb al-jaḥīm (tr. Muhammad Umar Memon) (The Hague: Mouton, 1976).

44. *Liberal Islam: A Sourcebook,* ed. Charles Kurzman (New York: Oxford University Press, 1998).

45. E. M. Wherry, *A Comprehensive Commentary on the Quran: Comprising Sale's Translation and Preliminary Discourse* (New York: AMS Press, 1975 [1896]); ʿAbd Allah b. ʿUmar al-Baydawi, *Baidawi's Commentary on Surah 12 of the Qur'an* (Oxford: Clarendon Press, 1963); Tabari, *The Commentary on the Qur'an,* trans. J. Cooper (London: Oxford University Press, 1987); Mahmoud Ayoub, *The Qur'an and its Interpreters* (Albany: State University of New York Press, 1984).

46. *Islamic Legal Interpretation: Muftis and their Fatwas,* ed. Muhammad Khalid Masud, Brinkley Messick and David S. Powers (Cambridge, Mass.: Harvard University Press, 1996).

47. Uris, *The Haj.*

48. S. Abul Aʿla Maududi, *Purdah and the Status of Woman in Islam* (Lahore, Pakistan: Islamic Publications, 1972).

49. *The Koran Interpreted,* trans. Arberry.

50. Neuwirth, "Images and Metaphors in the Introductory Sections of the Makkan sūrahs."

51. Brown, "The Apocalypse of Islam."

52. Ibn Hisham, *The Life of Muhammad* (London: Oxford University Press, 1955).

53. F. E. Peters, "The Quest of the Historical Muhammad," *International Journal of Middle East Studies* 23 (1991): 291–315.

54. Ibn al-Naqib, *The Reliance of the Traveller: A Classic Manual of Islamic Sacred Law*, trans. N. Keller (Evanston, Ill.: Sunna Books, 1991).

55. First Run/Icarus Films.

56. From Muhammad b. Muhammad Mufid, *The Book of Guidance into the Lives of the Twelve Imams: Kitab al-Irshad.*

57. From John Alden Williams, *The Word of Islam* (Austin: University of Texas Press, 1994). An excellent anthology; if I hadn't already assembled my own, this is the anthology I would use.

58. M. Ayoub, *The Qur'an and Its Interpreters* (Albany: State University of New York Press, 1984).

59. A. Kevin Reinhart, "Islamic Law as Islamic Ethics," *Journal of Religious Ethics* 11/2 (Fall 1983): 186–203.

60. G. M. Wickens, "al-Jarsifi on the Hisba," *Islamic Quarterly* 3 (1956–7): 176–187.

61. Ghazali, *Freedom and Fulfillment: An Annotated Translation of Al-Ghazali's al-Munqidh min al dalal and Other Relevant Works of al-Ghazali*, trans. Richard Joseph McCarthy (Boston: Twayne Publishers, 1980).

62. Farid al-Din Attar, *Muslim Saints and Mystics: Episodes from the Tadhkirat al-auliya' ("Memorial of the saints")*, trans. A. J. Arberry (Chicago: University of Chicago Press [1966]).

63. Shihabuddin Yahya Suhrawardi, *The Mystical and Visionary Treatises of Shihabuddin Yahya Suhrawardi*, trans. Wheeler Thackston (London: Octagon Press, 1981).

64. Ibn 'Arabī, "Ibn 'Arabī's Own Summary of the Fuṣūṣ: The Imprints of the Bezels of Wisdom," *Sophia Perennis* 1 ii (1975): 88–128; 2 ii (1976): 67–106.

65. From Carl W. Ernst, *The Shambhala Guide to Sufism* (Boston: Shambhala Publications, 1997).

66. Ibn al-Jawzī, "The Devil's Delusion," trans. D. Margoliouth [and Muḥammad Asad]. *Islamic Culture* (1935–48).

67. G. Makdisi, "Hanbalite Islam," in *Studies on Islam,* ed. M. Swartz (New York: Oxford University Press, 1981), 216–74.

68. Trans. by Michael Cooperson.

69. Khayr al-Din Tunisi, *The Surest Path; the Political Treatise of a Nineteenth-Century Muslim Statesman* (Cambridge: Distributed for the Center for Middle Eastern Studies of Harvard University by Harvard University Press, 1967).

70. Both from Kemal Karpat, ed., *Political and Social Thought in the Contemporary Middle East* (New York: Praeger, 1982).

71. Christian W. Troll, *Sayyid Ahmad Khan: A Reinterpretation of Muslim Theology* (New Delhi: Vikas Publ. House, 1978).

72. Frank E. Vogel, ed., *Islamic Law and Finance: Religion, Risk, and Return* (The Hague: Kluwer Law International, 1998).

73. Sayyid Qutb, *Social Justice in Islam* (London: Amana Books, 1993). It is regretable that William Shepard's translation is not available in an affordable edition from Brill.

CHAPTER THREE

Recent Critical Scholarship and the Teaching of Islam

KEITH LEWINSTEIN

A s ISLAM HAS BECOME A LARGER PRESENCE in Religious Studies departments, the resources for teaching it have likewise expanded. We now have undergraduate textbooks and anthologies which were unavailable to our own teachers, and this simplifies matters considerably both for specialists and the many nonspecialists who offer survey courses in the Islamic religious tradition. At least for those who take a historical approach to the tradition, the material has been neatly arranged in any number of textbooks published in the last fifteen years, reflecting a growing consensus about what an introductory course taught in a Religious Studies department should look like. Leafing through these books, one suspects that despite the increased attention they pay to popular practices and postclassical Islam, it is still early Islamic thought and piety which are expected to serve as the basis for such courses. If this requires justification beyond the fact that origins are intrinsically interesting to many of us, it can be found in the importance which the Muslim tradition itself attaches to the earliest period. The personalities and events of formative Islam have always been central to Muslim identity and thought; even in the late twentieth century, Muslim thinkers continue to express their political and social views through particular interpretations of early Islam.

Given the importance of the early period, it is unfortunate that it is precisely there that the parameters of acceptable discussion are narrowest and most out of line with developments in other fields. Many of our colleagues in Religious Studies (and the more experienced among our students) are likely to be struck by the reluctance of our textbooks to confront issues commonly met elsewhere in the discipline. Fundamental problems concerning the emergence of a scriptural canon and the crystallization of a communal identity are not in most textbooks and courses on Islam, given the attention they receive in analogous fields. As such, students who have done work in Biblical Studies, earliest Christianity, or early rabbinic Judaism can be forgiven for concluding that the text-critical questions central to these fields are not relevant to formative Islam. The result is a widespread assumption within Religious Studies that Islam is the one monotheism whose origins are clearly visible to the modern historian.

If most of our textbooks give this impression, it is because they accurately reflect the state of Orientalist scholarship as it has built up over the past century and a half. While close textual study is a hallmark of this work, it has for the most part been accomplished within the historical framework set by the Muslim tradition. Western philological and historical analysis of texts has not altered the basic facts which the tradition itself insists on. Nearly all scholars take for granted that Muhammad and his followers moved from Mecca to Medina in 622 C.E., and that this was Islam's prototypical emigration [ḥijrah]; that Muhammad's followers in Arabia considered themselves "Muslims" (distinct from Jews and Christians); that these Muslims were in possession of a scripture revealed in pieces over the course of Muhammad's career, and which would be collected and canonized within two decades of Muhammad's death in 632; and that the moral center of the movement was from Muhammad's day the traditional Arab sanctuary at Mecca. In short, both the Muslim and Orientalist traditions agree that Islam was made in Arabia and emerged chiefly out of a contest between Muhammad's monotheist teachings and traditional Arab paganism. However Islam may have evolved in the centuries following Muhammad's death, the fundamental issues of religious practice and identity are widely assumed to have been in place before the Arab conquests of the Near East.[1]

Although a few so-called revisionist scholars have sought to question these assumptions, their work has neither reached a wide audience within the field nor become part of the stock-in-trade transmitted to our students and shared with our colleagues in Religious Studies.[2] When mentioned at all, such scholarship is often dismissed as extremist and out of keeping with the irenic outlook preferred by many American Islamicists.[3] As a result, advances in the critical study of early Islam have not had much of an impact on what we offer our undergraduates or colleagues in other areas of Religious Studies. This is the problem I would like to address here, in the belief that we benefit as a field by exposing our students and colleagues to the sort of critical thinking taken for granted elsewhere in the discipline. I do not, of course, mean to suggest that there is only one correct line to take in teaching Islam, or that our courses ought to include whatever the latest academic heresies might be. I want simply to point to some alternative directions of thought, not normally integrated into the textbook canon, but which might profitably be communicated to our students. After offering some (necessarily) general remarks on certain key points raised by this scholarship, I shall discuss a few of the ways in which I have tried to integrate these questions into my own introductory course.[4]

The scholarship under discussion here is frequently called "revisionist," at least by those who find it objectionable. The term often serves as a *nomen odiosum* applied to those who challenge the traditional account of Islamic origins. As such it lumps together and dismisses scholars whose assumptions, methods, and conclusions might, in fact, be widely different. Despite some discomfort with the label, and with the idea that one can point to a single "revisionist" sect, I shall myself have to do some lumping together and rough generalization in the course of this essay. If this does some injustice to the complexity of the situation, it at least permits us to speak in general terms of a new critical orientation within Islamic Studies. And it is not too much to suggest that all of this scholarship shares two fundamental premises: a deep skepticism about the historicity of the Muslim sources, and a conviction that the traditional view of Arabia's role in Islamic origins ought to be reexamined.[5]

Western scholars have conventionally based their accounts of Muhammad and the rise of Islam on two types of Muslim literary sources: scripture (Quran) and the narrative accounts (the biography [sīrah] of Muhammad), treating the earliest history of the Muslim community. The sirah offers a narrative of Muhammad's life, much as the gospels do for Jesus. It is composed largely of anecdotal material arranged, at a secondary stage, into a roughly chronological framework. The form in which we have it dates, at the earliest, to the middle of the eighth century; that is, a century-and-a-half after the traditional date given for Muhammad's death. The chief sirah texts we have are nevertheless widely believed to preserve faithfully earlier material which goes back to Muhammad's own day or not long afterward. The Quran is different in every way. For one thing, it is believed by Muslims to have assumed its present shape within only 25 years of the Prophet's death; that is, before the center of Muslim power had shifted from Arabia to the more established areas of high civilization in the Near East. The tradition presents it as a purely "Arabian" text. Unlike the sirah texts, the Quran is not formally a historical narrative, but rather a collection of generalized sermons held to have been delivered (revealed) over the course of the Prophet's career. These sermons make little direct reference to the names, places, and events of Muhammad's time. As the Quran is assumed to be contemporary with the Prophet, traditional Orientalists have tried to exploit it both as a means of independently controlling the data in the sirah texts and as a source of information in its own right.[6]

Islamicists, then, have available to them a wealth of sources which their colleagues in search of the historical Jesus could only envy. Islam, unlike Christianity, is sometimes said to have been born "in the full light of history," as Renan famously observed.[7] But critics have begun to question just how bright that light actually is. While few if any question Muhammad's actual existence, most critical scholars remain unconvinced that the historical Muhammad is to be found in this material and have lately raised fundamental questions about its origins and historicity. The role of storytellers and popular preachers in producing the sirah texts generations after Muhammad has been increasingly emphasized, and scholars have noted that some of the sirah materials seem to have been produced not independently of the Quran, but in exegetical elaboration of it. Scriptural and sirah texts may not after all offer two independent witnesses to the "facts" of Muhammad's career.[8] Furthermore, "revisionists" have generally taken a skeptical view of the traditional dating of the Quran and have proposed a more extended period of time before the text achieved its canonical status as the exclusive Muslim scripture.[9] If this was, in fact, the case, it becomes even more difficult to associate the Quran directly and exclusively with Muhammad's career.

Such thinking has been inspired directly or indirectly by the work of John Wansbrough. It was his critical insights, eventually published as *Quranic Studies* (Oxford University Press, 1977) and *The Sectarian Milieu: Content and Composition of Islamic Salvation History* (Oxford University Press, 1978), that initially helped create a small community of "revisionist" scholars, chiefly in Britain, who have since taken the implications of his work in various directions. If they have failed to win many adherents, part of the blame doubtless lies with Wansbrough's writing style: his prose is famously turgid, overloaded with technical terms in several different languages and alphabets, and his reasoning is often opaque, even to many attentive, specialist readers. As one reviewer put it at the time, "Here is Anglo-Saxon revenge with a vengeance for every dense and massive tome of Germanic erudition ever published."[10] Both of these books ironically exhibit that same "Deutungsbedürftigkeit," that same inherent need for exegesis, that Wansbrough attributes to the Quran. It is to be hoped that his thinking will gain a wider audience from the recent efforts of several scholars to provide readable commentary.[11]

His prose aside, it is really Wansbrough's radical hypotheses about the origins of Islam that have led so many to dismiss his work out of hand. These hypotheses derive from (and in turn help shape) his skeptical approach to the Arabic source materials. For Wansbrough, Islamic history begins only in the late eighth century, the point at which a canonized scripture, a doctrine of prophetology, and a sacred language can be securely attested. The Arabic Muslim texts, which assume that all three existed from the early seventh century, cannot serve as evidence for anything occurring before the date of their final redaction, which he estimates to be 800 C.E. Even if these texts do (as they claim) preserve older materials, such materials are unlikely to have survived intact the vicissitudes of transmission. Explanatory glosses, expansion and excision, and other textual corruptions make it difficult if not impossible for historians using these sources to see clearly before 800. But beyond these technical problems, scholars confront an obstacle of another sort: what we have in the sirah texts, according to Wansbrough, is less history in the modern sense of the word than a "salvation history" designed to legitimate a new Muslim faith and communal identity. This *"Heilsgeschichte,"* he implies, was constructed by the religious scholars of Iraq almost two centuries after the events they purport to describe. It may tell us what Muslims had by that time come to believe about their prophet, but it does not form an archive from which we can reconstruct what really happened during the first two Islamic centuries. The Muslim account of Islamic origins is, in fact, a theological statement about God's guidance of Muhammad and his community; it is part and parcel of the faith and ought to be analyzed in those terms rather than taken simply as a tendentious but basically accurate account of the rise of Islam.

For Wansbrough and his followers, Islam as a distinct religion, with its own literature and ritual, did not crystallize before 800. There is, according to them, no distinctly Muslim theological or legal writing from before that time; even the received text of the Quran cannot be said to have acquired its final form and canonical authority much before 800. If Quranic material existed in the previous two centuries, it was only in the form of bodies of "prophetical *logia*," themselves born of various cultic and polemical practices in the Near East. In analyzing the text from a literary and form-critical standpoint, Wansbrough has argued that the Quran is likely to be a composite document containing various collections of prophetical sayings, stitched together into a single work only after being transmitted orally for an extended period of time while used liturgically by various proto-Muslim communities in the Near East. In Wansbrough's account, the Quran was not produced in pagan Arabia, but rather, emerged out of a sectarian monotheist milieu in the Near East. The same goes for Islam itself, which he sees as entirely a product of the diverse religious world of eighth-century Iraq.

What all this suggests is that the traditional account of Islamic origins is in need of revision. Rather than a tale of epic conquest followed by the diffusion of an Arab religion throughout the Near East, we instead have a new religion and scripture distilled from a world of sectarian monotheist polemic in Iraq and put to use to legitimate an Arab political domination throughout the area. In other words, Islam grew organically out of the religious world of late antique Mesopotamia; it was not a new religious departure brought to the Near

East from pagan Arabia. Islam's Arabian origins are on this reading little more than a foundation myth, a literary back-projection which served to distinguish Islam from its monotheist competitors. The basic elements of Muslim identity (Arab prophet, scripture, and sanctuary) were not carried out of the Hijaz by tribal conquerors, but were instead acquired later, lending an Arabian veneer to what was essentially a Near Eastern religious development. Remote and distant, seventh-century Arabia served to legitimate a religious and political identity emerging elsewhere.

Wansbrough's followers would concede that much of this is speculative and intended more as a working hypothesis than as a set of final conclusions. Still, Wansbrough's literary analysis of the texts and some of his claims about Islam's formation can be quite compelling: the notion that Islam (like rabbinic Judaism and Christianity) emerged as yet another refinement of the monotheist tradition (rather than as a direct break with paganism) is extremely attractive and pedagogically useful in a Religious Studies classroom; it also seems likely that the Quran's final form and exclusive canonical authority did emerge later than the traditional account allows.[12] But at the same time, Wansbrough's dating of canonical scripture and community to as late as 800 is untenable. The process cannot have taken 200 years. Wansbrough's theory is undermined by evidence which he and many followers either do not seriously consider (e.g., theological epistles likely to date from the early to mid-eighth century and which are clearly post-Quranic)[13] or do not consider at all (e.g., material evidence identifying Muhammad as "Messenger of God" as early as the 680s). Furthermore, without at least some germ of an ethno-religious identity in place during the early seventh century, it is hard to imagine how the Arab conquests of the Near East could have occurred, or how the Arabs themselves could have escaped rapid assimilation into the dominant cultures of the conquered territories.[14]

These and other problems were taken up by P. Crone and M. Cook in *Hagarism* (Cambridge University Press, 1977). This represents a very different line of critical thinking, even if its skeptical approach to the Muslim tradition was inspired by Wansbrough, and even if many critics of "revisionist" scholarship do not see much light between them.[15] In this work, Crone and Cook dispense entirely with the Muslim tradition and instead seek to reconstruct early Islamic history on the basis of a few non-Arabic sources closer in time than their Muslim counterparts to the events they describe, and not subject to the same biases. The resulting picture of the rise of Islam is completely inconsistent with the standard one. Here, the conquerors emerge from a Jewish messianic context, their eyes set on Jerusalem. It was only in the latter decades of the seventh century (and not in Arabia itself) that the conquerors began to dissociate from this Jewish messianism by equipping themselves with their own scripture, their own prophet on the Mosaic model (complete with Exodus and Sinai), and an Arabian sanctuary.[16] According to the authors, certain features of Samaritan Judaism provided the conquerors with an important model in constructing their own identity, and a large share of the weight was initially carried by the Umayyad Caliphs of Syria.

For all its powerful argument, *Hagarism* is best seen as an experiment which points up the problems of working entirely within the traditional paradigm, as well as the value of using sources external to the Muslim tradition. In method, it has the great advantage of outflanking the Muslim tradition's own biases and allowing us to view the rise of Islam with fresh eyes. But the approach is not without its drawbacks, chief among them being the polemical biases and problematic dating of these non-Muslim sources.[17] Whatever the many intellectual merits of the argument for historians, the book is less a reading of the Muslim tradition than a displacement of it (or rather, its reading of the tradition is very much implicit); apart from the Jewish messianism argument of the first part of the book, those teaching "Introduction to Islam" courses will not find much to work with here.[18]

In the Classroom

Does any of this belong in the classroom? Does it make pedagogical sense to offer our undergraduates a revised version of a story which they are only just beginning to learn? And if it does, how, practically speaking, can such material be incorporated into an introductory class?

Most of us would agree about the answers to the first two of these questions: of course, alternative hypotheses (if serious) belong in the classroom, and of course, our students are capable of keeping more than one possible interpretation in their heads. But at the same time, this kind of material is obviously sensitive to many students. It goes right to the most basic teachings and practices of Muslims, and certain students (both Muslim and non-Muslim) are liable to find it objectionable for just that reason. The first challenge for the teacher, I think, is to render the material less toxic by placing it in the context of variant Muslim and Western interpretations. The second is to find a practical way of incorporating it so that it becomes an integral part of the course rather than a mere curiosity, easily dismissed by students.

One approach that has worked for me is to structure the entire course around the problem of constructing and interpreting the Islamic tradition. While the syllabus is organized topically (Muhammad and the Quran, ritual, law, sects, etc.), I alert my students at the outset that lectures and discussion will explicitly treat each topic from a number of different interpretive angles.

Along with the syllabus, I distribute what will be the principal essay question on the final exam: students must teach (on paper) a number of the course topics from a variety of perspectives (e.g., traditional Muslim, modernizing Muslim, orthodox and/or "revisionist" Western scholar, in some cases as a Sufi shaykh or a Shiʻi). The risk here, of course, is that Islam may dissolve into nothing more than a set of contested interpretations, without any positive content for students to grab hold of. In my experience, though, the result is that students simply become more alive to how a religious tradition explains itself at different stages, and how scholarship might variously be able to interpret those explanations. By the end of term, students are less likely to ask such questions as "What does Islam say about X or Y?"; instead, their thinking is focused on the different ways a tradition might have handled such a problem, and in some cases on possible continuity between Muslim and other monotheist solutions.

Just about any feature of Islam (law, theology, sectarianism) can fruitfully be analyzed against a wider monotheist background. Here, I would like to indicate briefly how two particular subjects, scripture and ritual practice, might be presented along these lines.

Our textbooks typically set the origins of both the Quran and Muslim ritual against an Arabian backdrop. The Quran is said to represent a sudden explosion of monotheist polemic directed at contemporary pagans, perhaps drawn, in part, from monotheist teachings which had begun to appear in Arabia. Many basic practices and rituals, for their part, are said to have arisen as modifications of living pagan customs. The swearing of oaths and vows, inheritance regulations, and certain features of Islamic marriage law, to take just a few examples, are commonly presented as Muslim modifications of traditional Arab law. The Muslim pilgrimage is typically characterized as an adoption of several pre-Islamic Arab rituals. Muslims themselves understand these to have been Abrahamic (monotheist) in origin; as the Arab descendants of Ishmael fell into paganism, they continued to maintain these ancient rituals in a corrupt form until Muhammad and his followers eventually restored their proper monotheist character. Conventional Western scholars naturally dismiss the Abrahamic pedigree of the pilgrimage, but also insist that Arab Muslims directly adopted the rituals from their pagan predecessors.

Both the Muslim tradition and orthodox Western scholars, then, take the Quran and basic rituals such as the pilgrimage to have been fixed by Muhammad's death or shortly thereafter. Muslims, in other words, brought their own scripture and their own sanctuary rituals out of Arabia, uncontaminated by the religious culture of the late antique Near East.

Other explanations are available, although students generally do not find them in their textbooks. Large chunks of the Quran can be analyzed against a monotheist, rather than a primarily pagan, backdrop. Much of the text can be read as a response to a world of monotheist polemic, with the Quran serving almost as a kind of Arabic midrash on earlier monotheist scripture. Wansbrough's analysis of the Quran's formal and thematic content very much points in that direction. He identifies several Quranic motifs drawn from the traditional stock of monotheist imagery and conveyed through the rhetorical conventions of Near Eastern monotheism. These motifs (divine retribution, sign, exile, and covenant) can be said to express the basis of the Quranic message and are apparent throughout the text.[19] I have found it a worthwhile exercise to have students go through pieces of the Quran and identify these four motifs, paying special attention to the language and imagery surrounding them and discussing how they promote the book's monotheist agenda. At the very least, students become more attuned to the dominating presence of literary stereotypes and formulaic language in the Quran and perhaps gain a better sense of how this might serve to generate meaning for its audience.

Approaching the text from the beginning with literary questions in mind, students quickly see for themselves the Quran's fragmented and referential quality. (This is an undeniable feature of the text; Wansbrough's analysis of it is extremely useful, even if one disagrees with the conclusions he puts on it.) Almost any passage from the Quran might be used in the classroom to illustrate the text's referential (rather than expository) style. The accounts of Moses and other biblical figures require a biblical or midrashic context to be understood. Even the Joseph story (Surah 12), the most coherent piece of biblical narrative in the Quran, is essentially a skeleton which takes for granted audience familiarity with biblical or extrabiblical versions of the story. For example, the apparently obscure reference to another brother of Joseph at Q 12:59 presupposes a knowledge of Genesis 42:3–13 (or a Jewish interpretation [midrash] thereto), where Benjamin does not accompany his brothers into Egypt; the reference at Q 12:31 to women cutting their hands at a banquet makes sense only in light of a Jewish midrash, in which the women are so astounded at Joseph's beauty that they accidentally cut themselves.[20] Such examples are easily multiplied, particularly in passages concerning Moses and Abraham. In connection with the Abrahamic sacrifice, for example, the Quran's portrayal of the son as a willing victim (Q 37:101–109) manifestly reflects what the Jewish and Christian exegetical traditions had already done with the biblical narrative.[21]

If none of this actually requires our students to conclude that the Quran was born somewhere other than pagan Arabia, it does at least raise the possibility that large parts of it might have developed substantially once in a monotheist environment. It becomes easier to see the Quran as a reading of the living biblical tradition known among Near Eastern monotheists at the time of the rise of Islam, a reading through which older materials were rendered meaningful to a new monotheist community. If this did indeed take place over several generations, as Wansbrough suggests, with a single (if composite) text emerging only at the end of the process, one can make good sense of many of the Quran's distinctive literary characteristics: namely, its pronounced repetition, redundancy, parallelism, and inconsistent legal content. All are well-known features of the text. But analyzed without granting in advance the tradition's own account of the Quran's origins, these qualities might suggest a composite text hammered together from several independent (or partially independent) traditions, with the final redaction cautiously preserving variants.[22] Whether or not one cares to draw such a conclusion, this is at least the kind of examination students with any experience in Biblical Studies would expect, and it brings the teaching of Islam more into line with parallel subjects.

Something similar can be done with ritual, and here our best guide is the work of G. R. Hawting. What Hawting has tried to suggest in his studies on this subject is that Muslim ritual practices, far from being simple modifications of pagan Arab predecessors, may, in fact, have been produced in a Jewish matrix before being grafted onto Arabia at a later stage. Hawting has developed his argument along two lines. For one thing, he has tried to break the connection between Islam and Arabian paganism by suggesting that the Muslim accounts of the latter (our only real sources), while possibly containing some real information, can be read as stereotypical monotheist polemic against idolatry and polytheism. The Muslim descriptions of Arabian idolatry are decidedly formulaic and preserve (in Hawting's view) less an authentic picture of the pagan past than a typical monotheist construction of it. The Arabic sources owe more to a literary tradition of antipagan polemic than to any authentic memory of pre-Islamic [jāhilī] Arabia. Whatever concrete information the sources contain is presented in a manner typical of Jewish, Christian, and Stoic polemic against idolatry. Many of the examples Hawting adduces may profitably be offered to students alongside selections from the Quran and Ibn al-Kalbi's *Book of Idols,* an exercise which challenges students to consider how "Arabia-specific" our sources really are.[23]

For another thing, Hawting has argued (with particular reference to the Meccan sanctuary) that certain inconsistencies in the Arabic literary sources are difficult to account for if one assumes an early codification of ritual practice. Even the terminology which the Muslim tradition applies to parts of the sanctuary does not quite fit as it would had it developed exclusively in connection with Mecca.[24] A good example of this terminological instability would be the "place" or "standing place of Abraham" [maqām Ibrāhīm]. The term is in classical Islam applied to a stone situated a short distance from the northeast wall of the Ka'bah; during the pilgrimage ritual, Muslims perform two bowings there after completing the circumambulation of the Ka'bah. The Muslim tradition offers several different reasons for the sanctity of the stone, all having to do with the Abrahamic origins of the sanctuary. The Orientalist tradition seeks mainly to uncouple it from monotheist foundation myths and to explain it in the context of Arab paganism: the Muslim practice is a direct descendant of the pagan. Hawting, however, has noted that the term is not consistently used in the Muslim sources to refer to a particular location in the sanctuary: it sometimes seems to refer to the sanctuary as a whole. There is even a passage in the Quran which seems at odds with the classical understanding of the *maqām Ibrāhīm*: "Take for yourselves a place of prayer *from* the *maqām Ibrāhīm*" (2:125), which seems to suggest that the "place of Abraham" was at one time understood to be a larger area, perhaps the entire sanctuary. English translations of the Quran often obscure the problem by omitting the preposition "from" [min],[25] but the early Muslim commentators could not so easily dispense with it. Many of the earliest exegetes quoted in the classical collections apparently understood the term *maqām Ibrāhīm* to refer not to a stone at all, but to Mecca or to the sanctuary as a whole. This lexical instability, Hawting argues, suggests that the phrase arose in another context altogether and was only secondarily attached to the Meccan sanctuary. An origin in Jewish usage is possible, where a *maqōm* [Ar. maqām] is a place where the divine presence can be found. (At Gen 18:22, Abraham is shown to stand before the Lord in the *maqōm*.) For whatever reason, when the term *maqām Ibrāhīm*, having wide monotheist reference, was transferred to the Meccan sanctuary, it came to be understood as designating only a part of that sanctuary. From there it generated its own foundation myths, although the older meaning was never entirely displaced from the Muslim tradition.

Like the antipagan polemic in the Quran and other Muslim sources, the pilgrimage ritual might have been located in Mecca only at a secondary stage in the tradition's development. With further research, similar conclusions might well be drawn about the ritual prayer (we know, for example, that the number of daily prayers was contested even toward the end of the seventh century) and almsgiving. While both undoubtedly were among the earliest Muslim practices, it may be doubted that they achieved their classical form in predominantly pagan Arabia.

Conclusions

Naturally, introductory classroom presentations of the Quran or Muslim ritual cannot focus chiefly on their origins. But since few of us ignore the issue of origins, it makes sense to offer students a wide variety of scholarly opinion on the matter. Introducing them to the basics of modern critical scholarship not only gives our students fresh insight into Islam and Islamic Studies, but it also helps students connect with work they are doing in other Religious Studies courses. While no one would suggest making this perspective fundamental to an introductory course, my own experience tells me that it can be effectively integrated into a broad survey without either cultivating disrespect for the Muslim tradition or intellectually overwhelming our students.

NOTES

1. Where the Orientalist and Islamic traditions differ, of course, is on the question of influence. Believing Muslims insist on the Prophet's originality and the tradition's uniqueness, while even the most empathic of Islamicists, if forced to take a position, would concede at least an indirect Jewish or Christian influence on Muhammad's own teachings.

2. Most of the textbooks in common use make no mention of this scholarship; the notable exceptions are the first volume of A. Rippin's *Muslims: Their Religious Beliefs and Practices* (London: Routledge, 1990) (which is informed throughout by a "revisionist" outlook), and D. Waines's *An Introduction to Islam* (Cambridge: Cambridge University Press, 1995), which is traditional in approach but nevertheless includes a discussion of the modern critical scholarship in its last chapter ("Excursus on Islamic Origins," 265–79). It is telling that even R. Martin's *Islamic Studies: A History of Religions Approach*, 2d ed. (Upper Saddle River, N.J.: Prentice Hall, 1996) has no use for the revisionists, despite the author's methodological sophistication and unique organization of the material. The final chapter of the book, entitled "Whither the Study of Islam," focuses solely on the criticisms leveled at Orientalism by Edward Said and ignores recent critical scholarship altogether.

3. For a discussion of irenic approaches to Islam, see C. Adams, "Islamic Religious Tradition," in *The Study of the Middle East,* ed. L. Binder (New York: Wiley, 1976), 38–41; on the problems presented by such an approach, see the (somewhat intemperate) comments of J. Baldick, "Islam and the Religions of Iran in the *Encyclopedia of Religion*," *Religious Studies* 24 (1988): especially 47–50; as well as A. Rippin, "Literary Analysis of *Qur'ān, Tafsīr,* and *Sīra:* The Methodologies of John Wansbrough," in *Approaches to Islam in Religious Studies,* ed. R. Martin (Tucson: University of Arizona Press, 1985), 159.

4. Because I have had to keep the discussion here at a general level, it will appear largely, though not entirely, uncritical of this scholarship. The reader inclined to be skeptical of this "revisionism" should take heart that when such material is brought into the classroom, many students are both willing and able to raise their own sound objections to it, given at least minimal guidance.

5. In the early to mid-twentieth century, Goldziher and Schacht helped establish the need for a critical approach to the Muslim tradition; neither, however, dissented as

sharply from the traditional view of Arabia and Islamic origins as the more recent critical scholarship has done. Their work remains central, even beyond "revisionist" circles. As it is so well known, and already a part of most textbooks on Islam, I leave it out of consideration here.

6. For attempts to write history solely from the Quran, see W. Watt, *Muhammad's Mecca, History in the Quran* (Edinburgh: Edinburgh University Press, 1988); A. Welch, "Muhammad's Understanding of Himself: The Koranic Data," in *Islam's Understanding of Itself*, ed. R. Hovannisian and S. Vryonis, Jr. (Malibu, CA: Undena, 1983), 15–52. It will be noted, though, that both of these works take for granted the general outline of Muhammad's career as provided by the sirah texts, they do not, despite their claims, uncover much history in the Quran itself.

7. For a comparison of the problems encountered in the study of earliest Christianity and early Islam, see F. Peters, "The Quest of the Historical Muhammad," *International Journal of Middle East Studies* 23 (1991): 291–315. The article nicely situates some of the directions taken by modern critical scholarship.

8. For clear and accessible discussions of these source-related issues from a critical standpoint, see M. Cook, *Muhammad* (Oxford: Oxford University Press, 1983), 61–76; and P. Crone, *Meccan Trade and the Rise of Islam* (Oxford: Blackwell, 1987), 203–30. Cf. also the historiographical introduction to Crone's *Slaves on Horses* (Cambridge: Cambridge University Press, 1980), 3–17.

9. One notable exception is J. Burton, whose critical approach to the material led him to conclude that the Quran was actually put together *earlier* than the tradition claims (i.e., during the life of the Prophet himself); see his *The Collection of the Quran* (Cambridge: Cambridge University Press, 1977). The issue of the Quran's dating has now begun to receive attention beyond narrow professional circles; see T. Lester, "What Is the Koran?," in *The Atlantic Monthly* (January 1999): 43–56. The article serves as an exciting and useful introduction to recent critical work in early Islamic Studies, and is well worth assigning undergraduates.

10. W. Graham, review of *Quranic Studies*, in *The Journal of the American Oriental Society* 100 (1980): 138. The entire review is well worth consulting as an introduction to the book.

11. See the special 1997 issue of *Method and Theory in the Study of Religion* devoted to Wansbrough's work. Particularly useful introductions (which can be assigned in class) are the articles by C. Adams, G. Hawting, and H. Berg. The Adams article ("Reflections on the Work of John Wansbrough," 75–89) is especially valuable as a broad introduction to all the issues surrounding Wansbrough's work. Cf. also A. Rippin, "Literary Analysis of *Qur'ān, Tafsīr*, and *Sīra*: The Methodologies of John Wansbrough," in *Approaches to Islam in Religious Studies*, 159.

12. See esp. P. Crone, "Two Legal Problems Bearing on the Early History of the Qur'ān," *Jerusalem Studies in Arabic and Islam* 18 (1994): 1–37.

13. The dating and authenticity of this material is the subject of M. Cook's *Early*

Muslim Dogma (Cambridge: Cambridge University Press, 1981). The epistles are probably not as early as some have claimed, but they are certainly not as late as Wansbrough's theory would require.

14. The reality of the conquests (or at least of the stories telling of major battles won by an organized Arab army) has been called into question by J. Koren and Y. Nevo, "Methodological Approaches to Islamic Studies," *Der Islam* 68 (1991): 100–01. They seem to prefer a model of demographic shift and small-scale raiding, with the mass of Arabs still pagan by the end of the seventh century. For a more convincing interpretation, one that emphasizes the fit between monotheism, tribal power, and conquest, see P. Crone, *Meccan Trade and the Rise of Islam,* 231–50. This chapter is well worth assigning undergraduates, especially alongside the more traditional approach found in W. M. Watt's *Muhammad: Prophet and Statesman* (and numerous other works of his).

15. See, e.g., F. Rahman, *Major Themes of the Quran* (Minneapolis: Bibliotheca Islamica, 1980), xv.

16. For the view that the exodus concept [ḥijrah] was applied only secondarily to a movement from Mecca to Medina, but in the first instance to the conquest of the Promised Land, see Crone and Cook, *Hagarism: The Making of the Islamic World,* 7–9. The argument is fleshed out in P. Crone, "The First-Century Concept of ḥijra," *Arabica* 12 (1994): 352–87.

17. For valuable critical reviews of *Hagarism,* see that of J. Wansbrough, *Bulletin of the School of Oriental and African Studies* 41 (1978): 155–56; and J. van Ess, *The Times Literary Supplement* (Sept. 8, 1978): 997–998. For descriptive analyses of many of the non-Arabic sources, see R. Hoyland, *Islam as Others Saw It* (Princeton: Darwin Press, 1997).

18. Subsequent work by both authors is, however, extremely helpful in this respect. See, for example, Cook's discussion of hadith in *Dogma,* 107–16, and Crone's broader discussion of the formation of law in *Roman, Provincial, and Islamic Law* (Cambridge: Cambridge University Press, 1987), 18–34. Cf. also P. Crone and M. Hinds, *God's Caliph* (Cambridge: Cambridge University Press, 1986), which offers a powerful argument (based on the Muslim sources) about the evolution of religious authority in early Islam. The book's conclusions make it difficult to present the evolution of Sunnism and the Shi'ah in quite the usual way.

19. These are described, and textual examples are given, at *Quranic Studies,* 2–12.

20. Last example noted at Cook, *Muhammad,* 78. On the Quranic Joseph story in general, see Wansbrough, *Quranic Studies,* 1, 136–7. As a counterpoint to all this, cf. M. Waldman, "New Approaches to 'Biblical' Materials in the Quran," in *Studies in Islamic and Judaic Traditions,* ed. W. Brinner and S. Ricks (Atlanta: Scholars Press, 1988), 47–64, where the author attempts to make sense of the Quranic Joseph narrative in purely "Muslim" terms, without reference to biblical or extrabiblical versions.

21. Rippin, *Muslims,* vol.1, pp.18f. See also on this passage N. Calder's essay, "The *sa'y* and the jabūn: Some Notes on Qur'ān 37:102–103," *Journal of Semitic Studies* 31

(1986), especially 22–26; and idem, "From Midrash to Scripture: The Sacrifice of Abraham in Early Islamic Tradition," *Le Muséon* 101 (1988).

22. A few examples discussed by Wansbrough himself: narrative parallels apparently preserved at different redactional stages (e.g., different versions of the Shuʿayb tradition at 7:85, 11:84–95, 26:176–90, 29:36–37; parallel descriptions of the two gardens at 55:46–61 and 55:62–76, possibly representing variants of a single tradition transmitted orally in different milieux); intrusion of commentary into scripture (e.g., 16:51, identifiable by a change in pronoun: "God has said: 'Take not to yourselves two Gods, *for He is one God,* so have fear of *Me*'"); variant positions on the drinking of wine or on the practice of night vigil.

23. See G. R. Hawting, "The Literary Context of the Traditional Accounts of Pre-Islamic Arab Idolatry," *Jerusalem Studies in Arabic and Islam* 21 (1997): 21–41; for the possibility that the Muslim polemic against paganism might, in fact, have had a monotheist referent, see idem, "*Shirk* and Idolatry in Monotheist Polemic," *Israel Oriental Studies* 17 (1997): 107–26.

24. That Mecca may not have been the first sanctuary in Islam is also suggested in Crone and Cook, *Hagarism,* 21–24. The relevant articles by Hawting are "The Origins of the Muslim Sanctuary at Mecca," in *Studies on the First Century of Islamic Society,* ed. G. H. A. Juynboll (Carbondale: Southern Illinois University Press, 1982), 23–47; "The Disappearance and Rediscovery of Zamzam and the 'Well of the Kaʿba,'" *Bulletin of the School of Oriental and African Studies* 43 (1980): 44–54; and "'We were ordered not with entering it but only with circumambulating it.' *Ḥadīth* and *fiqh* on Entering the Kaʿba," *Bulletin of the School of Oriental and African Studies* 47 (1984): 228–42.

25. E.g., "Take as your place of worship the place where Abraham stood [to pray]" (Pickthall [tr.], *The Meaning of the Glorious Koran* [London, n.d.], 44); "Make the place where Abraham stood a house of worship" (Dawood [tr.], *The Koran* [London, 1990], 22); "Take to yourselves Abraham's station for a place of prayer" (Arberry [tr.], *The Koran Interpreted* [New York, 1955], i, 43–44). All these translations reflect the classical Muslim understanding of the passage, but not necessarily the language of the Quran itself.

CHAPTER FOUR

Islamicate Civilization
The View from Asia

BRUCE B. LAWRENCE

I N FALL OF 1998, the recent winner of the Nobel Prize for Economics
came to Duke University to address the notion of cultural complexity or
multiculturalism. Amartya Sen was—and is—a Cambridge don. He is also
Bengali. As a Bengali, he closely identifies with the cultural history of the Asian
subcontinent, and so it was no surprise that in his talk at Duke, Amartya Sen
gave a tip of his hat to an earlier Bengali Nobel laureate, the poet, Rabindra-
nath Tagore. Yet Sen also noted two other figures, who projected multicultural and cosmopolitan thinking in South Asia. One was the eleventh-century
Ghaznavid polymath, al-Biruni, the other the sixteenth-century Mughal emperor, Akbar.

While both al-Biruni and Akbar made major contributions to the expansive
force of Islamicate civilization, neither would rank high in any estimate of
Islam as a religious or juridical system.

The cases of al-Biruni and Akbar raise a pivotal but often ignored question:
How does one recuperate Islamicate civilization without ignoring or misrep-
resenting Islam? It is a key question for all who reflect on the Muslim world
and try to impart its lessons in the classroom. It is the key question that absorbed Marshall Hodgson in his landmark, three-volume analysis of Islamic
or better "Islamicate" civilization. It is the question that will absorb me, as I
try to chart the continued relevance of Hodgson's work more than 25 years
after its initial publication[1] and more than three decades since Hodgson's own
premature demise: he died in 1968 at the age of 46.

Islamicate civilization defines the dominant cultural idioms within the
most heavily trafficked central zones connecting Africa to Asia. For short-

hand, Hodgson calls this large expanse of the Mediterranean or middle world, the Afro-Eurasian oikumene. The Afro-Eurasian oikumene is an interactive and cosmopolitan domain. It is a widely diverse, global complex of subtraditions and histories. Defined by cities and trade, it projects a vast network of commercial and military, political and religious urban nodes, stretching from the Mediterranean Sea to the Pacific Ocean.

Focus on Islamicate civilization requires a retelling of Islamic origins. While Islam originated in the seventh century from the Arabian Peninsula, it did not become a world civilization till it passed beyond the borders of Arabia to the major centers of the Afro-Eurasian oikumene. Encompassing Iran and South Asia, Egypt and North Africa, Islamicate civilization came to include Persians and Turks, Berbers and Circassians, as well as Arabs. By the twelfth century, Islamicate civilization had become a multitiered force, and it was not eclipsed till the period of European expansion and conquest in the eighteenth century.

Such a vibrant diversity defies inclusive cataloguing, whether one attends to languages or ethnic groups or regions. It also strains the limits of a functional undergraduate syllabus: How would one begin to enumerate all the regional and subregional foci that a genuinely comprehensive catalogue, or a fully defensible syllabus, of Islamicate civilization would have to provide? Not easily; and since I am concerned with undergraduate teaching in North American universities, I will restrict myself to analyzing frame issues. The first, inescapable frame issue is to make sense of Islam and Islamicate variables.

Islam and Islamicate variables?! Yes, because even more crucial than adequate coverage of geographical diversity and historical achievements is the need to confront age old problems of key terms. Is the key term of an undergraduate course Islam or Islamicate civilization? To announce the question is to invite a comparison, which is also a contrast, between the notions of Islam as a religion or faith system and Islam as a global force or civilization.

While Islamicate civilization derives from Islam, the two are neither synonymous nor interchangeable. Islamicate civilization relates to Islam but also exceeds it. Islamicate civilization is about the complex of social relations that comprise the vast historical canvas of Muslim peoples. While Islamicate civilization projects belief and ritual, doctrine and law, shaped by Islamic perspectives, it is not limited to them. It exceeds them especially in its concern for the often taken-for-granted ways that patterns of conduct emerge. Islamicate civilization is as much about implicit ethical norms [adab] as it is about explicit juridical codes [shari'ah]. It is as much about difference between regions and traditions as it is about sameness, collapsing geographical and cultural difference within an umbrella concept such as the "ummah." It is as much about discontinuity over time as it is continuity, whether between the seventh and the twenty-first century of the Common Era or between the first and the fifteenth century in the Hijri calendar.

The focus on historical forces and social relations embeds an even greater departure from Islam viewed as a universal religion with discrete beliefs, rituals, and laws. To teach Islamicate civilization is to recognize, explore, and celebrate an Asian dimension in the lived experience of Muslim peoples. For the Afro-Asian oikumene marked by Islam is predominantly Asian rather than Arab; it draws more on the experience of Mongols and Mughals than it does on the history of Maghribis and Middle Easterners.

To teach Islamicate civilization is to announce, then pursue a resilient and persistent Asian focus. Most Muslims are Asian, and Islamicate civilization, like Muslim demography, derives its central focus and determinative profile from Asia. The teaching of Islamicate civilization, therefore, fails to reflect its subject, unless one highlights the worldview of millions of Asians, from Central to South to Southeast Asia. To etch my project, which is itself a summary revisioning of Hodgson's project, I am advocating that one begin teaching Islamicate civilization by invoking a comparison between West Asian or Middle Eastern notions of Islam across time and Central or South Asian notions of Islam as a world historical force. The comparison immediately involves a contrast between, on the one hand, Arabs as the dominant group, with Arabic as the preferred language and, on the other hand, Central Asians (Turks, Mongols, Circassians) or South Asians (Afghans, Punjabis, Bengalis) as the dominant group, with Persianate norms as the core worldview, projected through several languages but especially Persian.

The reverse proposition will raise eyebrows but has equal cogency: if Islam is both Persianate and Central or South Asian in its major premodern profile, then one cannot teach or write the history of Asia without a recurrent and nuanced Islamicate component. Indeed, if one excludes Islamicate civilization from Asian history, the result is to orientalize and etherealize one of the major elements in world history during the long millennium just ended.[2]

Of course, not all Asians, not even all scholars of Asia, are willing to acknowledge Islam as a major civilization in the Afro-Asian oikumene. Islam competes with two other preeminent Asian civilizations: the Indic in the South and the Chinese in the East. Can Asia have three major civilizational forces? Yes, as one of the oldest and most continuously trafficked continents, it has shaped, even as it has been shaped by, three equivalent, if competitive, worldviews: the Indic, the Chinese, and the Islamic. Of the three, Islamicate civilization stands out as a transregional social construct, crossing and combining discrete regions more fluidly than do its adjacent rivals. Consider that neither Indic nor Chinese norms span the breadth of Asia through its central and southern regions to the extent that Islamicate norms do. Especially compelling is the contribution that Islamicate civilization made during the long first half of the second millennium of the Common Era, from roughly 1000 C.E. to 1600 C.E.

How can one begin to give the Islamicate contribution a proportionate place in the teaching of Asian history as world history? One must begin by retelling Islamicate civilization as an Asian tale of premodern multicultural-ism. It is a tale complicated by the ambivalence of its religious dimension. Islam does not cease to be an Arab religion when it becomes a civilization, yet one must account for how Islam was transformed from a tribal code, or Arab cult, to a civilizational force, pervading but also imbibing non-Arab cultural norms. These norms were both Asian and African, yet in the eastward expansion of Islam, they became predominantly Asian.

Others have argued for an Asia-specific focus to the representation of Is-lamicate civilization. Among the best is Richard M. Eaton, especially in his lucid essay, "Islamic History as Global History."[3] Like Eaton, I am calling for closer attention to the emergence of distinctly Asian social patterns that are also closely identified with Islamicate patterns of interaction between a vari-ety of groups, but especially rulers and ruled. At the least, an Asian accent requires mention of the following three traits in any broad historical survey of Islamicate civilization:

- The preference for a militarized society, with a standing army which re-quires regular use, often to invade and conquer adjacent regions;

- The likelihood of autocratic rule by a military leader invested with in-strumental power but often claiming divine authority and patronizing scholars to further that claim;

- The erection of monuments commemorating religious heroes, as well as rulers of the past, built by the military leaders to strike awe in the living.[4]

None of these three is limited to Asia in their historical expression, nor do they project an exclusive linguistic option, yet for much of Central and South Asia they are linked to a pattern of language preference and high cultural usage that is at once evident and persistent. The link has been, above all, to Persian. Persian becomes the bridge element, opening Islamicate civilization to new, powerful forces of transformation. While Islam as religion has been often identified with the Arabic language and Arab norms, Arabs were merely the initiating agents for the development of Islamicate civilization. It was Per-sians, and even more Persianate norms, that provided the major instrument in premodern Muslim learning. What Arabs began Persians continued and also modified.

It was no less a person than the Arab Prophet Muhammad who once observed: "If scholarship hung suspended in the highest parts of heaven, the Persians would attain it." So evident was this tradition to the universal historian Ibn Khaldun that he quoted it in the late fourteenth century to support his own observation, to wit, that "only the Persians have engaged in the task of preserving knowledge and writing systematic scholarly works."[5]

But already the terms "Arab" and "Persian" beg for qualification. Just as the Arabic language was not limited to Arabs, having been mastered and used by Berbers, Persians, and Turks, among others, so Persian was not a language only for inhabitants of the Iranian plateau. From Central to South to Southeast Asia, Persian was used as both a literary and cultural idiom for diverse groups. Its flexibility as well as its appeal are better etched in the related but not identical term "Persianate."

Why does one have to distinguish "Persianate" from Persian? Persianate is a neologism, a new term first coined by the world historian Marshall Hodgson in his monumental three-volume work, *The Venture of Islam*, referred to earlier.[6] Persianate depicts a cultural force linked both to the Persian language and to self-identified Persians. Yet Persianate is more than either a language or a people; it highlights elements that Persians share with other non-Persian Muslims. Persianate is allied with Islamicate, another neologism coined by Hodgson. Adab, or custom in the broadest sense, may illustrate their similarity while also underscoring their nonequivalence.[7] In examining a range of sociocultural norms lumped together under the term "adab," one might use the qualifier Persianate, if one wants to stress the importance of Persian as a linguistic component, or Islamicate, if one wants to acknowledge the way in which Islam itself is invoked even when the connection between cultural observance and religious loyalty proves to be very slim. Persian poetry written by Turks, Persian paintings produced by Indians, Persian monumental architecture built by Mongols—all have Islamicate dimensions, yet are not restricted to a specific religious audience or to a precise ritual usage. Even when Persianate and Islamicate seem to converge, they express complementary excesses: Persianate connotes more than linguistic usage, just as Islamicate connotes more than creedal commitment, ritual performance, or juridical loyalty.

I am the first to admit that communicating Persianate and Islamicate nuances to undergraduates is a challenge. One can duck it, but at the risk of oversimplification and reversion to stereotypes. One can take it up, but only with judicious use of sources that have appeared since Hodgson's *The Venture of Islam*. One might best begin by assigning the *Encylopaedia Britannica*. Don't go to the library, unless you crave the printed page, for you can now find *Britannica Online* at *http://www.eb.com:180/bol/topic?artcl=106443*. There you can access a masterful overview of Islamicate civilization written over a decade ago by an accomplished historian of premodern Afro-Asian Islam, Marilyn Waldman. Professor Waldman builds on the work of her own teacher, who was none other than Marshall Hodgson. Like the inventor of Islamicate and Persianate accents, Waldman tries to make sense of the actual stages of shift within Islamicate civilization.

Her prose not only mirrors Hodgson's but also simplifies and streamlines some of his major theses. Waldman begins by noting that already by the middle of the first millennium, before the Common Era, there already existed four cultural core areas: Mediterranean, Nile-to-Oxus (not Middle Eastern!), Indic, and East Asian (or Chinese). Two rivers, the Nile to the south and Oxus to the north, are a better way of etching the core area of Islamic civilization than Middle Eastern or Near Eastern. It was these two rivers, the Nile and the Oxus, that framed major developments characterizing the early three phases of Islamicate civilization. They are, according to Waldman's reckoning, best viewed in alliterative or assonant pairs:

- **Formation and Orientation** (500–634) is Phase One; it ends with the death of the Prophet Muhammad.

- **Conversion and Crystallization** (634–870) is Phase Two: though Islamic rule comes to prevail, there are not yet Muslim majorities in all regions under Islamic rule.

- **Fragmentation and Florescence** (970–1041) defines Phase Three, as Muslim polities splinter while Islam itself emerges as a major civilizational force for the first time.

Most students find it hard to grasp the notion that political disunity and cosmopolitan engagement occur during the same period of Islamic history. One can illustrate the paradox of this development through the life of Ahmad Raihan al-Biruni (d. ca. 1050). This is the same al-Biruni to whom Amartya Sen made reference in his 1998 address at Duke University. Al-Biruni is, as Sen correctly observed, a pivotal figure in the emergence of Asian-style Islamic cosmopolitanism.

The dynast who was his patron, Sultan Mahmud of Ghazna, was responsible for continuing the political disintegration of a centrally controlled Muslim empire. He was a Turkish military chieftain, committed to expanding his own territorial realm and dynastic power. Yet Sultan Mahmud was also wedded to Islamicate norms. He saw the Persian language, art, and architecture as the natural extension of his own authoritarian rule. He enlisted, supported, then controlled a coterie of talented intellectuals. Al-Biruni, like the poet Firdausi, author of the epic *Shahnameh,* chafed under Sultan Mahmud's edicts yet also benefited from his patronage.

How did al-Biruni become an exemplar of Islamicate civilization, an exponent of that Asian-based multiculturalism that was at once premodern and Persianate? His native tongue was a variant of present day Uzbek, yet he also spoke and wrote in Persian. He was familiar enough with *three* "classical" languages to write in one and to translate from the other two: Arabic, Greek, and Sanskrit. Yet he was not a literary scholar. Rather, he became an extraordinary scientist and is said to have produced some 138 books, treatises, and translations. Only 22 are known to have survived, most of them written in Arabic, though some also exist in Persian renditions.

One of al-Biruni's less well-known translations concerned perhaps the most famous classical Sanksrit text on meditation or yoga. He translated the *yogasutras* of Patanjali from Sanskrit into Arabic. Titling it the Book of Patanjali (*Kitab Batanjal*), he showed how many, and varied, were the connections between Hindu and Muslim spiritual practices.[8] The other, more famous, book dealing with Sanskrit texts was his wide-ranging examination of Indic scientific sources. It was supplemented by conversations with Hindu pandits, whom al-Biruni met while forced to accompany Sultan Mahmud on military campaigns in the Ganges region. Written in Arabic, its full title was *The Book Confirming What Pertains to India whether Intellectually Acceptable or Abhorrent* [kitāb taḥqīq ma lil-Hind min maqbūlah lil-'aql aw mardhūlah], but it is often simply known as the *India,* since the most complete English rendition, made by C. E. Sachau, was entitled *Alberuni's India.* First published in 1910, it has been often reprinted.[9]

While al-Biruni stands at the apex of pre-Mughal Islamic scholarship on *non*-Muslim religious traditions, he had few followers, ironically perhaps because his principal work was written in Arabic, not in Persian. During the following centuries leading up to the Mughal or Indo-Timuri period (1526–1857), both Islamicate and Persianate emphases expanded within Islamic civilization. Persian style as well as Persian language, customs, and arts were widely adopted throughout South Asia. Their impact was attested, above all, in the life and labor of Emperor Akbar (1555–1604).

Akbar embodied the three traits of Persianate society etched above. Each had developed during the twin periods that Waldman describes as the highwater mark of Islamicate civilization. Nor is it coincidence that these developments occurred after the time of al-Biruni and the Ghaznavids. Islamicate civilization witnessed the infusion of first Turkish, then Mongol elements into the Persianate spirit that had begun in the tenth and eleventh centuries. The two next phases are marked as:

- **Migration and Renewal** (1041–1405). It ends with the death of Timur, or Tamurlane, who is himself a Chaghatai Turk but sympathetic to Mongol ideals. Above all, Timur embodied a form of Islamic absolutism that prevailed in the next phase.

- **Consolidation and Expansion** (1405–1683). This period gave rise to three new forms of absolutist rule, each of them predicated on military dominance, bureaucratic centrism, and monumental art in the service of dynastic power. Indo-Timuris or Mughals shared center stage with Ottomans and Safavids. In terms of Persianate influence, all represented new levels of advance, but the Indo-Timuris were the only dynasty to flourish in an Asian environment that was not only non-Muslim but strongly Indic in its civilizational outlook.

It is undoubtedly due to the Indic element in Islamicate civilization as it evolved south of the Himalaya mountain range that one can see the influence of saints. Saints not only flourished and commanded popular devotion, but they also rivaled Persianate rulers, even the most powerful of dynasts, even the Emperor Akbar.

By the mid-sixteenth century, when a youthful Akbar ascended the throne vacated by his father, Humayun, saints had become the major custodians and transmitters of Turko-Persian Islamicate values. Akbar acknowledged the power of saintly figures, especially those identified with the Chishti order, but he subordinated them to his "superior" dynastic power, one that approached a quasi-divine status not unlike his famous ancestor, Timur or Tamerlane.

The Mughals were, in fact, not Mongols (as their name implies) but Indo-Timurids; they were the Indian legatees of Timur, the fourteenth-century military genius who, though not a Mongol, claimed Chingizid lineage. Timur, or Tamerlane, also projected Mongol military and ruling ideals. He combined in his person the notion of great military conqueror and supreme spiritual leader. His function was similar to that of the familiar Perso-Turkish kings, but his extensive conquests lent even more credibility to his claim of divine inspiration and support. Small wonder then that Akbar identified with Timur, at the same time that he raised the Indo-Timurid legacy to new heights as an emblem of Persianate cosmopolitanism.

Akbar began, as did all his most illustrious ancestors, with a stunning record of military success. Yet no one could have predicted that he would succeed to the extent that he did. At the outset of his rule, he faced major challenges. He ruled a circumscribed realm that hardly extended beyond the Indo-Gangetic plain of Northern Hindustan. His father Humayun, after succeeding Babur as the second Mughal dynast, had spent over 15 years in exile in

Safavid Iran (1540–1555). He left the reconquest of India to Babur's grandson, Akbar. Akbar spent almost all the early years of his reign engaged in military campaigning. Even though he combined military success with economic reform, even though he united the maritime, commercial province of Gujarat with the agricultural heartlands of the Punjab and Gangetic basins, making possible an enormous expansion of trade and production during his reign, it was Akbar's ability to conquer militarily and then to assuage his former enemies diplomatically that earned him the largest place in Mughal annals.

Akbar also succeeded in attracting able men, both Hindu and Muslim, to serve him as courtiers. His chief tax officer was Todar Mal, a Hindu whom Akbar recruited over objections from Muslim notables. Through Todar Mal, Akbar constantly experimented with tax reforms until he evolved a system of administration and extraction that optimized his resources; it remained in place till modern times.

Akbar had more trouble achieving control and accountability in the religious establishment. He strove to establish Sufi Shaykhs as an alternate source of authority to the 'ulama, guardians of everyday ritual and law in Islam, but he also tried to keep them subordinate to the Mughal court. Neither policy was fully successful.

Official Mughal accounts, our major source of data for the reign of Akbar and his Timurid relatives, do not explain the nature of the Sufi brotherhoods, nor do they expose the attitude of their legatees and devotees toward the emperor. We have to read between the lines, literally, in order to understand the social dynamics at work.

On the one hand, the Emperor Akbar was blessed by a Chishti master living near the capital city of Agra. The saint's name was Shaykh Salim Chishti. At age 28, Akbar had produced only daughters, yet in a visit to Shaykh Salim, Akbar was told by the saint that his favorite wife would produce a male heir; not just one but three male heirs. Both predictions proved true, and in witness to the saint's power, Akbar's oldest son and future successor, the Emperor Jahangir, was named Prince Salim.

Nor did Akbar neglect to honor another saint, Shaykh Nizam al-Din Awliya (d. 1325). His was the dominant tomb complex of North India, located in the former capital city of Delhi. Akbar built a tomb honoring his father, Humayun, very near the tomb of Shaykh Nizam al-Din. Till today the tomb complex of Humayun remains a magnificent example of Akbar's attention to memorials for the dead. Though its actual designer may have been Humayun's widow, its patron and guiding force was the young emperor. Its central structure combines indigenous building traditions with familiar Persianate emphases. Just as white marble inlay in red sandstone lightens the octagonal formality of Humayun's tomb, so does its setting in a four-cornered garden on a vast plane augur a new tradition of tomb gardens known as the Mughal style.

Yet the building of Humayun's tomb near the tomb of Shaykh Nizam al-Din was an ambiguous gesture, for while his predecessors had favored Delhi, the young Akbar was suspicious of its past. In securing his own rule at Agra from 1556 to 1570, Akbar had to be aware of the tension between Agra and Delhi as rival imperial centers. It may have been, in part, due to their asymmetry (Delhi having the longer history, Agra the more immediate strategic advantage) that Akbar sought still another base from which to project his distinctive version of imperial authority. But one could not simply choose another site. The choice had to have symbolic and legitimating power such that others would be led to accept the rightness of the emperor's decision. By linking Sikri to the saint who predicted the birth of his heirs and successors, Akbar made its selection as a new imperial center seem logical, even compelling.

There were also other advantages that appealed to the spiritual dimension of Akbar's multifaceted personality. Having chosen Fatehpur Sikri, he was able to confirm and continue his affiliation with the tomb of Shaykh Mu'in al-Din in Ajmer while also drawing on the power of a living saint, Shaykh Salim, and through him on the spiritual *barakah* that derived from his ascetic patron, Shaykh Farid al-Din Ganj-i Shakar (d. 1265) in the Punjab. Through a twofold, redoubled Chishti loyalty, Akbar could spiritually anchor his imperial legitimacy in provinces adjacent to Uttar Pradesh, the Punjab, and Rajasthan. Both regions were crucial to the political-military ambitions of his reign.

Akbar had begun to sponsor monumental art on a new and expansive scale, even before the foundation of Fatehpur Sikri, and he continued to do so after his brief residence in that lustrous red sandstone city outside Agra. As important as Akbar's affiliation with Chishti saints was for the Fatehpur Sikri phase of his life, it became irrelevant during the final 20 years of his reign. His abrupt shift in loyalty had an impact on institutional Sufism that reverberated throughout the remainder of Mughal rule (till 1857 when the British assumed direct rule from Delhi). Just as neither Shaykh Salim nor Shaykh Mu'in al-Din remained a constant focus of Akbar's allegiance, so Fatehpur Sikri was sited as a temporary rather than a permanent capital city.

For Akbar, it was the emperor not a place nor a saint who was lauded as the apogee of authority—spiritual and temporal—in the Mughal polity. To the extent that his person became the metaphor for his realm, spiritual luminaries could only function by being linked to or subordinated within the aura of ultimate, imperial authority. The absolutist claims which were raised by Akbar, or by Abul-Fazl in Akbar's name, forced a redefinition of both sainthood and dynastic succession.

In 1577, Abul-Fazl's father, Shaykh Mubarak, drafted the decree [mahzar].

Its intention was to affirm the spiritual supremacy of the Emperor: he became officially superior to all religious functionaries and all religious institutions. By this time the Chishti *silsilah* had already lost whatever benefit its partisans—whether shrine custodians, living saints, or Hindu/Muslim devotees— may have gained by the favor that Akbar had showered upon them. Courtiers like 'Abd al-Nabi and Shaykh Mubarak were removed from active advocacy of either their own Sufi legacy or the active mystical interests of others. Nor did the construction of Shaykh Salim's tomb within the walled courtyard of the central mosque at Fatehpur Sikri promote the spiritual agenda of the Chishti lineage that he represented. Instead, the founding of Fatehpur Sikri affirmed Akbar—his brand of Islamic observance and his legitimate claim to rule as Timur's offspring.

Akbar's visit to saints' tombs after 1577 reveals his changed mood. He only visits Delhi once and spends most of his time at Humayun's tomb. When he does visit a couple of provincial saintly shrines, he uses these visits to draw attention to his own superior claims to spiritual favor. The Sufi exemplars, who shaped the first phase of his rule, were eclipsed, then gradually forgotten toward the final years of his life.

One of Akbar's most solemn acts of remembrance concerned his own burial site. He opted to plan for his own tomb in advance of his actual death. The site, named Sikandara, suggested the link between Akbar and another legendary military genius, Alexander the Great. It was located on the outskirts of Agra in a sumptuous garden complex. The actual construction, and perhaps even elements of the design, were left to Akbar's son and successor, Jahangir (1605–1627). The red sandstone forms the backdrop for intricate geometric patterns, including the reverse swastika, as well as delicate floral designs, all etched in black and white marble. Floating atop the entire edifice, almost suspended by their light surface, are four white marble minarets.

Its purpose was the same purpose as all Mughal art and architecture: to glorify the Emperor, imbuing his legacy with an aesthetic impress that no other human could rival or exceed. Except his own successors, of course, and it was the later Mughals—Jahangir with several monuments but especially I'timad al-Dawla built for his father-in-law, Shah Jahan with the triumphant tribute to his wife known as the Taj Mahal, and even Awrangzeb, the last of the Great Mughals, with his limp lookalike to the Taj Mahal, the Bibi ka Maqbara, built for his own favorite wife after her decease. In short, the Great Mughal, whether Akbar, Jahangir, Shah Jahan, or Awrangzeb, had more concern with his own office and image than with loyalty to another authority— spiritual or temporal.

Beyond the Mughal court and its artistic legacy, Persianate concepts were reflected in regional courts and the self-conception of their ruling elites.

Whether Kashmir or Gujarat, the Deccan or Bengal, one finds the traces of this same vibrant pattern of military control, spiritual dalliance, and monumental architecture. Bengal remains one of the showcases of Persianate culture in the premodern Muslim world. As Richard Eaton has argued in his brilliant monograph, *The Rise of Islam and the Bengal Frontier, 1204–1760*,[10] it is impossible to understand the most populous Muslim region of the subcontinent without resorting to Persianate concepts. Some conceal hierarchy by depicting all socioeconomic relationships as codependent, such as the famous Circle of Justice. Attributed to two prominent Persian adibs, Fakhr al-Din Razi (d. 1209) and Nasr al-Din Tusi (d. 1274), it was widely used by Turko-Persian elites in Bengal, as was the parallel but explicit theory of hierarchy, which placed certain spiritual masters or Sufi saints at the apex of collective wisdom, paralleling yet also rivaling the hierarchy of political rulers.

Whether in Bengal or elsewhere in Muslim South Asia, there emerged a distinctive Turko-Persian Islamicate culture. None of us like to use hyphenated multisyllabic neologisms when trying to communicate with cyberspaced undergraduates. The latter prefer a single click to a mouth-twisting phrase, yet it is Turko-Persian Islamicate culture, or Turko-Persianate Islamic culture, that best characterizes not only medieval Bengal but also other regions of Sultanate, then Mughal, and finally British India.

The major lesson may be about periodization. According to Waldman, in her synoptic overview of Hodgson cited above, there was *no* medieval period in Islamicate civilization. When the last of the major Persianate Empires, the Ottoman, was defeated at Vienna in 1683, there began the modern period that can be labeled: Reform, Dependency (on European colonial powers), and Recovery (following independence) (1683–present).

After the Classical Phase, which ended with al-Biruni in the mid-eleventh century or else with the death of Timur some 250 years later, there came the period of the Persianate Empires that built on classical features but also adapted to novel technologies, especially but not exclusively gunpowder. They were overshadowed, and also subordinated, to the ascendant European colonial powers, but without experiencing a medieval phase: the classical elided with the early modern which became the modern (and, some would argue, now the postmodern). What the emphasis on Turko-Persian Islamicate culture unfolds is a long prolegomenon to the advent of "modern" times, which also have tested the spirit and the resilience that were characteristic of Islamicate civilization in its earlier phases. Beyond the din of two World Wars, and beyond the technical/economic disparities that divide much of the modern Muslim world from Euro-American cybertopias, there remains the Persianate hope. It was etched by Marshall Hodgson when he wrote:

Islam as an identifiable institutional tradition may not last indefinitely [and the same may be said for Christianity and Judaism] . . . but Persian poetry will not die so soon as the disquisitions of fiqh or kalam. And Persian poetry may eventually prove to be as potent everywhere as among those who use language touched by the Persianate spirit, and so by Islam.[11]

As the twenty-first century dawns, Hodgson's project, cut short by his untimely death in 1968, remains the clarion cry or hope not only for Persian speakers but also for all who seek to identify the vitality and so the future resilience of Islamicate norms. One does not stop with Persian poetry but engages it in order to understand the further subtleties of cultural diffusion that continue to mark the persistence and the expansion of Islamic civilization. To move beyond Arabic and to include Persian as a foundational marker is merely to draw both together into a larger idiom, labeled by Hodgson the "Irano-Semitic." The accent is neither on Arabic or Persian alone, but on both together, as an interactive, dynamic construct that implies the variability, and also the creativity, of Islamicate civilization, from its earliest historical chapters to the present. Beyond the cultural specifier of any language or culture looms the adaptable, permeable quality of Islamicate civilization. The necessary lesson for undergraduates and for those who teach them, therefore, is that Islamicate civilization need not "confront" multiculturalism or adapt to it, for it is, of its essence, multicultural.

Amartya Sen was right to quote both al-Biruni and the Emperor Akbar as premodern multiculturalists. They, like many of their co-religionists, were forerunners to a world that includes Asians as well as Arabs, non-Muslims as well as Muslims touched by the Persianate spirit. That is a lesson worth teaching from the annals of Muslim history as world history.

NOTES

1. Marshall G. S. Hodgson, *The Venture of Islam: Conscience and History in a World Civilization,* 3 vols. (Chicago: University of Chicago Press, 1974). A useful collection of some of Hodgson's earlier essays has also been provided by Edmund Burke III. See Marshall G. S. Hodgson, *Rethinking World History: Essays on Europe, Islam, and World History* (Cambridge: Cambridge University Press, 1993).

2. If one were to tell the story of Islamicate civilization from the eighteenth century forward, then the key regional variable would be Southeast Asia rather than South Asia. I have provided a brief overview of the important Asian archipelago, which includes Indonesia and Malaysia, as well as the Phillipines, within the arc of Islamdom in an earlier essay. See Bruce B. Lawrence, "The Eastward Journey of Mus-

lim Kingship: Islam in South and Southeast Asia," in *The Oxford History of Islam,* ed. John L. Esposito (New York: Oxford University Press, 2000), chapter 9: 394–431, but especially 420–431. Leonard Y. Andaya, *The World of Maluku: Eastern Indonesia in the Early Period* (Honolulu: University of Hawaii Press, 1993) gives the most graphic account of how the extreme edge of the Asian or Malay archipelago became both a commercial frontier for Muslim traders and a cultural nexus of Islamicate with indigenous norms.

3. Richard M. Eaton, "Islamic History as Global History," in *Islamic and European Expansion: The Forging of a Global Order,* ed. Michael Adas (Philadelphia: Temple University Press, 1993), 1–36.

4. I have adapted this list from Robert L. Canfield, ed., *Turko-Persia in Historical Perspective* (Cambridge: Cambridge University Press, 1991).

5. Ibn Khaldun, *The Muqaddimah: An Introduction to History,* trans. Franz Rosenthal (Princeton: Princeton University Press, 1967/1981), 430.

6. Especially in volume 3 of *The Venture of Islam,* Hodgson characterizes the entire sixteenth century and early seventeenth century as a period of Persianate flowering. Its Persianate stamp was as evident in the Ottoman Empire under Suleyman the Magnificent (1520–1566) and in the Mughal or Indo-Timuri Empire under Akbar (1556–1605), as it was in Safavid Iran under Shah Abbas (1587–1629). See *The Venture of Islam* 3:46–52.

7. For a thorough study of *adab* in the Asian subcontinent, see Barbara D. Metcalf, ed., *Moral Conduct and Authority: The Place of adab in South Asian Islam* (Berkeley: University of California Press, 1983).

8. There have been many general studies of al-Biruni, but concerning his exploration of Hindu-Muslim themes in classical texts, see Bruce B. Lawrence, "The Use of Hindu Religious Texts in al-Biruni's *India* with Special Reference to Patanjali's Yoga-Sutras," in *The Scholar and the Saint: Studies in Commemoration of Abu'l-Rayhan al-Biruni and Jalal al-Din Rumi,* ed. Peter J. Chelkowski (New York: New York University Press, 1975), 29–48.

9. The most accessible translation of al-Biruni's classic is provided by Ainslee Embree in his abridgement of Sachau, *Alberuni's India; an account of the religion, philosophy, literature, geography, chronology, astronomy, customs, laws and astrology of India, about* A.D. *1030* (New York: Norton, 1971).

10. Richard M. Eaton, *The Rise of Islam and the Bengal Frontier, 1204–1760* (Berkeley: University of California Press, 1993).

11. Hodgson, *The Venture of Islam,* 3:441.

Part Two

DIMENSIONS OF MUSLIM FAITH,
COMMUNITY, AND ORDER

CHAPTER FIVE

The Essential Shariʿah
Teaching Islamic Law in the Religious Studies Classroom

JONATHAN E. BROCKOPP

WHEN I WAS IN CAIRO IN SPRING OF 1995, I regularly engaged in conversation with the men who gathered at the café next door to my apartment. Over time we came to know one another, and after they learned about my research into the manuscripts of early Islamic jurisprudence, our conversation frequently turned to religions. The discussion was often fervent, sometimes strident, as we covered the now familiar territory of the divinity of Christ, the imperialism of the West, and so on. One evening, though, toward the end of my four-month stay, they became quite serious when one of them asked me how I would teach Islam in the United States. Their concern was that Islam be taught within its own frame of reference, not merely as a foil for proving, for instance, that Christianity is a better religion or that Egypt's poverty is due to Islam's influence. However much these attitudes are ghosts of the past century, they still haunt my Egyptian friends, and they still influence our students. More often than not, students enter the classroom with a negative attitude toward Islam, as compared to, for instance, the overwhelmingly positive attitude they have toward Buddhism.

In my classes, therefore, I include a variety of texts written by Muslims themselves, not because I believe that Muslims can more accurately represent their tradition than non-Muslims, but because students need to learn that Muslims can also be sociologists, historians, religious scholars, and feminists. With my five courses a year on Islam, I have the luxury of examining a broad range of texts with students in a seminar setting. I know, though, that many colleagues struggle to discern the "essential" elements of Islam within a "world religions" classroom, where a fourteen-hundred-year-old tradition must be whittled down to three weeks. It seems to me, though, that each of us has the same problem. Both through voluntary and involuntary choices, reflecting personal competencies or availability of suitable texts, the instructor determines which aspects of the Islamic tradition will be considered. As a result, the presentation of Islam in the classroom is necessarily partial and incomplete—precisely the problem that worried my café cohorts. While a great deal of harm can be mitigated by emphasizing the incomplete nature of the presentation to the students, the search for the essence of Islam continues.

Shortly before his death in 1988, Fazlur Rahman wrote an important piece on the study of Islam, in which he largely argued against the primacy of the insider's view of Islam.[1] In this article, though, Rahman also argues for the necessity of a normative "anchoring point," which "must modify the phenomenological approach which otherwise tends to be incurably relativistic" (p. 197). Rahman's appeal for a normative Islam may seem out of date, but his argument has merit. On the scholarly plane, we still need the construct of normative Islam to speak effectively about movements and sects which use a variant norm. As for the classroom, we often have time to present only one view of the Islamic tradition, one which some of our students will invariably understand as normative. Where I differ from Rahman is in choosing the basis for this anchoring point. He chooses Quran and Sunnah, since any Muslim "will readily admit that what he considers true or correct Islam is to be judged (solely) by the Quran and Sunnah" (p. 197). But I find this definition problematic, since it suggests the existence of a Quran and Sunnah which is immutable, fixed in time as it were for all believers to consult. In fact, these sources must necessarily go through a level of interpretation, and it is the "proper" exegesis of these sources which is central to their normative value, not their authoritative status. Furthermore, Rahman is a modernist, following in the intellectual tradition of Muhammad Abduh and Iqbal. Naming Quran and Sunnah alone as normative, effectively wipes the slate clear for individual Muslims to exercise their own *ijtihād,* that is, to apply the principles of faith to their modern lives as they see fit. In other words, Rahman wants to "free" Muslims of their dependence on centuries of interpretation, allowing them to go back to the original sources.

I agree with Rahman that a norm is useful, but I believe that the addition of Islamic law to the Quran and Sunnah would make a more effective anchoring point. In studying the history of Islam, for instance, one cannot look at the Quran to understand the establishment of Islam in North Africa.[2] Law, however, necessarily includes this important element of interpretation. While the Shari'ah, God's path for humankind to follow, exists fully only in the mind of God, the application of that law in jurisprudence [fiqh] has been the subject of Islamic jurists in every time and place. Fiqh in its essence is mutable, incorporating the opinions of scholars in a continuous record of jurisprudential activity. Sources are available in English for the study of this activity in the early, medieval, and modern eras. For the early period, one can establish a clear picture of the ways in which the jurists [fuqahā'] perceived Islam; that is, one can reconstruct a theoretical norm, however sporadically it may have been applied. From the fourteenth-century onward, one can also consult books of legal opinions from actual cases and, in the Ottoman period, actual records of court proceedings. In our own time, the workings of the Islamic court system can be studied effectively as an important intersection between the demands of Islamic religion and the burdens of modern society.

Setting up a normative anchoring point does not mean that teaching Islamic law and Quran is a sufficient presentation of the Islamic religion, or that either of these is the essence of Islam. Rather, Islamic law provides a lens through which one can observe the rich variety of phenomena in the Islamic world. Even so, there are limitations. First, the study of Islamic law can solidify the characterization of Islam as a rigid system of rules which restricts free expression and change. Such a characterization is a particular danger among students who may seek to portray Christianity as a religion of love and Judaism and Islam as religions of law. Along the same lines, one should not use Islamic law as a litmus test, against which one can determine the relative "Islamness" of any particular group or ideology. Rather, a Muslim's relationship to Islamic law is only one of several key elements in the formation of their identity as Muslim.[3] On the other hand, the very fact that most Americans connect Islamic "fundamentalism" with the establishment of the Shari'ah argues for the need to teach Islamic law in the classroom. Before turning to a review of several new resources for the teaching of Islamic law, I will briefly cover some of the most important features of early Islamic legal development, particularly since our understanding of the early history of Islam has improved dramatically in recent years.

A Brief History

Before incorporating Islamic law into the syllabus, there are a number of misconceptions which still survive in the secondary literature on Islam and which must be challenged. These misconceptions are based on three basic errors: the treatment of the first two centuries of Islam as a type of "dark ages," of which we know little; the assumption of rigidity in the application of law; and the use of Christian categories to characterize Islamic law. The best background sources are somewhat dated and often out of print, but all provide a solid foundation for lectures. I would especially recommend works by Joseph Schacht and Noel Coulson.[4] Ignaz Goldziher's *Introduction to Islamic Theology and Law* (Princeton, 1981) was originally written almost 100 years ago, yet his explanations are so lucid I still use his text in my courses. These books, and especially those of Joseph Schacht, have been subjected to significant criticism in recent years,[5] and none take into account the impressive advances made in the last thirty years, in fields ranging from paleography to anthropology.

New scholarship on the earliest period of Islamic history, for instance, has allowed scholars to clarify some aspects of the early development of Islamic jurisprudence. Most important, Islamic jurisprudence is now known to have undergone a long period of development during the first 300 years of Islam. As a result, it is misleading to assume that categories from later periods typify early law. In fact, several of the standard features of medieval Islamic law, including the five Shariʻah values [aḥkām], the four schools of law, and the four roots of law, are unknown in the earliest centuries of Islam. As for the aḥkām, the division of acts into categories of required [wājib], recommended [mandūb], permitted [maʻdhūn], reprehensible [makrūh], and forbidden [ḥarām] does not appear at all in legal sources of the second and third Islamic centuries. Rather, a looser form of categorization appears to have obtained, rendering acts as good, bad, or indifferent. While use of intermediate terms (like desirable [mustaḥabb]) can be found, they are not used systematically. Along these lines, early texts show no systematic use of what came to be known as the four roots of jurisprudence, in which the Quran would first be consulted, followed by recourse to the Sunnah of the Prophet, and finally, consensus of the scholars or reasoning by analogy if the other sources failed. Instead, these texts utilize a broad range of authority, with Quran and hadith only one voice among others, and with dependence on scholarly opinion particularly obvious. The use of multiple systems in these texts is striking, with some texts treating hadith as primary, while others are predominantly dependent on opinion. Substantial variations are even seen among supposed representatives of the same school of law, which also calls our conception of the four orthodox schools into question. While definite regional tendencies can be observed, including a dichotomy between Iraqi and Hijazi law, each of the eventual four schools had an independent process of development and coalescence, so that the dates of their "founding" are still debated.[6] The history of the development of these concepts reveals a flexible system, able to adapt to local custom and necessity.

As an example of the way recent scholarship has affected the field, consider that until recently, the *Muwaṭṭaʼ* of Malik b. Anas (d. 179/795) was thought to be the earliest example of systematic legal writing in Islam. However, scholars are beginning to close the 150-year- gap between the organized, thorough presentation of the *Muwaṭṭaʼ* and the hodgepodge array of legal exhortation found in the Quran (compiled sometime around the Prophet's death in 10/

632). Already, the thoughts of some pre-Muwaṭṭa' scholars, such as al-Awza'i (d. 157/774), al-Majishun (d. 164/780), and 'Abdallah b. Lahi'a (d. 174/790), have come to light. Their texts begin to provide a context within which we may better understand Malik's *Muwaṭṭa'*.[7] Malik has usually been portrayed as the defender of hadith in law, while the Hanafis supposedly defended personal opinion. But the *Muwaṭṭa'* is much more than a hadith collection, as comparison with Ibn Lahi'a's text readily reveals. On the other hand, much more attention is paid to the chain of transmission [isnād] in Malik's work than in al-Majishun's, where out of five Prophetic hadith, none are found in the familiar *isnād/matn* format. Finally, it may be said that for both Malik and al-Majishun, hadith did not determine law but was subordinate to it, especially if it came in conflict with the customary practice of Medina.[8]

Although one may see a definite tendency to limit this subordination of hadith to local practice in the third and fourth Islamic centuries, it would be wrong to characterize Islamic jurisprudence of the middle periods, from roughly the fourth/tenth centuries to the twelfth/ eighteenth centuries, as ossified. It is true that Islamic law is based on the absolute authority of God as lawgiver, but the discovery of that law, through interpretation of the sources and application of their principles, remains open.[9] Moreover, the canon of texts which formed the basis of every jurist's course of study varied from place to place and never resulted in a codified law. Therefore, on the most fundamental level—the application of the law in the court system and in individually requested opinions [pl. fatāwā, sing. fatwā]—Islamic jurisprudence retained and continues to retain a remarkable level of flexibility.

The fact that Islam never developed a legal code (that is, until the nineteenth century in some areas) reveals several fascinating aspects about this religious tradition. One could argue that lack of a code is simply an accident of history, since there were only a few, limited opportunities for a law code to form in Islam on those rare occasions when political power joined together with legal authority. The 'Abbasid Caliph Harun al-Rashid, for instance, is said to have attempted to promote Malik's *Muwaṭṭa'* as a code, but Malik refused. While these stories of great personality clashes are entertaining, I find a systemic explanation more satisfactory. It seems that the very methods of collecting hadith from many individual sources promoted a view of legal authority which enshrined decentralization. This diffusion of authority among a broad base of individual jurists [fuqahā'] made the work of Umayyad and 'Abbasid caliphs difficult, as they tried to establish a codified form of the law. Their attempts at political control, through appointments and inquisitions, ultimately failed and only served to demonstrate the power of the legal community in resisting centralization of authority.

In retrospect, this system of decentralized authority was surprisingly effective. For instance, it promoted long years of study, providing the populace with well-trained scholars learned in all aspects of legal thought. This community regulated itself, with effective methods for weeding out incompetent or undesirable members. Moreover, through the promoting of individual choice in seeking a legal opinion [fatwā], or in choosing a teacher, popular scholars remained accessible to the public, regardless of the political choice for judge. In addition, the system probably benefited the scholars. By refusing to allow political authority over the Shari'ah, the jurists maintained both their own integrity and the integrity of the religious law. Only in this way could they be sure that rulings would be made on the basis of the Shari'ah and not merely on the whim of the ruler. The result of this lack of codification was not injustice, but a limitation on centralized power.

Finally, it is always worthwhile to maintain a healthy skepticism toward "common facts" about Islamic law. For instance, it is often stated, quite incorrectly, that there is no separation between "church and state" within Islam. Civil and spiritual authority have never been combined in Islam, not even during most of the Prophet's lifetime, and with no organized clergy there never has been a cognate institution to the Christian Church. Moreover, whenever a caliph, sultan, or imam has attempted to combine these realms, his rule has not long been tolerated by his subjects.[10] A similar point can be made about commonplace assertions that Shi'i law is more draconian than Sunni law, and that interpretations of Islamic law by Muslim revivalists are authoritative.

Teaching Islamic Law

The above points are meant as a guide for advanced reading in Islamic law, but for the undergraduate classroom I would especially recommend concentration on three specific areas: (1) the development of Islamic law in the earliest period, (2) the court and fatwā systems, and (3) the role of Islamic law in Muslims' lives today. I choose these areas both for their importance within the Islamic tradition and for their relevance for the broader study of religion; also, sufficient resources are available for classroom texts and further consultation. These three areas could be used to structure a series of lectures or seminar discussions if time allows; at the end of this essay, I have appended my own syllabus to show how these areas may be used to structure an entire seminar. Alternatively, one might suggest that students concentrate on one of these areas in an independent research paper.

Beyond the older texts outlined above (see n. 4), there are few secondary works on early Islamic history suitable for undergraduates. Bernard Weiss's excellent new book, *The Spirit of Islamic Law* (Athens, GA, 1998) may be useful for those considering the relationship of law or philosophy, but it is probably too demanding for most undergraduates. Likewise, the pro-misingly titled *Islamic Law: Theory and Practice* is of little help.[11] Coulson's *Conflicts and Tensions in Islamic Jurisprudence* (Chicago, 1969) is surprisingly accessible, however, and can be used effectively with other primary sources. In a series of short chapters, Coulson address the complex problems of inheritance law as they appeared in traditional commentary and hadith literature. His occasional references to "modern" British and Islamic law effectively contextualize the issues (though they also clearly date the book). The negative aspect of Coulson is his lack of historical context and criticism of the sources, but if combined with excerpts from early Islamic legal texts themselves, this book can serve as a fine teaching tool. To highlight the variability of early texts, I would recommend a thematic approach, illustrating Coulson's discussion of inheritance, marriage, and divorce law with examples from Quran, the *Muwaṭṭa'*, al-Risālah by al-Shāfi'ī (d. 204/820), or the *Ṣaḥīḥ* of al Bukharī (d. 256/870).[12] Since these sources are so rich in detail, excerpts need not be large.

As an example of the way this type of comparison can be done, take the Islamic law of slavery. The Quran retains a remarkable amount of legal material on slavery, for instance, most of which has to do with rules on emancipation and sexual relations.[13] These rules are found in some thirty verses and appear to regulate several pre-Islamic practices, but the main thrust of this material is to ameliorate the position of slaves and offer them some protection. Slavery was therefore fully acceptable in the Quran, though the slave is always categorized as a human being, not a mere piece of property. By the time Malik formulated his juristic dicta in the second Islamic century, Muslim jurists had greatly increased the legal material on slaves, developing both a sophisticated structure for discussion of slave law and a common vocabulary. The early jurists reserved as many as five chapters in their multivolumed law books particularly for slaves: emancipation ['itq]; the relation of the freed slave as a client of his or her former master [walā']; the slave who is promised freedom upon the master's death [mudabbar]; the one who enters into an emancipation contract [mukātab]; and the one who bears her master a child [umm walad]. The material on these subjects in the *Muwaṭṭa'* is substantial and deals with a broad range of distinct concerns, both in terms of general rules and specific cases. In other words, during the 150 years between the recording of the Quran and the *Muwaṭṭa'*, Islamic law moved from modification of a preexisting system to establishment of whole new categories of law, including increased regulation of the status of a slave's children; new rules on slaves and business transactions; and expanded rules on emancipation. In general, Quranic rules are concerned primarily with ameliorating the position of slaves in the context of accepted societal norms, while early Islamic law fo-

cuses on the details and ramifications of slave emancipation in the context of
a developed legal system.

In a course on comparative law or comparative ethics, concentration on
the primary sources is the only basis for comparative work, since there are almost no secondary sources available.[14] Nevertheless, comparative work can
provide a contextual base for understanding Quranic and early legal rules. In
the case of slavery again, comparison with legal codes from other Near Eastern cultures, including Judaic, Christian, Byzantine, and Sasanian, demonstrate that Malik's *Muwaṭṭa'* is addressed to a vastly different audience than
that which received the Quran: first, to a society that has assimilated numerous cultures, along with their practices; and second, to jurists who seek to
bring these practices in line with Islamic sensibilities. For instance, while certain emancipation practices have roots in the Quran and early Muslim practice, their particular mode of application could vary widely, depending on the
practices of the preexisting local cultures, which also had long traditions of
emancipation. I would particularly recommend comparative readings in Talmud, Byzantine law, and Sasanian law.[15]

Just published is a helpful new teaching resource for the comparison of
Jewish and Islamic law. In *Comparing Religions through Law: Judaism and Islam*
(London, 2000), Jacob Neusner and Tamara Sonn discuss many of the most
important theoretical aspects of law in Judaism and Islam. While the authors'
choice of sources limits the scope of their discussion, they are able to make
some substantial discoveries about the nature of religious law. A companion
volume, *Judaism and Islam in Practice: A Sourcebook,* has also appeared (London, 2000). This volume contains extensive excerpts from the classical legal
texts, as they struggle with common questions of prayer, marriage, charity,
and the community. Together, these two texts can provide the basic reading
for a whole course on the subject of comparative religious law.

The benefit of focusing on original sources in translation is to give students
first-hand experience working with the authoritative texts which have helped
define Muslim thought over the centuries. Legal handbooks, however, are
best understood as theoretical expressions of the law, as a guide to correct behavior with no guarantee as to how closely such suggestions were followed.
A balance to this material can be found in collections of official legal opinions
[fatāwā] and other court documents. These texts are usually tied to specific
cases and when combined with historical contextualization, provide a rich
slice of Muslim life in various times and places. While it is true that the vast
majority of the populace would not go to court to solve legal problems, and
that therefore the documents cannot be said to be representative of all Muslim society, they offer rare insights into the way Islamic law could be applied.

Tales of courts, judges, and famous cases are found throughout Islamic historical texts, but fatāwā were not actually collected until much later. For instance, *Kitab al-mi'yār* is a collection compiled by Ahmad al-Wansharisi (d. 1508 C.E.), which contains fatāwā dating back centuries earlier. In a series of articles, David Powers has traced dozens of fatāwā from al-Wansharisi's collection, providing much historical and legal background in the process.[16] Any of these articles would serve as an excellent introduction to the topic for undergraduates. For instance, in *"Kadijustiz* or *Qadi*-justice?"[17] Powers outlines the facts of a case in fourteenth-century North Africa, in which a politically well-connected family is embroiled in an inheritance lawsuit. It seems that the deceased may have adopted his bastard child Salim as a son, and now Salim has sued the family for a portion of the estate. In telling this tale, Powers uses historical and legal sources to provide rich detail on fourteenth-century politics and jurisprudence, bringing this 700-year-old court document to life.

Other work on fatāwā includes articles by Peters, Hallaq, and Tucker,[18] as well as an edited volume by David Powers, Muhammad Masud, and Brinkley Messick (*Islamic Legal Interpretation: Muftis and Their Fatwas*, Cambridge [Mass], 1996). This book can serve as an excellent teaching source, taken either as a whole or as selections from its twenty-eight articles. Divided into sections on premodern, early modern, and modern periods, the book covers a wide range. Nevertheless, a clear focus is maintained on the court and its documents, including numerous translations of fatāwā from Andalusia to Indonesia. For instance, Mohamad Mudzhar's contribution on the Council of Indonesian 'Ulamā' (pp. 230–241) includes a four-page fatwā from 1981, which explains in great detail why it is forbidden for Indonesian Muslims to attend Christian celebrations of Christmas. Mudzhar provides extensive background material on this declaration, describing the political and religious reasons that Muslim and Christian relations have recently been primarily characterized by rivalry. He also reflects on the ways in which changes in the nature of issuing fatāwā (from a central institution like the Council of Indonesian 'Ulamā' as opposed to the individual who issued the fatāwā [muftī]), result in substantial changes in the application of Islamic law. Other fatāwā in this collection include such issues as child marriage in seventeenth-century Palestine (pp. 131–132), postmortem examinations in 1940s Egypt (pp. 279–282), and Operation Desert Storm (pp. 279–300). Each of these fatāwā is placed in its historical and social context, providing an excellent resource for students. The benefit of working with such documents is to see both the range of material covered under Islamic law, and the methods employed by the lawyers in making their arguments.

Nonetheless, *Islamic Legal Interpretation* is rooted in the methodology of studying other cultures primarily through the documents they produce. While this is an appropriate method for a document-oriented field like law, the impact of Islamic law on the lives of modern Muslims may be best explored by the participant observation of anthropologists. Several recent contributions to the field of legal anthropology make excellent resources for studying the role that Islamic law has in modern Muslim societies. Moreover, the theoretical maturity of this field makes for some fascinating comparative possibilities, as well as useful material for courses focusing on gender, postcolonial societies, or religious revival.

Brinkley Messick's recent book, *The Calligraphic State* (Berkeley, 1993) forms a bridge between studies of past societies through documents alone and studies of present societies. Combining local-level ethnography and textual analysis of the works of Islamic jurisprudence, Messick analyzes the role played by formal textual language and thought in the town of Ibb, Yemen. His book covers a variety of subjects, from the way the scribe records court proceedings to the politics of the Yemeni judges, drawing on theories of Geertz and Foucault. Yet in spite of the complexity of the subject matter, the book remains highly readable. For instance, Messick begins his chapter on "Judicial Presence" (p. 167) with a fascinating description of the physical format of a typical Shari'ah court session held in front of the qadi's residence. Shifting to a criticism of old Orientalist snipes at qadis sitting under palm trees, Messick explains the particular way that this format promotes accessibility of justice. Furthermore, Messick places these practices within their historical and religious context, drawing on texts and philology to enrich the reader's appreciation of the event. In short, the book exemplifies Geertz's call for a "thick description" of events, and in Messick's hands simple, everyday occurrences are infused with a rich profusion of meaning. Messick's is only one of a number of recent studies on Yemen that can be used to complement a study of Islamic law.[19]

Two other works of legal anthropology focus on Islamic family law and its impact on women. *Marriage on Trial* by Ziba Mir-Hosseini (London, 1993) is a comparative study of Moroccan and Iranian family law courts based on information collected from 1985 to 1989. Although too expensive for the undergraduate, the valuable case studies in this book make it an excellent library resource. Mir-Hosseini's introductory chapter is also an important and accessible statement on methodology. Shahla Haeri's *Law of Desire* (Syracuse, 1989) also looks at Iran but concentrates solely on temporary marriage [mut'a or sigheh]. Based on a series of interviews with both men and women, this book is particularly interesting as it tracks the differences in people's attitudes to temporary marriage both before and after the 1979 revolution. In addition to general courses on Islam, Haeri's book is strongly recommended for courses dealing with pilgrimage, prostitution, or Shi'ism; it is both highly readable and theoretically sophisticated.

A Seminar in Islamic Law

In my opinion, it is important to avoid the temptation to concentrate only on these anthropological studies. While students are naturally attracted to the personal narrative of "real" Muslims, these studies are sophisticated examples of the use of traditional sources in daily life, and presume a significant background in Islamic history. Moreover, examination of one or two "real lives" of Yemeni women in divorce courts could lead to mistaken generalizations about the nature of Islamic law. As Messick's book demonstrates, these two sources are best used together to complement one another, revealing both the depth and the relevance of the tradition. As I think back to my friends at the café, I realize that it was my knowledge of the classical texts that comforted them most. As difficult as they may be, the ancient sources play an essential role in defining the Islamic religion.

In the syllabus that follows, these classic sources form the core, and I address anthropological studies only after establishing a solid foundation in these sources. As may be gleaned from the introductory paragraphs, I change much of the course every year to reflect the interests of particular students, but the first six weeks remain constant. The course is run as a near-graduate seminar, in which one student takes responsibility for initiating discussion every week with a formal class presentation. The extensive recommended readings in the syllabus are designed to help this discussion initiator and also to provide preliminary bibliographies for research papers.

Religion 321: *Seminar in Islamic Law*

Part of our task in this class is to criticize misconceptions of Islam and its holy law by examining the historical roots, early development, and application of Islamic Law in the modern world. As a 300-level course, familiarity with the basic history and institutions of Islam is assumed, and integration of your expertise in other fields is encouraged. Our emphasis will be on engaging original sources in a careful, thematic study which will follow the topics we agreed on last semester. When the course is finished we may not have all the answers, but we should be able to frame the right questions.

This course is conceived as a seminar, in which the arts of discussion and criticizing ideas are nearly as important as the material itself. Each week we will deal with a short primary text, which students are expected to prepare intensively—that means reading the material several times, taking notes, and coming to class with specific questions; part of this preparation should include consultation with recommended readings and standard reference works in order to fully understand the arguments in the text. In addition, students will have the opportunity to set the agenda for a session by presenting a paper to the class on a topic of their choosing. Class participation will be evaluated on the basis of preparation of texts and a brief oral exam; it will account for 25 percent of the final grade. There will also be two papers: one to serve as the basis for class discussion (7–10 pp., 20%), and a research paper (20–25 pp., 45%). A bibliographical essay, on the same topic as your research paper, will be worth 10 percent.

REQUIRED BOOKS (AVAILABLE FOR PURCHASE IN THE BOOKSTORE)

Haeri, Shahla. *Law of Desire.*
Khadduri, Majid. *Islamic Jurisprudence: Shāfiʿī's Risāla.*
Maududi, A. A.. *Purdah and the Status of Women in Islam.*
Messick, Brinkley. *The Calligraphic State.*
Schacht, Joseph. *Introduction to Islamic Law.*

RECOMMENDED FOR PURCHASE

Quran [Arberry's edition is available in the bookstore].
Hourani, Albert. *A History of the Arab Peoples.*

ON RESERVE IN THE LIBRARY

Calder, Norman. *Studies in Early Muslim Jurisprudence.*
Coulson, Noel J. *Conflicts and Tensions in Islamic Jurisprudence.*
Coulson, Noel J. *A History of Islamic Law.*
Crone, Patricia. *Roman, Provincial and Islamic Law.*
Gibb, H. A. R. *Muhammedanism.*
Goldziher, Ignaz. *Islamic Theology and Law.*
Malik b. Anas. *al-Muwaṭṭa',* Aisha Bewley, Translator.
Masud, Powers, Messick. *Islamic Interpretation: Muftis and Their Fatwas.*
Mir-Hosseini, Ziba. *Marriage on Trial.*
Watt, W. M. *Islamic Philosophy and Theology.*

STANDARD REFERENCE WORKS IN LIBRARY

The Encyclopedia of Islam (EI), new edition
Shorter Encyclopedia of Islam (SEI)
Encyclopedia of Religion (ER)

SYLLABUS

After a first week of essays from modern Muslim jurists, designed to demonstrate the wide variety of current thinking on Islamic law, I delve into a swift review of the first centuries. In the syllabus, I make use of the above abbreviations in reference to various encyclopedia articles.

The Discourses of Islamic Law

Prepare: Abdullahi al-Na'im (Sudan/Emory): "The dichotomy between religious and secular discourse"; Fazlur Rahman (Pakistan/Chicago): excerpt from *Islam and Modernity;* Fatima Mernissi (Morocco): excerpt from *The Veil and the Male Elite*
Read: ER: "Islamic Law"; EI: "fiqh," "Sharī'a"; Coulson: *History:* 1–73; Schacht: 116–123

Muhammad and the Earliest Legal Institutions

Prepare: Quran: Surahs 74; 75; 2:157–200; 4:1–112; 17:80–91
Read: Schacht: 1–36; EI: "'Ibādāt," "Ḳur'ān," "Mu'āmalāt"; Quran: Surahs 2, 4, 5, 24
Rec: Hourani: 1–21; Gibb: 1–48

The Early Schools of Sunni Law

Prepare: Brockopp: "Early Islamic Jurisprudence in Egypt" in *IJMES* 30 (1998): 167–182
Read: Hourani: 22–58; EI: "Ibn 'Abd al-Ḥakam," "Muzanī"; Schacht: 37–48
Rec: Calder: *Studies;* EI: "Awzā'ī," "Ḥanābila," "Ḥanafiyya," "Mālikiyya," "Shāfi'iyya"; SEI: "Ẓāhiriyya"

Early Court System

Prepare: Schacht: 175–211
Read: Schacht: 49–56; EI: "Ḳāḍī," "Ḳaḍā," "Muzakkī," "Maẓālim," "Shāhid"
Rec: Coulson: *History:* 75–148

al-Muwaṭṭa', an Early Book of Jurisprudence

Prepare: Malik: 1–7; 24–35; 76–83; 173–183; 200–208
Read: Schacht: 37–85; EI: "Mālik b. Anas"; Malik: 209–220; 327–338; 355–357; 395–397
Rec: Gibb: 49–85

Shafi'i's Risāla—a treatise on the sources of jurisprudence?

Prepare: Khadduri: 81–104; 154–163

Read: Khadduri: 3–54; 67–80; 179–229; 252–304
Rec: Hallaq: "Was al-Shāfiʿī the Master Architect . . ." in *IJMES*; EI: "Shāfiʿī"

Usually, I like to include a substantial section on medieval Islamic law, focusing on the social realities in a particular location, like Cairo, Baghdad, or Istanbul. Often, I include a more extensive discussion of Islamic theoretical jurisprudence (uṣūl al-fiqh), but in this year, students were particularly interested in modern applications and theological issues; therefore, the medieval period was limited to one week. The text here, A.J. Arberry's Theology of Avicenna, *is unfortunately now out of print.*

Theology

Prepare: Arberry: *Avicenna,* 25–76
Read: Arberry: *Avicenna,* 1–25; Hourani: 59–79; Watt: *Islamic Philosophy:*
     56–74
Rec: Goldziher: *Islamic Theology and Law*

A bridge to the modern period is formed by the Masud, Messick, and Powers book, which contains cases from medieval and modern law. This excellent resource is described in detail above.

Early Cases in Islamic Law

Prepare: Masud et al.: 47–86
Read: Coulson: *History:* 149–181; Schacht: 89–111; Masud: 1–43
Rec: Hourani: 81–205

Islamic Law in the Early Modern Period

Prepare: Messick: 1–131
Read: Hourani: 207–298
Rec: Masud: 151–220

The final section of the course focuses on modern cases from three localities: Iran, South Asia, and Yemen. These advanced texts worked well with my students, many of whom had done significant work in Asian Studies. The Haeri text is particularly challenging as a complex anthropological study of "temporary marriage" in modern Iran. In contrast, Mawdudi's text is prescriptive, not descriptive, and demonstrates the way some reformers attempt to reclaim early Islamic history, proving the value of a solid grounding in the classic sources.

Iranian Application of Islamic Law

Prepare: Haeri: 1–102
Read: Haeri: 105–211

Rec: Mir-Hosseini: *Marriage on Trial;* Momen: *History of Shiʻi Islam;* Hourani: 299–415

Islamic Law in South Asia

Prepare: Mawdudi (entire)

Read: Peter J. Awn, "Indian Islam: The Shah Bano Affair," in *Fundamentalism and Gender,* ed. J. Hawley (Oxford, 1994), 63–78; Rafiuddin Ahmed, "Redefining Muslim Identity in South Asia," in *Accounting for Fundamentalisms,* ed. M. Marty and Scott Appleby (Chicago, 1994), 669–705; Shahla Haeri, "Obedience versus Autonomy," in *Fundamentalisms and Society,* ed. Marty and Appleby (Chicago, 1993), 181–213.

Rec: Gibb: 113–131; Hourani: 299–349

Studies from Yemen

Prepare: Messick: 135–255
Read: Masud: 310–320
Rec: Hourani: 416–458

NOTES

1. Fazlur Rahman, "Approaches to Islam in Religious Studies: Review Essay," in *Approaches to Islam in Religious Studies,* ed. Richard C. Martin (Tucson: University of Arizona, 1985. Reprinted, Oxford: Oneword Publications, 2001), 189–202.

2. One could, of course, use interpretations of the Quran [tafsīr] for the same purpose. In fact, legal and mystical *tafsīr* are particularly important resources for students of Islam and the work of probing this material has only just begun.

3. In my opinion, an introductory course in Islam would be incomplete without some consideration of Baha'is or Nizari Shiʻis who consider themselves free of the bonds of Islamic law. On the other hand, the central role for Islamic law in twelver Shiʻism forms an effective tool for questioning the common appellation of this sect as heterodox.

4. Coulson, *A History of Islamic Law* (Edinburgh: Edinburgh University Press, 1964); and idem, *Conflicts and Tensions in Islamic Jurisprudence* (Chicago: University of Chicago Press, 1969). Schacht, *The Origins of Muhammadan Jurisprudence* (Oxford: Clarendon, 1950); and idem, *An Introduction to Islamic Law* (Oxford: Clarendon, 1964).

5. For some recent criticism of Schacht's theories, see Wael Hallaq, "Was the Gate of *ijtihād* Closed?" *International Journal of Middle East Studies* 16 (1984): 3–41; and idem, "Was al-Shāfiʻī the Master Architect of Islamic Jurisprudence?" *International Journal of Middle East Studies* 25 (1993): 587–605. Baber Johansen updates Schacht's theoretical dependence on Weber in *Contingency in a Sacred Law: Legal and Ethical Norms in the Muslim fiqh* (Leiden: E.J. Brill, 1999).

6. For the latest installment of this debate, see Christopher Melchert, *The Forma-*

tion of the Sunni Schools of Law: 9th–10th centuries C.E. (Leiden: E.J. Brill, 1997), and the major reviews of this book in scholarly journals.

7. For a more extensive discussion of this point, see chapter 2 of my *Studies in Early Mālikī Law* (Leiden: E.J. Brill, 2000).

8. Miklos Muranyi writes on page 36 of *Ein altes Fragment medinensischer Jurisprudenz aus Qairawan* (Stuttgart: Franz Steiner, 1985): "Daß die Rechtsgelehrsamkeit der Frühzeit sich wenig um das *ḥadīt* kümmerte, das seinerseits noch in der Umgebung von al-Māgišūn, Mālik und ihrer Nachfolger zunächst Gestalt annehmen und auch dann dem anerkannten *'amal* entsprechen mußte, um sich im *fiqh* als Quelle behaupten zu können, ist im vorliegenden Werkfragment über Ḥaǧǧ-Bestimmungen direkt belegt."

Although it is an interesting study of the *Muwaṭṭa'*, Yasin Dutton's *Origins of Islamic Law* (Surrey: Curzon, 1999) cannot be recommended due to its prejudicial attitude toward the sources.

9. In *A History of Islamic Legal Theories* (Cambridge: Cambridge University Press, 1997), Hallaq demonstrates the flexibility and creativity of medieval and modern jurists, although his first chapter on early developments takes an uncritical stance toward the sources.

10. There are many examples in Islamic history of such rulers, who have been portrayed as despots, among them: the caliphs 'Uthman b. 'Affan (d. 34/656) and al-Mu'tasim (d. 258/842), the sultan Abdülhamid (d. 1909), and Ruhollah Khomeini (d. 1989).

11. This book (ed. Robert Gleave and Eugenia Kermeli [London: I. B. Taurus, 1997]) contains an uneven collection of essays, most of which are quite specialized.

12. All these sources are available in translation. Aisha Bewley's translation of *Al-Muwatta of Imam Malik ibn Anas* (London: Kegan Paul, 1989) is not a scholarly translation and not based on a scholarly edition. While her English is usually accurate, there are some misleading and incorrect translations; a helpful index is included. Majid Khadduri has produced a very useable translation of al-Shāfi'ī's *Risālah* (*Islamic Jurisprudence: Shāfi'ī's Risāla* [Baltimore: Johns Hopkins Press, 1961]; now available from the Islamic Texts Society in Cambridge), with a fine historical introduction. The *Ṣaḥīḥ* of al-Bukharī is available in several English versions, some of which are summaries of the original. Hadith collections can now be searched on-line at *http://www. usc.edu/dept/MSA/reference/searchhadith.html*, though the results are dependent on the vagaries of the English translation.

13. For background on this subject, see W. 'Arafat, "The Attitude of Islam to Slavery," *Islamic Quarterly* 10 (1966): 12–18; R. Roberts, *The Social Laws of the Qorân* (London: Williams and Norgate, 1925); and chapter 3 of my *Early Mālikī Law*.

14. Though see Daniel Brown, "Islamic Ethics in Comparative Perspective," *The Muslim World* 89 (1999): 181–192. This whole volume of *The Muslim World* is devoted to the Islamic ethics of abortion and euthanasia.

15. Translations of Talmud and the Justinian Code are readily available. For Sasanian law, see Maria Macuch, *Das Sasanidische Rechtsbuch "Mātakdān i Hazār Dātistān"* (Wiesbaden: Franz Steiner, 1981); for provincial Roman law, see Patricia Crone, *Roman, Provincial and Islamic Law* (Cambridge: Cambridge University Press, 1987). For slavery, see also the important study by William Westermann, *The Slave Systems of Greek and Roman Antiquity* (Philadelphia: American Philosophical Society, 1955).

16. See particularly "The Mālikī Family Endowment," *International Journal of Middle East Studies* 25 (1993): 379–406; also: "Fatwās as Sources for Legal and Social History," *al-Qantara* 11 (1990): 295–341; "The Islamic Inheritance System," *Arabic Law Quarterly* 8 (1993): 13–29; and "Legal Consultation (*futyā*) in Medieval Spain and North Africa," in *Islam and Public Law,* ed. Chibli Mallat (London: Graham & Trotman, 1993), 85–106.

17. *Islamic Law and Society* 1 (1994): 332–366.

18. W. Hallaq, "Murder in Cordoba," *Acta Orientalia* 55 (1994): 55–83; R. Peters, "Muḥammad al-ʿAbbāsī al-Mahdī (d. 1899), Grand Mufti of Egypt and his *al-Fatāwā al-Mahdiyya*," *Islamic Law and Society* 1 (1994): 66–82; and J. Tucker, "*Muftīs* and Matrimony," *Islamic Law and Society* 1 (1994): 265–300. Other issues of *Islamic Law and Society* are also recommended.

19. See, for instance, Anna Würth, "A Sanʿa Court: The Family and the Ability to Negotiate," *Islamic Law and Society* 2 (1995): 320–340.

※

CHAPTER SIX

※

Disparity and Context

Teaching Quranic Studies in North America

JANE DAMMEN McAULIFFE

T O BEGIN WITH A CLARIFICATION: I speak of "teaching Quranic Studies" rather than of "teaching the Quran" in order to emphasize the range and complexity of this subject field. The Quran, like the New Testament, is not a big book, but Quranic Studies, like Biblical Studies, is a vast, multilayered discipline, one which no single scholar can hope to master in all its intricacy and diversity. Within the field of Religious Studies, the status and scope of Biblical Studies are readily manifest. In North America, the Society for Biblical Literature (SBL), with a membership of nearly 7,000, almost equals the size of the American Academy of Religion (AAR), a professional organization that purports to represent scholars of all other scriptural and religious traditions combined.[1] The AAR and SBL share the program book for their huge, jointly sponsored annual meeting, mounting roughly equal numbers of panels. All of this is well known to academics in the field of Religious Studies, but I repeat it here in order to draw your attention to the immense disparity that exists between North American Biblical Studies and North American Quranic Studies.

To provide some evidence of that discrepancy, let me describe my own, admittedly limited, attempts to explore the field of Quranic Studies in situ. A few years ago, courtesy of a fellowship funded by the Mellon Foundation, I spent a semester at the University of Jordan's Faculty of Islamic Law [Kulliyyat al-Sharīʿah]. I went to Jordan because I wanted to find out how the Quran was studied in a contemporary Muslim university. Having long rubbed shoulders with biblical scholars, both as colleagues and as friends, I had a fair

94

sense of the graduate preparation required by the field of Euro-American Biblical Studies. But I was eager to experience the analogue—the range of offerings available in a university program of Quranic Studies. The Kulliyyat al-Sharī'ah, with its extensive range of courses, afforded an excellent venue for this exercise. Although I could only sample a portion of the courses offered in Quranic Studies, in the hope that even that sampling will prove instructive, I shall briefly sketch the syllabus of my semester's work.

Quranic Studies [Dirāsāt qur'āniyyah], taught by Dr. Muḥammad al-Majālī, was the primary foundation course for the more specialized aspects of Quranic Studies. Dr. al-Majālī moved rapidly through the standard loci of the Quranic sciences, that is, the phenomenon of revelation [waḥy], the formation of the 'Uthmānic codices [maṣāḥif], textual or semantic variation [al-aḥruf al-sab'a], the designation of Meccan and Medinan verses, the abrogating and abrogated verses [al-nāsikh wa-l-mansūkh], and the occasions or circumstances of revelation [asbāb al-nuzūl]. Professor al-Majālī, who has a Ph.D. from the University of Edinburgh, was a popular teacher and his classes were always packed. Students were occasionally quizzed orally in class and were free, time permitting, to raise questions. They were formally tested on the material and these exams [imtiḥān] were, quite expectedly, the source of considerable student anxiety.

Prescriptive Verses [Āyāt al-aḥkām], also taught by Dr. Muḥammad al-Majālī, concentrated on those verses of the Quran that carry legal implications. Dr. al-Majālī's lectures presented exegetical analyses of specific passages. My notes for the course record remarks on Q 2:102–103, 106–108, 114, 154, 172–73, etc. In fact, the formal lectures never went beyond the second "chapter" [sūrah] of the Quran [sūrat al-baqarah] because of the high degree of detail that the professor wished to convey to his students. While the focus was on the main legal norm or rule [ḥukm] of the verse, attention was also paid to such legally significant issues as *asbāb al-nuzūl, nāsikh/mansūkh,* and matters of jurisprudential disagreement [ikhtilāf]. Professor al-Majālī's intention was to model a method of studying the prescriptive verses, one the students could then extend to other parts of the Quran, once they had thoroughly assimilated the procedures as applied to the relevant portions of the second surah. The basic texts for this course were a twentieth-century *aḥkām* textbook by Muḥammad 'Alī al-Sāyis[2] and the important twelfth-century source by Muḥammad b. 'Abdallāh b. al-'Arabī.[3] The al-Sāyis text itself provides a convenient summarization of noteworthy elements of earlier legal exegesis, while current, well-printed editions of Ibn al-'Arabī offer students direct access to a widely cited classical source. The lectures, however, made frequent reference to other major *aḥkām* works, especially those of al-Qurṭubī, al-Jaṣṣāṣ, and al-Harrāsī,[4] as well as the standard, full-scale [musalsal] Quran commentaries.

Recitation and Memorization I [al-Tilāwah wa-l-ḥifẓ I] was taught by Mrs. Amal al-Naʿīmma, and *Recitation and Memorization II* [al-Tilāwah wa-l-ḥifẓ II] was taught by Dr. Aḥmad al-Quḍāh. As the Roman numerals indicate, these titles represent two levels of Quranic recitation courses. Normally students would take these courses in sequence, but I audited both simultaneously in order to assess the different levels of instruction and of student development in the theory and technique of Quranic recitation. Students at the primary level began with memorization and recitation of the final section [juzʾ] of the Quran. They were introduced to the rudiments of correct articulation and vocal conveyance [tajwīd] and were frequently quizzed on their understanding of these principles. The fundamental classroom procedure, however, was straightforward recitation of memorized or previously prepared passages. For me, participation in these classes took on a timeless quality. I could well imagine hearing these sounds and seeing the same tightly concentrated student faces in any Islamic land and in any century of the Islamic era.

The second level of this course sequence reviewed tajwīd theory in more detail, elaborating all aspects of physical sound production [makhrūj al-ḥurūf] and concentrating attention on the finer points of consonantal assimilation [idghām], vowel lengthening [madd], mandated or recommended pause points [waqf], etc. Developing genuine skill in the "science of recitation" [ʿilm al-tajwīd] is a complex and exacting task, one that requires many hours of focused attention and practice. At this second level, students were expected to memorize and correctly recite significantly longer portions of the Quranic text, and their precise pronunciation and full employment of principles of articulation [aḥkām al-tajwīd] were judged more stringently. Again, the majority of class time was taken up with prepared recitation. Students were usually called on by row and desk order and the instructor expected to move quickly from person to person. I noticed that the religious etiquette [adab] of recitation was followed scrupulously. Each new reciter began with the compulsory prayer formulas [taʿawwudh and basmalah] and during periods of ritual impurity, students followed a neighbor's copy, taking care to avoid any direct contact with the text.[5]

It is worth mentioning that tajwīd classes in the Kulliyyat al-Sharīʿah, unlike other courses, are sex-segregated and, obviously, I was permitted to attend only those for females. The reasons most often cited by students for this mandatory segregation was that women's voices would be too spiritually distracting for male classmates. While this is a common viewpoint in many parts of the Muslim world, it is not universally shared. Women have achieved prominence as professional reciters, sometimes international prominence.[6]

Textual Study of Quran Commentaries [al-Dirāsat al-naṣṣiyyah fī kutub al-tafsīr], taught by Dr. ʿAbd al-Jalīl ʿAbd al-Raḥmān, was an upper-level exegesis course that involved close textual analysis of a selection of exegetical works. The course began with a section from a twentieth-century Shiʻi commentary, al-Ṭabāṭabāʻī's *Mīzān*,[7] and ranged through a number of works, both classical and modern, with particular attention to al-Qurṭubī and Abū Suʻūd.[8] The class format entailed virtually all lecture with very little student interaction. The lectures themselves tended to range broadly and, occasionally, verge on a sermon-style. Professor ʻAbd al-Jalīl has written a book on *tafsīr mawḍūʻī*, a method of contemporary exegesis that treats Quranic material thematically rather than sequentially, and, understandably, this focus shaped much of the course content.

Principles of Quranic Exposition [Asālīb al- bayān], taught by Dr. Faḍl Ḥasan ʻAbbās, was a packed-house, upper-level course taught by one of the most revered faculty members in the Kulliyyat al-Sharīʻah. His lectures, delivered in impeccable Arabic [fuṣḥā], were riveting. The basic text was the professor's own two-volume work on rhetoric [balāghah], and students were expected to master substantial sections of this in preparation for each class session.[9] The material was densely detailed and accessible only to those students with a strong preparation in both the Quranic text and in classical grammatical and rhetorical analysis.

Hermeneutical Methods of the Commentators on the Quran [Manāhij al-mufas-sirīn], taught by Dr. Muṣṭafā al-Mashnī, was a graduate seminar conducted on the student-presents-paper model. But Dr. al-Mashnī, who has written exten-sively on Andalusian tafsīr,[10] would frequently interrupt with his own insight-ful reflections or challenge the students on issues of research methodology. For this auditor, class arrangement presented a problem, an unanticipated consequence of gender segregation in the classroom. The six male students sat facing the instructor in the front row. As was expected in the Kulliyyat al-Sharīʻah, I sat several rows behind with the only female student in the class. The effect on seminar dynamics was quite marked. Not only was female par-ticipation marginalized, but also the expected cohesion of a graduate seminar never materialized.

I have described this semester at the University of Jordan in some detail— and I repeat that this selection of courses by no means represents the univer-sity's full offerings in Quranic Studies—for two reasons. First, this kind of in-formation is not easily available to Western-language readers. Rarely does non-Muslim scholarly literature allude to the contemporary reality of Quranic Studies as a multifaceted academic discipline in Muslim educational institu-tions. Second, I want to reinforce the point that the concept of Quranic Stud-ies as a subject within the undergraduate or graduate curriculum of a Euro-pean or North American university bears little resemblance to its counterpart within a modern Muslim academic institution. No North American university would hire a research scholar of "Biblical Studies." It would recruit a specialist in John or Luke-Acts or Christian origins. Or it would advertise for a biblical archaeologist, an authority in Israelite and Canaanite religion, or a scholar of northwest Semitic languages. That same university, however, would feel no hesitancy in advertising for a specialist in "Quranic Studies," if it were even willing to diversify its faculty beyond a single, all-purpose Islamicist. The situation within our major professional organizations is no different. A recent AAR/SBL directory listed 79 program units for Biblical Studies and none for Quranic Studies. There is but a single "study of Islam" unit which in any given year may or may not choose to include Quranic Studies among its program offerings.

The Quran, then, cannot be studied within North American universities and colleges in a manner either commensurate with its biblical cognate or with its equivalent mode of instruction in a Muslim university. The frank acknowledgment of this fact can serve as a useful prelude to another important qualification: Any course on Quranic Studies must inevitably be shaped by the academic context in which it is offered. Naturally, both the diversity and the orientation of the offerings in Quranic Studies at a Muslim "seminary," such as the Kulliyyat al-Sharī'ah of the University of Jordan, or comparable faculties at institutions like Egypt's al-Azhar, India's Aligarh, or Malaysia's International Islamic University, will be different than those forged within a Western academic heritage. But even within the latter category, significant variation will occur. Again, I can best explain this by reference to my own experience.

The first course devoted solely to the Quran that I developed was a graduate offering in the Ph.D. program at Emory University. While at that time the Graduate Division of Religion was not yet admitting doctoral students in Islamic Studies, it had—and continues to have—a very strong program in Biblical Studies. Consequently, most of the graduate students in my course were doing advanced work in either Old or New Testament. For the most part, their interest in the Quran was comparative. They were curious about the genesis and development of the Quranic text, and they brought to their study the perspectives and preoccupations of contemporary biblical study. Because they were already quite sophisticated in textual and exegetical investigations, they were able to probe the Quranic corpus with developed analytical skill. These students, however, had no training in classical Arabic—although a number of them subsequently enrolled in my graduate Arabic course—so there was no opportunity to do comparative philology or to address the lexical and grammatical conundrums of the Quranic text.

Nevertheless, these students generated stimulating seminar sessions and wrote some exceptionally interesting graduate essays. They were capable of absorbing and discussing dense and detailed material and, given the strong theological focus of Emory's graduate program, they were especially interested in Quranic themes that drew upon the scriptural commonalities of Judaism, Christianity, and Islam. With such interests in mind, I allowed these aspects of the Quran to occupy more space on the syllabus than would be the case in other teaching contexts. Yet I felt it was also important to highlight significant differences between the Quran and its biblical "cousin." An example of this would be the role of orality in both the formation of the Quranic text and its subsequent religio-social function. Here I found the works of William Graham and Kristina Nelson, among others, to be particularly useful.[11] Another example would be the pronounced continuities of classical and contemporary Quranic exegesis, continuities which have not sustained the kind of intellectual rupture represented by post-Enlightenment skepticism and secularity.

Moving from Emory University to the University of Toronto in 1992 meant changing my pedagogical contexts in a significant way. (In 1999, I left Toronto for Georgetown University in Washington, D.C.) The University of Toronto is a very large, publicly supported institution situated in the center of one of the most ethnically diverse urban areas on the globe. Just as in the United States, revisions made to Canadian immigration legislation within about the last thirty years, have dramatically altered the older religious demography, particularly in major metropolitan regions. Consequently, the university student body, which draws largely upon the population base of both the greater Toronto area and southern Ontario more generally, has experienced recent and profound demographic shifts. Although no completely accurate statistics are available, surveys within the last few years indicate that the undergraduate population at the University of Toronto now approaches 50 percent Asian in ethnic origin, including West, South and Southeast Asia, as well as the Pacific Rim countries. For about 40 percent of the undergraduates, English is a second language.

My appointment at the University of Toronto was shared between two departments, the Department for the Study of Religion and the Department of Near and Middle Eastern Civilizations. In each of these departments the results of this demographic shift were striking. Unlike the situation twenty years ago within the Department for the Study of Religion, now when the faculty offer courses in religious traditions such as Hinduism, Buddhism, and Islam, many—often, most—of the students are either themselves adherents of these traditions or come from families with a cultural practice of adherence. I would argue that this change raises some basic pedagogical issues for the field of Religious Studies, a subject to which I will return shortly. For the moment, it is enough to note some of the ways in which changing classroom demography affects pedagogical expectations and strategies.

In the Department for the Study of Religion, I regularly offered an under-graduate course entitled "Revelation and Interpretation in Islam." Initially, I structured this as a historical and thematic exercise. A variety of questions generated the course's topical outline: How do Muslims understand the pro-cess of Quranic revelation? Is the Quran a book or a sound? Can different lit-erary genres be found in the Quran? How did the Quran achieve its present format? Can the Quran be translated? Why are there so many exegetical books on the Quran and why do they continue to be produced? What is the Quranic understanding of God, human nature, revelation, etc.? How should one explore a particular topic in the Quran? How does the Quran function in diverse Muslim societies? What role did/does the Quran play in shaping both the aesthetic environment and responsive human sensibilities?

In this course students combined their study of particular Quranic surahs with other readings which explored the history and the structure of the text. They traced some of the Quran's principal themes or topics and examined various ways in which the Quran functions within contemporary Muslim so-ciety. In some iterations of this course, I reduced the amount of secondary scholarship with which students were asked to acquaint themselves and fo-cused their attention on a close, analytical reading of the Quranic text itself. In preparation for each class session, students read assigned surahs in at least three different English (and/or French) translations. Such comparative read-ing quickly highlights textual differences and discrepancies and pushes stu-dents to acknowledge the inherently interpretive nature of both translation and reading. Often these students struggled to wrest a preunderstood or pre-explained meaning from the text. Frequently, they confronted rhetorical and stylistic elements that ran counter to the expectations created by their own Western educations. Inevitably, they brought to the text ideological forma-tions that had been constructed within the family and community or that were being freshly created within the confines of their university experience.

At Toronto, my graduate teaching in Quranic Studies was done through the Department of Near and Middle Eastern Civilizations (NMC). Until the 1996–97 academic year, the university had two separate departments, a Department of Near Eastern Studies and a Department of Middle East and Islamic Studies. While budgetary concerns were yoked to academic justifica-tions in creating the amalgamated department, the union offered particular benefit to students of Quranic Studies as they became, through both formal course work and informal conversations, more conversant with the Near Eastern literary heritage.

During my time there the graduate students in that department were drawn from a wide range of religio-cultural and academic backgrounds. Some had a fairly standard North American undergraduate and master's level education, while others had attained an equivalent stage of preparation in European, Middle Eastern, Asian, or African universities. The courses which I offered in NMC were also cross-listed with the Centre for the Study of Religion and the Centre for Medieval Studies. Students from these programs added to the intellectual diversity of my graduate classrooms.

The majority of these graduate students had commenced doctoral level work in some aspect of Islamic studies, such as history, literature (Arabic, Persian, or Turkish), philosophy, art, and archaeology or the "religious sciences." Because of this range of concentrations, one of my graduate courses on the Quran attempted to introduce students to the whole field of contemporary Quranic Studies, with primary concentration on the development of Western scholarship in this area within the last century and a half. This was not done, however, to the complete neglect of classical and contemporary Muslim scholarship on the Quran, although the latter was less prominent in my planning for this course because I did not assume source-language fluency on the part of all the students. (Of course, those students who could read one or more of the languages of Islamic scholarship were encouraged to pursue work utilizing such sources.)

With this graduate course, I wanted to open students to the ongoing "conversation" of contemporary Quranic Studies and to equip them to access this conversation for their own areas of specialization and, eventually, to participate in it. An important aspect of this approach involved guiding students to the recognition that this "conversation" is not monovocal: actually, it is a whole congery of conversations, some of which complement each other and some of which are mutually exclusive or contradictory. Representative readings for this course ranged from Norman Calder's "*Tafsīr* from Ṭabarī to Ibn Kathīr" to Patrick Gaffney's *The Prophet's Pulpit*, from Estelle Whelan's "Writing the Word of God" to Barbara Stowasser's *Women in the Quran, Traditions and Interpretation*.[12] I gave anthropological research on the Quran's social function a good deal of attention, as I feel that this remains a range of Quranic Studies that has yet to be integrated adequately into our understanding and appreciation of the total field.[13] As a graduate seminar, this course also provided students with an opportunity to explore an aspect of the contemporary conversation of Quranic Studies and to present the results of their research for mutual discussion and critique.

For those students with a sufficient preparation in Arabic, I also offered a course of "Readings in Quran and tafsīr (Quranic exegesis)." Texts selected for this ranged from representative passages drawn from classical commentaries [tafāsīr] to contemporary textbooks of the Quranic sciences ['ulūm al-Qur'ān]. Through this course I wanted to provide students with exposure to a variety of materials so that they could develop familiarity with the technical vocabulary of Quranic interpretation and with the common rhetorical patterns of classical exegetical discourse. With this background the vast literature generated by the Quran became more accessible to them for their own, individual research purposes. Because this was a semester-long rather than a full-year course I could incorporate only selective reading of the Quranic text itself, but I began with tutelage in the basic rules of tajwīd. This permitted students to recognize the orthographic particularities of the Quranic corpus and to produce a reasonable approximation of the correct oral conveyance of the text.

It may now be useful to broaden this discussion of the contextual shaping of courses on the Quran by raising some issues that concern the field of Religious Studies more generally. As I mentioned earlier, the major changes produced by the contemporary religious diaspora may be seen in the classrooms of those departments of Religious Studies to be found in large, urban universities. Faculty who teach non-Euro-American traditions, that is, religions other than those of the earlier European immigrants, have experienced a startling change in their classroom demographics. Fifteen, or even ten, years ago most of the students in courses on Hinduism, Buddhism, Islam, or Chinese and Japanese religions were students of Judeo-Christian or secular backgrounds, who wanted to learn something about these "other" religions. Now, as they scan the class list and look out at the faces gathered for the first day of lectures, faculty of Religious Studies in these large urban universities find that most of the students in the courses on Islam are Muslims, most of those in courses on Hinduism are from South Asian Hindu families, the majority of those enrolled for the course on Sikhism have Punjabi surnames, etc.

Several factors can be cited to explain this striking alteration. Universities, particularly publicly accessible universities, are a primary focus of immigrant aspiration. Many studies mention access to advanced education as a major motivation for emigration. Urban universities, furthermore, have long operated as, at least in part, commuter-schools, that is, institutions which draw a significant segment of their undergraduate population from their respective metropolitan areas. Patterns of immigration have intensified this tendency because now large numbers of students come from families, where both financial and cultural considerations mandate their living at home during their university years. Ordinarily, students from recent South Asian, East Asian, and Middle Eastern backgrounds are not encouraged to follow the North American model of dormitory student life, of "going away to college."

The degree of change doubtless varies from one educational institution to another. Prestigious private universities in the United States, such as Georgetown, which has long attracted an international student body, may be somewhat sheltered from the full impact of these recent demographic shifts. Large urban universities, whether Canadian or American, are not. Conversations with colleagues on both sides of the border have simply reinforced my sense of the speed and scope of this change. These changes in classroom demographics have been so sudden that the field of Religious Studies has not even begun to address them in any comprehensive fashion. The prevailing assumptions which undergird the teaching and research functions in Euro-American universities follow the post-Enlightenment ratification of academic secularism. Scholars in the field generally envision their research as the descriptive analysis of religious phenomena surveyed from a "neutral" perspective, despite the massive attack on such assumptions mounted by feminist, Marxist, postcolonialist, etc., critiques. The field seeks to maintain careful distinctions between the confessional and the cultural study of religion, distinctions undergirded by the separation of church and state common to much Western political philosophy. The prevailing classroom model, whether explicitly acknowledged or not, assumes students of Judeo-Christian or secular backgrounds, students whose previous religious education, if any, has been conducted within the context of church/state separation and of religion understood as a private and individual affair.

But these assumptions are changing, that framework is shifting. Inevitably, the question must arise: How should this field of study address these shifts both theoretically and pedagogically? Some would argue that changes in religious demography, both global and as reflected in the university classroom, remain irrelevant to the theories and methodologies which inform the discipline of Religious Studies. Following this line of argument, scholars in the field should not change their methods and theories in order to accommodate their teaching and research to students who do not share their Western cultural formation. They should simply insist upon academic assimilationism. By this model, Religious Studies treats all religious traditions as equally "other," and matters of proximity or distance, whether cultural or geographical, are simply irrelevant. One might call this—while acknowledging the exaggeration—the "physics model" of Religious Studies, because the reactions and sensibilities of religious adherents to being the focus of such study or the recipients of its associated pedagogy are of no more concern than that of subatomic particles under an electron microscope.

Conversely, other scholars in the field would look at the epistemological questions being raised in such ancillary disciplines as anthropology and sociology, as well as at recent work in the academy's understanding of scientific "objectivity," for clues with which to begin a reexamination of the grounds upon which research and teaching is conducted in the field of Religious Studies. These remarks do not seek to prejudge the results of this debate but simply to stress its contemporary inescapability. Distinctions which seemed largely settled (i.e., that between Religious Studies and Confessional Theology) have reemerged in quite different guise now that scholars and teachers in the field can no longer assume the homogeneity of Judeo-Christian or Western secular academic and cultural formation.

For many students of East Asian, South Asian, and Middle Eastern backgrounds, courses in university departments of religious studies are their first, formal religious education. Although they may have had some exposure, via mosque, temple, or gurdwara, to lectures or sermons, very few of the more recently arrived religious communities have yet had the time or the accumulation of resources necessary to develop programs or schools of religious formation. Furthermore, such programs and schools may not be part of the social fabric in the countries of emigration. For North American Christians and Jews, however, there exist an array of seminaries, divinity schools, rabbinic institutions, and theological faculties that provide a forum for intellectual reflection on religion. Such facilities have mediated between the strictly academic study and research of the universities and the pastoral concerns of the adherents of these religious traditions. There are as yet virtually no comparable institutions, and few of the appropriately trained personnel, among the more recently arrived religious traditions and thus no institutional structures available to serve the mediating function. Rather, university departments of Religious Studies have, by default, begun to function in ways unforeseen by those who first founded them.

To bring the focus back to the specific case of Quranic Studies, I can attest to the tensions and dilemmas created by this rapidly changing university demography. It has become common for faculty in Islamic Studies, when they cluster in the conference coffee room, to complain about their more "fundamentalist" students. Colleagues recount stories of being challenged and upbraided during class sessions, of being confronted with angry (but often ill-informed) rebuttals that such-and-such a teaching, practice, or institutional configuration is "not Islam." Behind the fussing—and one hears it from both non-Muslim and Muslim university faculty—lies a deeper dismay, a sense of sadness at the premature closure of intellectual horizons and at the unwillingness or inability to recognize the stunning variety and vast richness of the Islamic religious tradition. Sometimes when I taught my undergraduate course on the Quran, I was the only non-Muslim in the room. This created a peculiar classroom dynamic, at least in the initial sessions, and I found myself quite sympathetic to the plight of those students who felt uncomfortable with the situation, who were confronted with a sharp challenge to their common religio-cultural assumptions. I also found that it helps to acknowledge the possibility of this student unease, without necessarily assigning it to specific individuals, and to let students express concerns if they feel inclined to do so.

Of course, the adherent versus nonadherent professor conundrum has long plagued the field of Religious Studies. In the last twenty years, it has been interesting to watch the same issue come to the fore in such emerging academic fields as Women's Studies, African-American Studies, Latino Studies, Gay and Lesbian Studies, etc. The provisional settlement of this problem, reached by Religious Studies in the fast-growth period of the sixties and seventies, may be starting to unravel under the combined forces of rapid demographic change and the identity politics of the turn-of-the-century North American academy. Many Muslim students come into the Islamic Studies classroom, especially a course on the Quran, looking for religious formation. Their expectations reflect both generalized cultural presuppositions, as well as an understanding of the function of such instruction in the country of origin. When such expectations meet the prevailing praxis of university Religious Studies programs, issues of what I would call epistemological hegemony are likely to erupt. Within the ensuing fray, basic changes may emerge as quite diverse interests and orientations compete for position in the newly reconfigured spectrum of academic options.

Some individuals and groups, for example, feel that a publicly supported institution can no longer justify offering a privileged place to the post-Enlightenment secular ideology that grounds both the particular field of Religious Studies and the Western academic enterprise more generally. These voices are pressing for a change in academic culture which would accommodate their visions of religious education and would enable them to remold Religious Studies programs to embrace far greater pluralism of both guiding principles and operating practices. The strict division between the "seminary" and university department of Religious Studies, a division which is basic to the way many of our colleagues define their disciplinary identification, could begin to blur. The last thirty years has produced profound changes in university departments of Religious Studies. The next thirty may witness equally momentous ones. Teaching Quranic Studies in this fast-evolving context will undoubtedly present opportunities and challenges far different than those imagined when most of us embarked upon our own studies of this time-sanctified text.

NOTES

1. The current AAR membership, according to its website, is about 8,000. Of course, many SBL members also belong to the AAR.

2. Muḥammad ʿAlī al-Sāyis, *Tafsīr āyāt al-aḥkām*, 4 vols. in 1 (Cairo: al-Azhar, 1953).

3. Muḥammad b. ʿAbdallāh Abū Bakr b. al-ʿArabī, *Aḥkām al-Qur'ān*, 2nd ed., 4 vols. (Cairo, 1392/1972).

4. Abū ʿAbdallāh Muḥammad b. Aḥmad al-Qurṭubī, *al-Jāmiʿ li-aḥkām al-Qur'ān*, ed. Aḥmad ʿAbd al-ʿAlīm al-Bardūnī et al., 20 vols. (Cairo, 1371–87/1952–67); Abū Bakr Aḥmad b. ʿAbdallāh al-Jaṣṣāṣ al-Rāzī, *Aḥkām al-Qur'ān*, 3 vols. (Istanbul, 1335–8/1916–9); Ilkiyā Abū al-Ḥasan al-Ṭabarī al-Harrāsī, *Aḥkām al-Qur'ān*, ed. Mūsā Muḥammad ʿAlī, 4 vols. (Cairo, n.d.).

5. During their menstrual periods many Muslim women will avoid touching a Quran. Among some Muslims, concerns about ritual purity make them reluctant to see a Quran in any non-Muslim hands.

6. A recent edition of *The Chronicle of Higher Education* (November 24, 2000; 48:A72) included an article by Andrea Useem about Maria Ulfah, an outstanding Indonesian reciter and teacher, who has toured the United States as a guest of the Middle East Studies Association. I was particularly pleased to see this article because when I lectured in Indonesia a few years ago, I had the chance to meet Maria Ulfah, to hear her recite, and to talk to her about the study of Quran recitation.

7. Muḥammad Ḥusayn Ṭabāṭabāʾī, *al-Mīzān fī tafsīr al-Qur'ān*, 20 vols. (Beirut, 1393–4/1973–4); vol. 21 (Beirut, 1985).

8. Abū al-Suʿūd Muḥammad b. Muḥyī al-Dīn al-ʿImādī (d. 982/1574), *Tafsīr Abī al-Suʿūd aw Irshād al-ʿaql al-salīm*, 5 vols. (Riyadh, 1971).

9. Faḍl Ḥasan ʿAbbās, *al-Balāghah, funūnuhā wa-afnānuhā*, 2 vols. (Amman, 1405/1985). ʿAbbās has also written a book that assesses and responds to the article on the Quran written by Helmer Ringgren for the fifteenth edition (1974) of the *Encyclopaedia Britannica*. Cf. *Qaḍāyā Qur'āniyya fī l-mawsūʿa al-brīṭāniyya* (Amman, 1410/1989).

10. Muṣṭafā Ibrāhīm al-Mashnī, *Madrasat al-tafsīr fī al-Andalus* (Beirut, 1406/1986) and *Ibn al-ʿArabī al-Mālikī al-Ishbīlī wa-tafsīruhu Aḥkām al-Qur'ān* (Beirut, 1411/1991).

11. W.A. Graham, *Beyond the Written Word. Oral Aspects of Scripture in the History of Religion* (Cambridge: Cambridge University Press, 1989); Kristina Nelson, *The Art of Reciting the Qur'ān* (Austin: University of Texas Press, 1985). While Nelson's book offers an accessible explanation of Quranic recitation, the more comparative study by Graham highlights its importance in Muslim societies both present and past.

12. Norman Calder, "*Tafsīr* from Ṭabarī to Ibn Kathīr: Problems in the Description of a Genre, Illustrated with Reference to the Story of Abraham," in *Approaches to the Qur'ān*, ed. G. R. Hawting and Abdul-Kader A. Shareef (London: Routledge, 1993), 101–40; Patrick D. Gaffney, *The Prophet's Pulpit: Islamic Preaching in Contemporary Egypt* (Berkeley: University of California Press, 1994); Estelle Whelan, "Writing the Word of God: Some Early Qur'an Manuscripts and Their Milieux, Part I," *Ars Orientalis* 20 (n.d.): 113–47; Barbara Freyer Stowasser, *Women in the Qur'ān, Traditions and Interpretation* (New York: Oxford University Press, 1994).

13. Representative examples of this syllabus are John R. Bowen, *Muslims through*

Discourse (Princeton: Princeton University Press, 1993); Dale F. Eickelman, *Knowledge and Power in Morocco: The Education of a Twentieth-Century Notable* (Princeton: Princeton University Press, 1985); C. B. M. Hoffer, "The Practice of Islamic Healing," in *Islam in Dutch Society: Current Developments and Future Prospects,* ed. W. A. R. Shadid and P. S. van Koningsveld (Kampen, the Netherlands: Kok Pharos, 1992); Frederick M. Denny, "Qur'an Recitation: A Tradition of Oral Performance and Transmission," *Oral Tradition* 41 (1989): 5–26.

CHAPTER SEVEN

Between Orientalism and Fundamentalism
Problematizing the Teaching of Sufism

CARL W. ERNST

IN LATE TWENTIETH-CENTURY AMERICA, teaching or writing about Islamic religion is inescapably caught up in political controversy. Everyone who has taught a class on Islam has had to deal with the powerful stereotypes of terrorist violence and gender inequality that pervade media representations of Islamic societies. In the academy, it has long appeared that a conveniently nonpolitical alternative subject could be framed in terms of the study of Sufism or Islamic mysticism. Many Islamicists have offered courses on Sufism at North American colleges and universities or have discussed Sufism in their classes on Islam, and a number of academics who offer courses on mysticism have attempted to incorporate some Sufi material into their surveys on this topic. Despite lively debates over the nature of mysticism in recent years, there has been hardly any reflection on the category of Sufism, considered as Islamic mysticism. This means that courses dealing with Sufism have been unable to provide any problematization of this concept—and that sort of reflection is necessary for any course in Religious Studies that aspires to be critical.[1] In this essay, based on a 1997 study of Sufism, I would like to argue that the nonpolitical image of Sufism is illusory.[2]

The history of the study of Sufism shows how powerfully the Orientalist discourse on religion reformulated aspects of Islamic culture into a separate category called Sufism. At the same time, growing "fundamentalist" movements in Muslim countries have isolated and rejected many aspects of what we call Sufism, as part of a struggle over the ownership of Islamic religious symbolism. The fact that these debates have taken place in the colonial and postcolonial periods indicates that modernity is crucial to the understanding of Sufism. Yet the classicist bias of Orientalism, and the strikingly similar "golden age" historiography of fundamentalism, have conspired to keep Sufism separate from modernity. Here I would like to show how it is possible to deal with Sufism critically in terms of Religious Studies, by introducing to the classroom some of the highly charged ideological interpretations of Sufism that have been offered by Orientalists and fundamentalists. When juxtaposed with the ways in which Sufis themselves have actively engaged with the ideologies and technologies of modernity, these "political" readings of Sufism make the subject far richer than the default hagiographic approach that limits itself to "classical" texts.

I would like to frame this discussion in terms of several outcomes that seem to me important in teaching courses relating to Islam:

- To acquaint students with religious practice, not just theological doctrine;

- To illustrate the contemporary relevance of the religious tradition, not just its "classical" past;

- To create an immediacy for students by employing multimedia resources (film, music, and internet) in addition to written texts;

- To complicate the picture of monolithic Islam by illustrating difference through categories such as ethnicity, gender, class, and nationality;

- To avoid privileging one Islamic perspective over another as being "orthodox," while clarifying the issues under debate;

- To problematize the study of Islam as an example of the modern conceptualization of religion.

It is still necessary to provide a synthetic textbook presentation and some primary texts in translation, and my syllabi and readings still contain the standard narratives on the importance of the Quran, the Prophet Muhammad, etc. But a course on Sufism or Islam can end up being an Orientalist catechism, rather than a critical course in Religious Studies, unless objectives like these are part of the picture. The following remarks sketch out ways in which the modern ideologies surrounding Sufism may be integrated into the subject.

Sufism as an Orientalist Category

The standard presentation of Sufism as Islamic mysticism can be easily recognized in the venerable textbooks and anthologies that have been in use for decades in North American universities. A. J. Arberry's *Aspects of Islamic Civilization* as presented in the *Original Texts* (1956) is one of the best examples. It presents Sufism as a classical literary phenomenon best illustrated by the great Sufi poets (Rumi, Ibn al-Farid, etc.) or by prose works on discipline and metaphysics. This portrait was an intellectual achievement made possible by the deep erudition of sympathetic Orientalists who specialized in the study of Sufism (R. A. Nicholson, Arberry, Louis Massignon). Yet this concept of "Islamic mysticism" had a genealogy worth considering.

The term and category "Sufism" was first coined for European languages by British Orientalists based in India, particularly Sir William Jones.[3] Before the nineteenth century, many European travelers had remarked about "fakirs" and "dervishes," but only as exotic curiosities. Orientalists applied the term "Sufi" primarily to the literary phase of Sufism, particularly as expressed in Persian poetry. These European scholars were uniformly persuaded that the elegant poems of Hafiz and Jalal al-Din Rumi could have nothing to do with the Islamic ("Mahometan") religion. The so-called Sooffees were poets, after all, and they composed odes to the joys of wine-drinking, something no pious "Mahometan" would do. Furthermore, as anyone could see from their poems, they were fond of music and dance, they were great lovers, and their bold declarations were an open affront to the Quran. The Orientalists saw them as freethinkers who had little to do with the stern faith of the Arabian Prophet. They had much more in common, so went the argument, with true Christianity, with Greek philosophy, and with the mystical speculations of the Indian Vedanta. Until rather recently, it was unanimously believed that Sufism was derived from Indian sources.[4] Thus the term "Sufi-ism" was invented at the end of the eighteenth century, as an appropriation of those portions of "Oriental" culture that Europeans found attractive. British colonial officials, who were the main source of European studies of Sufism in the nineteenth century, thus maintained a double attitude toward Sufism: its literary classics (part of the Persian curriculum required by the British East India Company until the 1830s) were admired, but its contemporary social manifestations were considered corrupt and degenerate in relation to what was perceived as orthodox Islam.[5] Thus, the essential feature of the definitions of Sufism that appeared at this time was the insistence that Sufism had no intrinsic relation with the faith of Islam.

The literary aspect of Sufism was thus considered by Orientalists to be separate from its contemporary institutional base, which was consigned to colonial administrators to worry about. In many Muslim regions, the Sufi orders, often referred to as "brotherhoods" or "confreries" by Europeans, were the only local organizations to remain intact after the onset of colonial rule. In North Africa, French officials paid close attention to "marabouts" (from Arabic murābiṭ, a resident in a Sufi lodge known as a ribāṭ), fearing charismatic leaders who might organize local tribes. In places like the Indian Punjab, the descendants of Sufi saints were caretakers of what had become popular pilgrimage sites, and the British concocted a strategy of coopting them into the system as influential landlords. In other cases, Sufi leaders who had extensive followings led resistance to European conquest. In Algeria, the Emir 'Abd al-Qadir fought the French for years until his defeat in 1847; in his exile in Syria, he wrote extensively on Sufism and supervised the publication of important Arabic Sufi texts. In the Caucasus, Shaykh Shamil of the Naqshbandi Sufi order set up an independent state that frustrated Russian attacks until 1859. The messianic movement of the Sudanese Mahdi, destroyed by British forces in 1881, originated from a Sufi order; British accounts of the defeat of the "dervishes" at the battle of Omdurman formed one of the high points of colonial triumphalism.

By the end of the nineteenth century, the study of the "brotherhoods" had become a necessary subject for European colonial administrators. In these circles the study of Sufism became a cross between the assembly of police dossiers and the analysis of dangerous cults. Sufi leaders like the Pir Pagaro in Sind were described as hypnotic demagogues whose fanatic followers would kill themselves at a hint from the master. In Somalia, the British dismissed the conservative Sufi leader Shaykh Muhammad 'Abd Allah Hasan as "the mad mulla," though he was neither mad nor a mulla (traditional religious scholar); he is remembered today by his countrymen as the father of the Somali nation. In any case, there is considerable proto-anthropological material on Sufi saints and shrines compiled by British and French colonial officials, often drawing upon local oral tradition.

Neither the Orientalist nor the colonial-administrative approach to Sufism was very close to the sense of the word "Sufi" in Arabic and allied languages. The literature of Sufism that began to be produced in the tenth century C.E. employed the term Sufi in a deliberate and self-conscious fashion to orchestrate the ethical and mystical goals of the growing movement in a prescriptive fashion. A series of writings, primarily in Arabic, expounded the ideals of the Sufis and explained their relationship to other religious groups in Muslim society. The term "Sufi" in this way took on a didactic rather than an informational purpose. Answers to the question "What is Sufism?" multiplied and began to take on a new importance, as they nearly always were placed prominently at the beginning of every new treatise on Sufism. All these "definitions" are elusive from the perspective of descriptive history and social science. They do not have any clear reference to a defined group of people. Instead, they accomplish a powerful rhetorical transaction; the person who listens to or reads these definitions is forced to imagine the spiritual or ethical quality that is invoked by the definition, even when it is paradoxical. Definitions of Sufism are, in effect, teaching tools. References to individuals as being Sufis are comparatively rare. The actual terminology for different Islamic mystical vocations covers a wide range of semantic fields.

In the academy today, there is accordingly a fair degree of ambiguity attached to the concept of Sufism. As with other terms coined during the Enlightenment to describe religions, Sufism has now become a standard term, whether we like it or not. I would suggest that "Sufism" can best be used as a descriptive term of the "family resemblance" variety, to cover all the external social and historical manifestations associated with Sufi orders, saints, and the interior practice of Islam. Since this lacks the normative and prescriptive force of the ethical term "Sufi," it is important to point out to students the gap between outsider and insider perspectives and to point out the objectives that govern any presentation of the subject.

Sufism, Fundamentalism, and Islam

While Islamic fundamentalism is certainly the aspect of Islam most frequently discussed in the Western media, it is unfortunately not much better known than other aspects of Islamic culture. The vagueness with which these terms are thrown around makes the average reader suspect that they are synonymous; one would assume that all Muslims must be fundamentalists. While it is usually recognized that there are Christian fundamentalists as well (indeed, the term originated in Los Angeles early in this century), the press have nearly given Muslim fundamentalists a monopoly over the term. Since the term has a fairly negative air, probably dating from the time when it was associated with anti-evolutionist forces at the time of the Scopes trial, Muslims who are tarred with this brush rightly resent it. Nonetheless, if it is carefully defined, "fundamentalism" can be used as a descriptive term with a specific meaning in a variety of religious contexts. Bruce Lawrence defines it as an anti-modernist ideology based on selective interpretation of scripture, used largely by secondary male elites in an oppositional role against the state.[6] It is important to note that anti-modernist does not mean anti-modern; fundamentalists are very much at home with modern technology and modern techniques of political struggle. Fundamentalists are instead opposed to the secularist ideology that has banished religion from public life; in this respect they are inescapably modern.

The relevance of fundamentalism for Sufism comes at the root of their belief systems. The selective interpretation of scripture that underlies the central authority of fundamentalism cannot afford to tolerate alternate interpretations. Since fundamentalists typically portray their interpretations as literal and hence unchallengeably true, any kind of psychological or mystical interpretation of the sacred text is a basic threat to the monopoly that they wish to claim over tradition. Western journalists are too often content to accept the self-interpretation of Muslim fundamentalists as the sole authentic custodians of tradition. One would never guess from most media reports that fundamentalists usually constitute no more than 20 percent of any Muslim population, and that in this respect they are likely to have the same proportion as fundamentalists in Christian, Hindu, or Buddhist societies.

Like the spin doctors who attempt to mold public opinion through commentary, fundamentalist spokesmen attempt through their rhetoric of total confrontation to claim representation of Islam. For this effort to succeed, they must discredit and disenfranchise all other claimants to the sources of authority in the Islamic tradition. There is no stronger rival claim on these sources than in Sufism. Modern studies of Muslim fundamentalism rarely point this out, preferring instead to dwell on confrontation with European colonialism and the secular state as the proximate causes of this ideology. But the principal early fundamentalist movement, the Wahhabism that swept Arabia in the nineteenth century, had nothing to do with responses to Europe. While resistance to the Ottoman empire may have been a factor, there was a basic religious struggle going on between Wahhabis and Sufis for the control of central religious symbols. Fundamentalists articulated their goal as the domination of the symbols of Islam.

The remarkable thing is that many of the leaders of Muslim fundamentalism were raised in social contexts where Sufism was strong. Both Hasan al-Banna, founder of the Muslim Brotherhood in Egypt, and Abu al-'Ala' Mawdudi, founder of the Indo-Pakistani Jama'at-i Islami, were very familiar with the authority structures of Sufi orders from their youth. From their writings it is quite clear that they admired the organizational strength of Sufi orders, and they acted in relation to their followers with all the charisma of a Sufi master in the company of disciples. They did not, however, adopt any of the spiritual practices of Sufism, and, in particular, they rejected the notion of any saintly mediation between God and ordinary humanity. In an attempt to destroy the accretions of history and return to the purity of Islam at the time of the Prophet, fundamentalists rejected the ritual and local cultural adaptations of Sufism as non-Islamic. From a political point of view, one must acknowledge that fundamentalists had sized up their opposition well. No other group held such a powerful hold on Muslim society and spirituality as the Sufi orders and saintly shrines.

Ironically, as a result of strategic successes by fundamentalist movements in certain key regions like Arabia, and the massive oil wealth that fell into the lap of the Saudi regime, many contemporary Muslims have been taught a story of the Islamic religious tradition from which Sufism has been rigorously excluded. It is ironic because as recently as the late eighteenth century, and for much of the previous millennium, most of the outstanding religious scholars of Mecca, Medina, and the great cities of the Muslim world, were intimately engaged with what we today call Sufism. It is doubly ironic because the fundamentalist story is belied by the religious practices of more than half of today's Muslim population. Veneration of the Prophet Muhammad and the Sufi saints is found as a major theme in every Muslim country from China to Morocco. On a more specialized level, millions have sought initiation in the multiple Sufi orders, which trace back a sacred teaching, generation after generation, all the way to the Prophet Muhammad. Techniques of meditation and chants of the names of God, sometimes in combination with music and dance, continue to be practiced as disciplines under the supervision of Sufi masters. Poetry, songs, and stories in dozens of local languages convey the lives and teachings of Sufi saints to a huge public. Despite the attempts of many postcolonial governments to regulate Sufi shrines and orders, because of their large followings and potential political clout, much of the activity connected with Sufism goes on regardless of attempts at interference.

The polemical attacks on Sufism by fundamentalists have had the primary goal of making Sufism into a subject that is separable from Islam, indeed, even hostile to it. This strategy permits fundamentalists to define Islam as they wish by selective use of certain scriptural texts. The novelty of this project has so far escaped the notice of most journalists and diplomats, since the study of Islamic cultures has not played a significant part in most Euro-American education. The Arabic term "islām" itself was of relatively minor importance in classical theologies based on the Quran; it literally means "submission" to God, and it denotes the minimal external forms of compliance with religious duty. If one looks at the works of theologians such as the famous al-Ghazali (d. 1111), the key term of religious identity is not "islām" but "faith" [imān], and the one who possesses it is the believer [mu'min]. Faith is one of the major topics of the Quran, mentioned hundreds of times in the sacred text. In comparison, "islām" is a relatively uncommon term of secondary importance; it only occurs seven times in the Quran. Since, however, the term "islām" had a derivative meaning relating to the community of those who have submitted to God, it became practically useful particularly in modern times as a political boundary term, both to outsiders and to insiders who wished to draw lines around themselves.

Historically, the term "Islam" was introduced into European languages in the early nineteenth century by Orientalists like Edward Lane, as an explicit analogy with the modern Christian concept of religion; in this respect, "Islam" was just as much a neologism as the terms "Hinduism" and "Buddhism" were. Before that time, Europeans used the term "Muhammadan" or "Mahometan" to refer to the followers of the Prophet Muhammad. The use of the term Islam by non-Muslim scholars coincides with its increasing frequency in the religious discourse of those who now call themselves Muslims. That is, the term "Islam" became popular in reformist and proto-fundamentalist circles at approximately the same time, or shortly after, it was popularized by European Orientalists. Both the outside "scientific" observers and the internal ideologues had found an ideal tool in the term Islam. Treated simultaneously as a set of changeless religious doctrines and as a sociological unit (now usually assimilated to the Arab minority), Islam became the eternal other opposing European civilization. The fact that much of Islamic history and culture was left out of the picture was not too great a price to pay for either of these constituencies.

Despite these historicist cautions about the use of religious terms, it must be acknowledged that the Orientalist and fundamentalist concepts of Sufism have coincided with the possibility of new alignments of Sufism with respect to Islam; once the two concepts emerge as separable, anything is possible. Contemporary Sufi groups are now called upon to make an explicit statement regarding the relation of the Sufi group with "mainstream" Islam, which may take the form of a nonrelation. In premodern Sufism it was rare that any option but Islam could even be articulated. On the level of theoretical and literary mysticism, one can find some rare instances of Jewish Sufism, such as Maimonides' grandson Obadiah ben Abraham (d. 1265) or the Christian Sufism of Ramon Llull (d. 1316). In both these cases, the authors in question were powerfully affected by reading Arabic Sufi literature, which inspired them to write new works in the same vein addressed to their co-religionists. As far as Sufi orders are concerned, in India there were a few instances of premodern Hindus, who were initiated by Chishti masters without having to convert to Islam, but these were extremely few in number and by no means typical. On less formal levels, many non-Muslims have had contact with Sufi saints and have been impressed by them on a personal level. Such was the case, for instance, with the Christians and Jews who attended the funeral of Rumi; during the later Ottoman centuries, many Christians and Jews interacted with Sufism in this manner. Occasionally, Zoroastrians did the same in Iran. The same kind of relationship still holds today for many Hindus and Sikhs who visit Sufi shrines in India. All this was made possible by the inwardness of Sufism, which tends to make external boundaries less significant. But prior to the nineteenth and twentieth centuries, it was scarcely necessary for a Sufi, steeped in the Quran and the example of the Prophet Muhammad, to have to define him- or herself in terms of Islam. Once Islam had been narrowly redefined as a legal and ideological system, however, the dual critique of Sufism by Orientalists and fundamentalists forced Sufis to justify themselves in terms of scriptural sources. Certainly, there had been criticism of particular Sufi practices or doctrines prior to this, but never had the entire inner dimension of religion been called into question.

Today, particularly in Western countries, Sufi groups have to position themselves in relation to Islamic identity. Some are rigorous in following Islamic law and ritual, and this insistence is often combined with adoption of the clothing and manners of the group's country of origin. Other groups are flexible for newcomers, on the theory that they can be gradually introduced to the outer dimension of religion later on after the inner aspect has been first absorbed. Yet other groups frankly relinquish Islamic law and symbolism, defining Sufism as the universal aspect of all religions. The most striking example of this universalist tendency is Hazrat Inayat Khan, who came to the West in the early years of this century. Trained both as a musician and as a Sufi in the Chishti order, he traveled in Europe and America giving performances of classical Indian music. Faced with the need to articulate a religious position, he presented Sufism in terms of universal religion, detached from Islamic ritual and legal practice. The groundwork for this position had been partly established much earlier by European scholars who viewed Sufism as a mysticism comparable to any other. More important, there was a universalist dimension implicit in Sufism as there was in the Islamic tradition, which recognized that every people had been sent a prophet. In all Muslim societies, there were significant continuities with pre-Islamic cultures, which guaranteed that Islamic culture was never merely Islamic.

In any case, there are excellent pedagogical opportunities to be found in raising the issues surrounding Sufism, Islam, and the fundamentalist critique of Sufism. What is important in this series of contested issues is to awaken students to the historical contingency of religious terminology. The semibiological model of religious essences, which does not recognize significance in historical change, is simply inadequate to explain this sort of debate.

Sufism and the Modern World

Two major categories of modernity have already been touched upon in connection with the understanding of Sufism: Orientalism as the academic response to Europe's colonial expansion and fundamentalism as a rejection of secular modernism. To this a number of other categories can be added, particularly the nation-state, science, and mass communication. While these have not eliminated the traditions of Sufi teaching and practice, they have added new concepts, relationships, and activities that should be acknowledged in any account of Sufism.

Most Muslim-majority countries gained independence in the years following World War II, and the new regimes in many ways continued the policies of the colonial regimes that preceded them. Colonial governments had typically eliminated or neutralized other sources of authority, and they centralized all functions of government under their own control. Formerly colonized countries have inherited authoritarian government structures that did not welcome competing political forces. In many Muslim countries, one can see special government bureaucracies devoted to controlling Sufi institutions. In Egypt, this takes the form of a bureau called the Majlis al-Sufiya or Association of Sufis, which lists and supervises some eighty "official" Sufi orders. As Valerie Hoffman has shown, however, some of the most popular Sufi orders, such as the Sudan-based Burhaniyya with a membership of several million, are not recognized by the state.[7]

The attempt to control Sufi orders and institutions by the state should be seen in the context of nationalism. In Pakistan, political leaders such as Ayyub Khan and Z. A. Bhutto attempted to redefine Sufi shrines in terms of a national ideology. Festivals at the tombs of important Sufi saints are regularly graced by provincial governors and even the prime minister, who give speeches describing how these saints were forerunners of the Islamic state of Pakistan. On the bureaucratic level, this relationship is paralleled by assertion of the authority of the Department of Charitable Trusts over the operations and finances of major Sufi shrines. This same bureau is also responsible for a series of publications of official biographies of popular saints as well as devotional manuals, in this way indicating what constitutes officially approved forms of Sufism.[8]

Probably the most remarkable example of government conflict with Sufism occurred in modern Turkey, which banned all dervish orders in 1925; in a case of the internalization of European political anxieties, secular nationalism apparently attempted to eliminate a potential rival with strong claims on the loyalties of Turkish citizens. But after 1954, the Mevlevi or "Whirling Dervishes" were permitted to revive their ritual dance, on condition that it be a secular artistic performance and not a religious ritual. Rumi (Mevlana) is now celebrated as a hero of Turkish culture and religious tolerance. A similar case in the twentieth century was the attempt of the Soviet regime to control Sufism. With an official policy of promoting atheism, the Soviet government declared Sufi gatherings and rituals to be illegal. In the post-Soviet period, however, the Sufi shrines of Uzbekistan, particularly the tomb of Baha' al-Din Naqshband in Bukhara, have taken on considerable symbolic importance in the articulation of a new cultural and national identity.

Science looms large for Sufism in terms of the modernist critique of religion as superstition. This has been devastatingly effective in secularized circles in Muslim countries, where the issue of saintly miracles has come under attack. Modernist Muslim philosophers such as Sir Muhammad Iqbal and Mohamed Lahbabi blamed the mystically befuddled Sufi for the retrograde situ-

ation of Asian countries. It is instructive to offer to students a document that
shows the response to such arguments. The author of an English biography
of Shaykh 'Abd al-Qadir Jilani published in Lahore in 1953 addressed skeptical
readers by simply inviting them to apply scientific standards to these mind-
boggling events.[9] The defenders of Sufism replied to the threats of Orientalism and science on modern terms. Some Sufi leaders have taken the step of
undergoing university training in the sciences, particularly in the professional
discipline of psychology.

The Pakistani Chishti leader Capt. Wahid Bakhsh Sial (d. 1995) is an example of a Sufi treating both Orientalists and Western scientists with their
own medicine. In his English and Urdu writings he has systematically evaluated the theories and biases of European scholars of Sufism. On the one hand,
he has taken them to task for their tendency to separate Sufism from Islam.
Over one-third of his book *Islamic Sufism* is devoted to disproving "That Myth
of Foreign Origin of Sufism."[10] On the other hand, he has appropriated the
rhetoric of science and uses it to undermine secularists who criticize religion.
The first paragraph of his book's introduction announces this strategy:

> Sufism and science are striving for the same destination. Science wants
> to know: How did the universe come into being and what is its nature?
> Is there any Creator? What is He like? Where is He? How is He related
> to the universe? How is He related to man? Is it possible for man to ap-
> proach Him? Sufism has found the answers and invites the scientists to
> come and have that knowledge.

This is the rhetoric of authority, well established by the prestige of medicine,
science, and engineering. In Europe since the time of Comte, this rhetoric has
been used to make religion irrelevant. Like other Muslim apologists who appropriate the language of science, Capt. Wahid Bakhsh seeks to turn the tables.
While it has been possible for many Sufi leaders to accommodate their teachings in this way to the contemporary age, as will be shown below, modernism
(whether religious or secular) is not comfortable with the spiritual authority,
institutions, or practice of Sufism.

Perhaps the most remarkable aspect of the emergence of Sufism as a topic
in the nineteenth and twentieth centuries has been the publicizing of a previously esoteric system of teaching through modern communications media.
Today, Sufi orders and shrines in Muslim countries produce a continual stream
of publications aimed at a variety of followers from the ordinary devotee to
the scholar. Just as the recording industry democratized the private rituals of
Sufi music for a mass audience, the introduction of print and lithography
technology made possible the distribution of Sufi teachings on a scale far be-

yond what manuscript production could attain. As has been noted in the case of Ibn 'Arabi's Arabic works, when they first emerged into print in the late nineteenth century, suddenly a work that had existed in at most a hundred manuscripts around the world (and those difficult of access) was now made easily available at a corner bookstore through print runs of a thousand copies.[11] Evidence is still far from complete, but indications are that in the principal locations for print technology in Muslim countries in the nineteenth century (Cairo, Istanbul, Tehran, and Delhi/Lucknow), the main patrons of publication, aside from governments, were Sufi orders.[12]

Although little work has been done on this subject, biographical sources can furnish valuable information about the role of print media in the development of a modern form of Sufism. Here we can see, for instance, how the Chishti leader Dhawqi Shah (d. 1951) was a university graduate and a reporter for an English-language newspaper prior to becoming a Sufi. He continued to publish newspaper articles throughout his life, both in Urdu and in English. His writings deal with such modern topics as racial theory, fundamentalism, comparative religion, and the Pakistan nationalist movement. Most remarkably, his chief successor, Shaykh Shahidullah Faridi, was a British-born convert to Islam originally named Lennard, who came to Pakistan after reading English translations of works on Sufism. His Urdu discourses, dictated in Karachi in the 1970s, are still available in print. The international distribution of printed books and periodicals was a necessary element in the lives of both men. The dramatic effects of print technology on subjects such as the Protestant Reformation and the development of nationalism have been frequently discussed, but the role of printing in the development of contemporary Sufism, including such modern forms as the periodical and the novel, still needs to be investigated.

In the late twentieth century, the other forms of publicizing Sufism has been through visual and electronic media. Most professionally made films relating to Sufism have fallen into the category of ethnographic or cultural documentary, although some governments (Turkey, India, Uzbekistan) have produced films that appropriate Sufi saints and Sufi-related culture as part of the national image.[13] The availability of movie and video cameras has made it possible to record the talks of Sufi teachers for several decades. But the recent explosion of Sufi-related home pages on the internet and in on-line discussion groups indicates that Sufism is going to be a very public part of the electronic age. The World Wide Web permits anyone to set up a home page without having to seek authorization from any particular religious hierarchy. It is accordingly receptive to a cheerful anarchy and a generally anti-authoritarian attitude. The principal divide that separates Sufi groups on the internet is whether or not they identify primarily with Islamic symbolism and religious practice; while this was not even an option in the premodern period, it is a major issue in debates about the nature of Sufism conducted in internet discussion groups. The Internet is also a vehicle for advertising books and recordings relating to Sufism, so it continues to function as a marketing device.

The publicizing of Sufism through print and electronic media has brought about a remarkable shift in the tradition. Now advocates of Sufism can defend their heritage by publishing refutations of fundamentalist or modernist attacks on Sufism. In this sense, the media permit Sufism to be contested and defended in the public sphere as one ideology alongside others. At the same time, more personal forms such as the novel allow for an intimate expression of individual spiritual aspirations, which can be communicated to a large audience through the empathy created by the novelistic narrative. Biographies and discourses can also create an intimate relationship between readers and Sufi masters; although this was also the function of those genres in manuscript form, the wide distribution of print greatly enlarges the potential audience. Through these modern public media, Sufism is no longer just an esoteric community constructed largely through direct contact, ritual interaction, and oral instruction. Now it is publicized through mass printing, modern literary genres, and electronic technology, with all the changes in personal relationships that these media entail.

The transplantation of Sufism to Europe and America raises a number of issues, including the degree to which acculturation to a Middle Eastern or South Asian homeland is encouraged. One of the most distinctive developments of Sufism in the West is probably in the area of gender relations. Most Muslim societies where Sufism has been a living force have practiced some form of gender segregation. Female Sufi masters and saints, while known, have not been common in the past. But the social habits of the modern West are different, and it is not unusual to see men and women participating together in rituals, musical performances, and other gatherings held by Sufi orders. In some Sufi groups, women have quite naturally taken on positions of leadership. Just as American women are playing a notable and innovative role in the development of Buddhism in this country, so it may be expected that Sufism in the West will have to pay special attention to women's perspectives in order to succeed.

Above all, it must be pointed out that there are numerous points of contact between the Sufi tradition and the popular culture in which our students are immersed. Today, in any music store, one can buy fine audio recordings of music that originated in Sufi circles, now transformed into "world music" performances. The Pakistani qawwali singer Nusrat Fateh Ali Khan and the Moroccan musicians from Jahjouka have obtained the sponsorship of recording labels and the enthusiastic support of successful European and American musicians, and their music has appeared on recent motion picture soundtracks (e.g., *Dead Man Walking*). The Persian poet Rumi in multiple English versions is now the best-selling poet in America. The Whirling Dervishes from Turkey regularly perform tours in major concert halls in the West. There are dozens of Internet web sites linked to Sufi groups based in America. High-quality literary periodicals with glossy photographs and well-written articles are being produced by groups such as the Iranian Nimatullahi Sufi order, now based in London. I strongly urge that this kind of material (much of it easily available) be integrated into courses on Sufism and Islam, not only to provide access but also to stimulate debate on the nature of religion and culture in contemporary society.[14] Ignoring the contemporary dossier makes this subject a hermetically sealed vessel that is irrelevant to our students' concerns.

Problems with "Mysticism" as a Category

I would like to conclude with a brief reflection on how the study of Sufism can help alter the generic concept of mysticism with which it is often associated. Mysticism, although critically explored in a number of recent studies, is still often reduced to a bare universalism (with minor concessions to religious traditions) and, what is more, to the private experience of an individual. Not enough has been done to historicize and problematize the category of mysticism as it emerged around the turn of the century in Western thinking about religion. We still take for granted that terms such as "religious experience" are self-evident, though they, in fact, have historical genealogies.

It is important, for instance, to keep in view the political and social aspects of Sufism. Those who consider mysticism a private affair, and who view Sufism primarily through poetry or theoretical treatises, may feel that military and economic activities do not fit the picture of inner mystical experience. From this point of view, any accommodation with political power constitutes a fall from purity. It is difficult, however, to reconcile such a purely "other-worldly" perspective with either the history or the teachings of Sufism. As one famous saying has it, "Sufism is all practical ethics (adab)." The prescriptive ethics that are bound up in Sufi rhetoric cannot be put into effect by isolated hermits. Sufis are constantly reminded of this by the model of the Prophet Muhammad, who plays for them the role of social and political leader, as well as mystical exemplar. While there is certainly a tension between Sufism and "the world," illustrated most dramatically by the repentance that is the beginning of the spiritual stations, Sufism is also very much a community affair that is hard to separate from the rest of life.

Students of Christian mysticism are well aware of the political and social activities of mystics like St. John of the Cross and St. Catherine of Siena. How would the textbook definition of mysticism change if these activities were connected more fully with their mystical writings? Joining the critical dimension of the study of religion with the comparative aspect may prove to be the most useful future agenda for the teaching of Sufism.

NOTES

1. Critical reflection and problematizing of categories, in my opinion, should be part of even the most elementary introductory courses in Religious Studies. They are all the more necessary in specialized and advanced courses.

2. Carl W. Ernst, *The Shambhala Guide to Sufism* (Boston: Shambhala Publications, 1997). Further specific discussions of the problem of Sufism and modernity are to be found in Carl W. Ernst and Bruce B. Lawrence, *Sufi Martyrs of Love: The Chisti Sufi Order in South Asia and Beyond* (New York: Palgrave, 2002).

3. Sir William Jones, "The Sixth Discourse, On the Persians," and "On the Mystical Poetry of the Persians and Hindus," in *Works* (London: Piccadilly and Paternoster-Row, 1807).

4. Lt. J. W. Graham, "A Treatise on Sufiism, or Mahomedan Mysticism," *Transactions of the Literary Society of Bombay* 1 (1819): 89–119. This attempt to find an extra-Islamic origin for Sufism has had defenders as recently as R. C. Zaehner, *Mysticism, Sacred and Profane: An Inquiry into Some Varieties of Praeternatural Experience* (London: Oxford University Press, 1961). A detailed discussion of this issue will be presented in my *The Pool of Nectar: Muslim Interpreters of Yoga* (forthcoming).

5. Sir R. F. Burton, *Sindh* (London: W. H. Allen, 1851; reprint, Lahore: Khan, 1976), 198–231.

6. Bruce B. Lawrence, *Defenders of God: The Fundamentalist Revolt Against the Modern Age* (San Francisco: Harper & Row, 1989), 100–1.

7. Valerie J. Hoffman, *Sufism, Mystics, and Saints in Modern Egypt* (Columbia: University of South Carolina Press, 1995).

8. Katherine Ewing, "The Politics of Sufism: Redefining the Saints of Pakistan," *Journal of Asian Studies* 52 (1983): 251–68.

9. S. A. Salik, *The Saint of Jilan* (Lahore, 1953; reprint, Chicago: Kazi Publications, 1985).

10. Capt. Wahid Bakhsh Sial Rabbani, *Islamic Sufism: The Science of Flight in God, with God, by God, and Union and Communion with God, Also showing the Tremendous Sufi Influence on Christian and Hindu Mystics and Mysticism* (Lahore: Sufi Foundation, 1984), chapter 5, 112–249.

11. Martin Notcutt, "Ibn 'Arabi in Print," in *Muhyiddin Ibn 'Arabi, A Commemorative Volume*, ed. Stephen Hirtenstein (Rockport, MA: Element, 1993), 328–39.

12. Muhsin Mahdi, "From the Manuscript Age to the Age of Printed Books," in *The Book in the Islamic World: The Written Word and Communication in the Middle East*, ed. George N. Atiyeh (Albany: State University of New York Press/Library of Congress,

1995), 6–7. Mahdi suggests that the large followings of mystical orders made such publishing economically feasible.

13. Several documentary films on Sufism are available for loan to educational institutions from the Non-Print Section, Undergraduate Library, University of North Carolina, Chapel Hill, NC 27599. Some of these include *For Those Who Sail to Heaven* (about an Egyptian saint's festival at Luxor), *Saints and Spirits* (about Sufi shrines and spirit possession in Morocco), and two films about the Mevlevis, *Turning* and *Whirling Dervishes*.

14. My *Shambhala Guide to Sufism* includes a select discography.

CHAPTER EIGHT

Engendering and Experience
Teaching a Course on Women in Islam

ZAYN KASSAM

INSTRUCTORS EMBARKING ON TEACHING a course on women in the Islamic tradition often start out with questions such as: "How am I going to teach a course on Women and Gender Issues in Islam?" "How can I organize so much material into a one-semester format?" "How do I teach a course on women in Islam to students who may have very little exposure either to Women's Studies or to Islam?" Beth Baron's review article is an excellent starting point, and indeed she points out that "the scholarly literature on women in the Middle East has increased so rapidly in the past few years that it is almost impossible to keep up with this body of material."[1] As the 1991 publication of the Association for Middle East Women's Studies (AMEWS) attests,[2] the literature available in English with respect to Muslim women living in diverse societies has undergone a rapid and momentous increase over the last twenty years. The challenges facing instructors concern how to lend focus, cohesion, and integrity to the burgeoning and expanding realm of materials. This chapter will suggest some modular approaches that could be utilized by instructors within which currently available studies of Muslim women and gender issues may be set. Although this discussion is primarily situated within the interdisciplinary methodology of the History of Religions, it is hoped that each of these modules can be adapted to the specific needs and disciplines of instructors. The bibliographic references appended are provided as starting points and are not to be taken as exhaustive, especially more so given the robust rate of publication in the area of Muslim gender studies.

In devising my frameworks of enquiry, I sought to isolate some overarching principles that might organize the vast subject matter while simultaneously emphasizing the interconnections and intersections that exist in the realities of women's lives. Since it is impossible in the course of one semester to include all the modules suggested, it is possible to vary the emphases of the course from year to year and factor in additional modules that could conceivably emerge. For instance, students have come to me with requests to develop independent courses focusing solely on, say, "Contemporary Muslim Feminist Literature," "Writings by Iranian Women," "The Challenge of Muslim Feminist Activism," "Women and Politics in Muslim Societies," "Muslim Women as Other in Colonial and Post-Colonial Discourses," "Muslim Feminist Theology." The possibilities are endless. My rationale for isolating the frameworks of analysis and investigation is to examine the construction of gender and gender expectations in classical and medieval Muslim sources considered authoritative in Islamic societies and inscribed in social institutions aimed at prescribing women's comportment in the public sphere, the family, and women's rights. Simultaneously, we need to examine women's experiences, strategies, and discourses to understand how women have sought to name and define their own realities and negotiate their agency in contexts in which such agency is not explicitly recognized or is channeled or restricted by social and cultural custom and religious mores. Hence, the title of my course: "Engendering and Experience: Women in the Islamic Tradition."

Thus, under the rubric of Engendering, I have included four modules: (1) Women, Patriarchy, and Islam; (2) Authoritative Islamic Sources for Gender Roles; (3) Legal Discourses; and (4) Intersectionalities of State, Society, Economics, and Islamist Discourse. Under the rubric of Experience, I include four additional modules: (5) Feminist (or Woman-Sensitive) Critiques; (6) Women's Ritual Participation and Feminine Spirituality; (7) Recovering Herstories; (8) Women's Experiences. Although the two rubrics, Engendering and Experience, serve broadly to classify the material examined, they are by no means mutually exclusive. My rationales for each module are given under each heading.

Women, Patriarchy, and Islam

Many of my students enter with the assumption that Islam has the corner on discriminatory ideology and practices and express immediately their distaste at the sight of veiled women. This introductory module aims to expose students to a sampling of theoretical reflections on religion, society, and gender, such as those offered by Gerda Lerner, Rita Gross, and Katherine K. Young. The latter, for instance, draws attention, as a starting point, to the connection between patriarchal structures, the subordination of women, social organization, symbolic expression of gender, and female power.[3] Mary Daly's identification of patriarchal strategies employed to derail gender issues and concerns from becoming part of the social conscience is helpful in problematizing how discourses can perpetuate gender inequities.[4] I also call upon an essay by Deniz Kandiyoti that investigates different forms of male dominance and the manner in which these affect the actual practice of Islam and the ideological constructions of Islamic discourse.[5]

Such reflections enable the transition to materials specific to Islam, especially with respect to women's history prior to and during the founding phases of Islamic culture and society. Leila Ahmed's classic textbook for use in courses on women in Islam frames pre-Islamic society on the eve of Islam's appearance on the world stage within the context of Mesopotamia and the Mediterranean Middle East. She explores the argument that the exponents of Islam subsequent to Muhammad, the prophet of Islam, continued, and did not initiate, a patriarchal vision already dominant in the region.[6] Her work draws on the theories advanced by Gerda Lerner and Sarah Pomeroy, among others,[7] and these may be briefly discussed in class in order to give students some understanding of the structures and strategies of patriarchal institutions. Each of the above-mentioned studies provides ample references for further review. As with all suggestions made in this chapter, the instructor will add her/his own knowledge of sources germane to the issue.

Authoritative Islamic Sources for Gender Roles

Muslim students who take my course often conflate the Quran, the hadith literature, and Shari'ah law into one religiously authoritative source outlining normative behavior incumbent upon Muslim women. Non-Muslim students come in with the perspective that everything Muslim women are required to do is outlined in the Quran. Caroline Walker Bynum's short, but probing, essay examining the multivalency of religious symbols (whether oral, written, ritual, institutional) makes the case that a symbol may be polyvalent or polysemically read by different people in different contexts. This discussion is useful in questioning why so many Muslim women, when they read the Quran, come away with the defensive claim that "Islam" does not encumber them with many of the problems faced by their Western religious counterparts. For these women, the Quran speaks to them as affirming the spiritual and moral equality between men and women, a point underscored by Leila Ahmed. Ahmed, however, does make the point that we must turn to historical factors to understand the processes by which gender inequities crept into the social sphere, thereby setting the stage within the classroom for a connection between the cultural construction of gender and the rallying of scriptural support. Leila Ahmed nicely articulates some of these views in a video titled, *Islamic Conversations: Women and Islam,* produced by Films for the Humanities and Sciences.

The hypothesis that gender is culturally constructed may help to contextualize the discussion of authoritative Islamic sources on gender, and this hypothesis may, as part of class discussions, be tested against those very sources if desired. These sources comprise the Quran, the hadith literature, Quran commentaries [tafsīr], and, as a source which informs both popular conceptions as well as commentarial elaborations on prophets mentioned in the Quran, the stories relating to the prophets [qiṣaṣ al-anbiyā'] literature. The importance of these sources lies in their impact on the legal and cultural institutions which define the expected comportment of men and women as members of an Islamic society and also enforce the social view of gender. It is impossible to treat each of these literatures in depth in a one-semester course, even if English-language studies examining the gender issues in each of these categories had already been conducted and were available. An excellent work, both careful in its research and illuminating in its analyses, is that of Barbara Freyer Stowasser, titled *Women in the Qur'an, Traditions and Interpretations,*[8] recently released in paperback, thus making it eminently accessible and affordable as a classroom text. This work details the appropriation and utilization of Quranic figures and texts by classical, medieval, and modern commentators in designating paradigmatic models for women in Islamic societies. Stowasser also examines Muslim articulations of the need for reinterpretation of authoritative sources as a modernization effort. Amina Wadud-Muhsin's reexamination of scriptural verses pertaining to gender provides an example of Muslim activism with respect to grounding gender equity in reinterpretations of the Quran that accord with current hermeneutical tools.

The expected comportment of Muslim women in the modern world may also be examined in the conduct-manual writers' prescriptions for virtuous Muslim women. Attention can be drawn to writings such as those of Thanawi, brought within reach of the non-Urdu reader by the efforts of Barbara Daly Metcalf.[9] For an earlier perspective, Huda Lutfi in her article on fourteenth-century Cairene women presents a compelling rereading of a medieval prescriptive text by Ibn al-Hajj (d. 737/1336) that reveals the dissonance between the real and the ideal in Muslim women's lives.[10] To this instructors may, at their own discretion, add other normative writings such as those by Ayatollah Khomeini and Maulana Mawdudī, and Ali Shariati. Sometimes, in the absence of class time in which to read such works, I will ask students to "get on the Web" to see if they can find any directions on the rights, duties, and expectations made of Muslim women.

Legal Discourses

Chapters 5 and 6 of Ahmed's work provide the context within which the development and direction of Islamic law may be discussed. Her work draws attention to the "vital but more hidden role" played by "interpretation and the biases and assumptions" inscribed into the formation of legal codes in the Muslim world. Eleanor A. Doumato's thought-provoking essay points to the legal cohesiveness between pre-Islamic Christian society and the emerging legal discourse and may also be read in conjunction with chapter 5.[11] Until a full-scale study on the status of women in the classical and medieval Islamic legal schools is undertaken, recourse must be taken by and large to edited works for essays dealing with various historical phases, up to and including the modern. Among the many worthy of citation, attention may be drawn to two recent works edited by Sonbol and Yamani, despite the uneven quality of some of the essays.[12] A brilliant investigation of the problematic issue of temporary marriage in the Iranian context is offered by the cultural anthropologist Shahla Haeri, and students in my classes have benefited from the connections she draws between this institution and the socio-historical circumstances in which laws governing this practice are implemented.[13] The call for the reform of laws with respect to women has been investigated within the South Asian context by several works, and as a sample, one may refer in passing to Asghar Ali Engineer's study, in which he argues for a call to the use of fresh legal reasoning [ijtihād] in contrast to blind imitation of earlier precedents [taqlīd].[14] As counterpoint, a study of case law in Pakistan spanning the last 45 years asks whether there are, in fact, any trends in the interpretation of law that have benefited women.[15] Asifa Quraishi offers an insightful critique of rape laws in Pakistan,[16] as an instance of how woman-sensitive perspectives can open up the debate on redressing legal injustices toward women. Ziba Mir-Hosseini's work on divorce law may also be dovetailed with the film, *Divorce Iranian Style*, which is useful for talking about the context-sensitive interpretation of the Shari'ah in the cases profiled.

Much of the discussion regarding the legal status of women in the Islamic world is framed within the context of human rights, which is increasingly becoming an issue of concern to women globally, as evinced within forums such as the United Nations Conferences on Women. An additional source of concern is the growing trend in countries with majority Muslim populations (and significant minority Muslim populations) to enact Shari'ah legislation within their legal institutions. The concerns are twofold: one, that the growing number of Islamist women, while they have negotiated access to public spaces by adopting an Islamist ideology and the signifier of that ideology most prominently displayed through Islamic dress, may inadvertently perhaps weaken the significant gains that an earlier generation of Muslim feminists (including both men and women) were able to effect. The second concern is the implication that anyone interrogating current social arrangements with respect to gender must be tainted by Western ideology and hence be viewed as a traitor, or worse, a proponent of Western neoimperialism. The current environment of postcolonial rejections of Western values and lifestyles, brought about in part by the colonizing powers' strategic identification of women's dress and seclusion in Muslim societies as an indication of Islam's backwardness (and consequently, of Western moral and political superiority), has fueled this view. Thus, it is supposed, for a Muslim to engage in activism, whether intellectual or practical with regard to ameliorating women's status, results in the denunciation of such activists as non-Islamic and hence, inauthentic. As a result, ground-level organizations such as nongovernment agencies, who work with the practical dimensions of women's lives, have attempted to do so without engaging theological constructs regarding the place of women in society. In her work on pressing social issues such as violence against women in Pakistan, Riffat Hassan has drawn attention to the dire need to engage in theological constructs. This, she convincingly argues, must be undertaken in order to educate the public with regard to the rights women are accorded in the Quran, especially since much violence against women is conducted under the understanding that the Quran accords men the right to police women's comportment and agency. Some activists have tried to avert being labeled inauthentic by taking recourse to universalizing discourses, claiming that it is incumbent upon all nations of the world to treat women's rights as fundamental human rights. Such a position runs the risk of losing sight of the specificities pertaining to the lives of women in concrete contexts and of predicating this universalizing discourse on the concerns of its articulators. It is critical, however, to bring governments to the table for global cooperation on issues such as marriage age, access to reproductive technologies, violence against women and children, child labor, and access to education and the waged workplace. Kandiyoti, Karam, Sabbagh, and Afkhami may be singled out as introducing issues pertinent to the interconnections between the law, the state, the Islamist call for a society regulated by Shari'ah law, and the impact these exercise on women's rights.[17] They examine how current legal discourses in Muslim societies affect the lives of women and investigate the efforts undertaken by women, both locally and through international networks, to attain equitable treatment under the law.

Studies such as these are extremely valuable in their framing of issues and the concrete directions taken by activists so as to ameliorate the legal status of women in Islamic societies, or as minorities empowered to follow communal religious law in societies such as those of India.[18] Another field of enquiry concerns issues faced by immigrant Muslim communities in the European, North American, and Australian contexts.[19] Some of these communities have experienced challenges to the rights of Muslim women to wear the veil in public forums such as schools (France, Canada) and the workplace (North America). Other public concerns include the practice of female circumcision in North America; the perceived and/or substantiated poor treatment of Muslim women by their male counterparts, comprising spousal abuse, the necessity of a guardian to enact marital relationships, and the seclusion of women in public spaces (The Netherlands, Germany, Britain). Rather than reading materials on these issues, I often ask students, for the end-of-semester exam rituals, to find recent and relevant newspaper articles on which they write an intelligent commentary. Students are asked, for example, to identify any perceptible reporting biases, the background or history that someone who has not yet studied gender issues in Islam might need to know, and whether there might be a Muslim woman's viewpoint that could have been explored. All this in the hopes that students by the end of the semester will have a much more nuanced understanding of the issues at stake, when media stories relating to Muslim women enter the public forum.

Intersectionalities of State, Society, Economics, and Islamist Discourse

Much of the current Islamists' formulation of Islamic society cannot be understood apart from the legacy left by colonization and the internal upheavals witnessed in Muslim societies by what has been termed "the crisis of modernity." Insofar as this is relevant to women's status, it is necessary to understand both colonial constructions of the "other" and the Islamists' need to define an identity that stands apart from that of current hegemonies, the cultural construct known as "the West."[20] As Ahmed, among others, has pointed out,

> colonialism's use of feminism to promote the culture of the colonizers and undermine native culture has ever since imparted to feminism in non-Western societies the taint of having served as an instrument of colonial domination, rendering it suspect in Arab eyes and vulnerable to the charge of being an ally of colonial interests. That taint has undoubtedly hindered the feminist struggle within Muslim societies.[21]

Kandiyoti, in *Faith and Freedom*, makes the link between colonial discourses and the current preoccupation with women's status in Muslim societies:

The identification of Muslim women as the bearers of the "backward-ness" of their societies, initially by colonial administrators and later by Western-oriented reformers, is mirrored by a reactive local discourse which elevates the same practices into symbols of cultural authenticity and integrity. . . . The privileged sites for such assertions of authenticity are, once again, the dress and deportment of women.[22]

The classic feminist struggle to negotiate access to and fairness in the public, income-generating sphere, is thus rendered increasingly complex by the plethora of identity discourses.

Part 3 of Ahmed's study contextualizes the postcolonial discourses of Muslim reformers and conservatives. It also critically examines the efforts of modern Egyptian women to negotiate a more equitable space for women within the specificities of class, economic, cultural, religious, and historical situations. Other articulations by and about Middle Eastern women may be encountered in several edited works available,[23] the most familiar perhaps being *Middle Eastern Muslim Women Speak*.[24] An important agent of change in women's social status is the state, which is at best an unreliable ally,[25] in that it can both promote and derail women's legal, social, and economic status. The state's sometimes complicit, sometimes unwilling compliance with Islamist political agendas can translate into a retrenchant attitude toward effecting changes in the laws and social practices affecting women, and some of these issues have already been raised in the previous module.

Economic, political, and cultural realities have a role to play in affecting social change, as ably argued and substantiated by Valentine Moghadam. She asks whether women's status in any society can be reduced to its religiously authoritative discourse, or whether one must necessarily also examine the social and economic realities in which women live. Moghadam argues that Middle Eastern women "are not simply acting out roles prescribed for them by religion, by culture, or by neopatriarchal states; they are questioning their roles and status, demanding social and political change, participating in movements, and taking sides in ideological battles."[26] Her work also introduces students to economic and social-scientific data that can be used to arrive at a more realistic assessment of women's status in majority Muslim societies. Thus, in this module, I largely focus on exploring the nexus of state, society, and economics as an "engendering" frame within which women's practical lives are lived.

Feminist (or Woman-Sensitive) Critiques

Proceeding now to the "Experience" segments of the course, there are several recent Muslim critical writings on gender that participate in the broader reexamination and reinterpretation of historical materials informing social and legal constructs of gender. While such enterprises are termed feminist in the European and North American social and intellectual spheres, the term feminist is by no means appropriated by Muslim women, whether activists or academics, in its entirety, or at all. The Western term "feminist" has been questioned from various quarters regarding whether it adequately includes women of color, whether it perpetuates an anti-Semitic or Orientalist bias, whether it is representative of local concerns in non-Western contexts, or whether it is even relevant to the agrarian economies, rural bases, and diverse cultures of many parts of the non-Western world.[27]

The social inequality of women is hinted at within the Quran[28] if examined from a modern lens, even though the argument has been made that the verses in question allowed seventh-century Arab women rights unprecedented for the times. Mention has already been made of the notion that the Quran holds men and women to be equal before God with respect to their spirituality and their religious and moral obligations. Further indications of women's spiritual equality are found in reports following a complaint regarding the fact that revelations were addressed only to males. This complaint, made by one of Muhammad's wives, is offered, in part, to explain why subsequent revelations were addressed equally to men and women. Verses that assign to men greater inheritance and legal witness quotients than to women, and which are fully explicated by subsequent commentators and legislators, as well as those that indicate a preference for the male gender over the female have come under scrutiny by several scholars. Of these writings, I draw attention to Amina Wadud-Muhsin's slim but remarkable volume titled *Qur'an and Woman*,[29] which attempts to reframe some of the avowedly patriarchal readings of the Quran and raised, in my classes, discussions on whether her arguments are entirely convincing in dealing with problematic stances for women emerging from Quranic verses. Riffat Hassan's essays engage in theological reconstructions of gender based largely on a careful analysis of Quranic passages.[30] A critique of hadith transmissions that have served to proscribe Muslim women's access to the political realm, and the public sphere, by extension is to be found in Fatima Mernissi's *Women and Islam*,[31] which is published in the United States under the rather provocative title, *Women and the Male Elite*. In this work she also reexamines the medieval historical and commentarial literature detailing the context of the Medinan verses, some of which have proved problematic for Muslim women. Maysam al-Faruqi proposes that the legal identity of Muslim women must be understood from within the Islamic tradition, and not from the viewpoint of a universalizing feminism that argues that patriarchy dominates all women everywhere, nor from the lens of Muslim apologists or reformists. In her analysis she calls for a review of juristic rulings on women's rights "in the light of the Quran—this time a Quran read accurately."[32] All the above may be read and discussed within the context and parameters discussed in relevant chapters by Ahmed, if her work is being utilized as a class text.

These materials also probe issues such as whether gender is a category that can be applied to souls, since certain verses would appear to indicate that it is not; whether the term Adam as progenitor of humanity is a generically human rather than gender-specific term; what the precise role of Adam's unnamed mate is in the primordial events that led to the expulsion of the primary couple from the Garden, and what place women will have in heaven [jannah], since the reference to the doe-eyed maidens populating Paradise might seem to indicate that women end up as little more than objects of enjoyment for men.[33]

Women's Ritual Participation and Feminine Spirituality

Women's ritual participation within the context of the mosque—or their segregation within it—has been discussed in an early article by Leila Ahmed, titled "Women and the Advent of Islam" in the *Journal of Women in Culture and Society* (1986). Examinations of the intersections of sexual ideologies with ritual behaviors are found in the essays comprising part 4 in Lois Beck and Nikki Keddie, eds., *Women in the Muslim World* (1978). The expression of female spirituality in contexts other than the mosque, such as those of the saintly sanctuary and the home, is discussed in articles pertaining to Muslim women in works such as Nancy Auer Falk and Rita M. Gross, eds., *Unspoken Worlds* (1987). These articles explore, among other notions, the idea that women may develop their own rituals in addition to prescribed ritual practices in order to find avenues of religious expression by finding and keeping alive their participation in the extra-mosque dimension of religious life. Laal Jamzadeh and Margaret Mills's article titled, "Iranian Sofreh: From Collective to Female Ritual,"[34] is also noteworthy in exploring the connection between the use of the commemorative meal for both religious (ritual) and secular (social) purposes. For women's ritual participation in Shi'i *muḥarram* rituals, see Vernon Schubel's fine study on the subject.[35]

The subject of women as religious personages of note has been associated most commonly with the topic of noted Sufi mystics such as Rābi'a al-'Adawiyya (d. 801), details of whose biography and work can be found, for example, in Margaret Smith's classic study of Sufi women, and see Javad Nurbaksh, *Sufi Women* (1983). See also Jamal J. Elias, "Female and Feminine in Islamic Mysticism" in *Muslim World* 77: 3–4 (1988). Annemarie Schimmel's essay on "The Feminine Element in Sufism" is found in Appendix 2 of her landmark study, *Mystical Dimensions of Islam* (1975) and draws attention to female Sufis and to the "representation of the longing soul in the form of a woman." This latter notion is explored at length, in addition to the inscribing of the feminine in mystical discourse, in Sachiko Murata's erudite study titled, *The Tao of Islam: A Sourcebook on Gender Relationships in Islamic Thought* (1992). For the feminine element in Ibn al-'Arabī, who stands along with Rūmī among the seminal masters of Islamic mysticism, see Henry Corbin's chapter 2 in *Creative Imagination in the Sufism of Ibn 'Arabī* (1969). On the notion of the feminine as "the receptacle of the influx and effects of the celestial Spheres" in Shi'i mystical and philosophic thought, see Corbin's *Spiritual Body and Celestial Earth: From Mazdean Iran to Shī'ite Iran* (1977), especially chapter 2, on Fāṭimah.

Recovering Herstories

A reconstruction of gender history in the Middle East and North Africa has been undertaken by Guity Nashat and Judith E. Tucker,[36] a task that is no small feat given the propensity of historians, until recently, to concern themselves with the public sphere and the male point of view. Another useful source, despite its sometimes disparaging tone, for an investigation of women of note is Ruth Roded's *Women in Islamic Biographical Collections: From Ibn Sa'd to Who's Who* (1994). This work begs an extension of the investigation of biographical materials on women beyond the parameters she has drawn, namely, the Islamic heartlands, which are specified as being the Hijaz, Syria, Iraq, and Egypt. While these studies are valuable for providing background information to instructors, I have found that undergraduate students engage more readily with women's life histories, such as those of 'Ā'ishah, the youngest of the Prophet's wives,[37] and Nur Jahan, the fifteenth-century Mughal empress.[38] Fatima Mernissi's *The Forgotten Queens of Islam* (1993) attempts a recovery of some women who achieved notable political status (although her historical investigations sometimes rely too heavily on politically biased sources, especially with regard to the Shi'ah), and works well in the classroom to counter the stereotype of politically silent or inactive Muslim women. The recovery of sociological data from which to assess the historical role and status of ordinary women is, as Leila Ahmed notes, still in its preliminary stages; nonetheless, there are studies and articles to be found for those who wish to incorporate such data into their courses.[39]

Conclusions

I have found it an imperative in this course to allow women to speak for themselves, to provide space for articulations of their own experience in Muslim societies or as minorities elsewhere. Allowing women's voices to surface provides a lived counterpoint to the constructed discourses drawn from the religiously authoritative sources and the legal discourses mentioned above. While such sources define the gender role expectations and the proscribed limits of women's behavior, narratives that recount women's experiences reveal the extent to which cultural, social, legal, and religious expectations are internalized. Furthermore, such narratives enable students to explore how gender role expectations may or may not shape women's decisions or are drawn upon as sources of strength or are subverted, and also how women craft meaningful lives for themselves in their varying contexts. How do they negotiate space for themselves in the face of patriarchally inscribed institutions, the overwhelming forces of culture and tradition, familial expectations, economic limitations, and so forth? What are their issues, their hopes, their dreams, and their imagined realms of possibility? Drawing texts from different geographical and cultural locations also enables a comparative lens to come into focus, given the diversity of Islamic expression in various cultures around the globe.

There is a rich and ever-growing pool of resources to draw from with respect to this component of the course.[40] I change my selections from year to year, both in order to stay current and to keep expanding my own horizons. In terms of disciplinary focus, I have utilized texts emerging from anthropology and social studies, as well as literary texts and studies, journalistic literature, and edited texts representing a broad range of voices. While it is impossible to include more than one novel or study and a few short stories, each of the materials selected can be made to dovetail with other sections of the course. In order to underscore the point that women in the Islamic world are not a monolithic group, experiencing the same realities in monochrome, I find it essential to bring forward materials culled from different Muslim societies. For instance, Ismat Chughtai's work highlights a keen sensitivity to class and cultural issues in North India; Erika Friedl's sojourn among women in Iran provides a window into the courage and wiles of village women; Mariama Ba's work from western Africa underscores one view of living with polygamy and finding selfhood; Nawal el-Saadawi's work, which always evokes strong reaction, brings into focus women in the Egyptian context who struggle for self- expression and agency at the risk of social rejection; and Sherifa Zuhur's study examines veiling choices by Egyptian students. This is a rich literature, indeed, and some of the more well-known authors such as Alifa Rifaat, Salma Jayyusi, Hanan al-Shaykh, Ahdaf Soueif, Sahar Khalifeh, Assia Djebar, Qurratulain Hyder, and Simin Daneshvar have provided short stories that have sparked much discussion in class. Miriam Cooke's recent work, *Women Claim Islam*, provides some critical approaches to theorizing about some of this literature.[41]

Mention may also be made of another genre of works that is critical to include within this module, which details the transformation of consciousness accompanying the involvement of women in political or military struggles for freedom. The politicization of women consequent upon their participation in revolutionary struggles ironically has made women far more critical of restrictive measures relating to women's status in postrevolutionary societies, suggesting that the groundswell of women's voices has not yet attained its peak and will be heard ever more strongly in future decades.[42] Students have found especially valuable Miriam Cooke's studies on women and war.

The reader may wonder, at this juncture, why some of the problematic issues that fall under the larger rubric of violence against women have not explicitly been raised in this chapter. If there are three issues that most interest students in their exploration of gender inequities relating to the Muslim world, they are veiling, female genital mutilation (or modification or cutting), and honor killings. I will often weave these into the larger discourses of human rights or women's experiences and include works and films included in the notes.[43] My larger purpose in a course such as this is to introduce students to the complexity of the sources and the material and the methods or frameworks relevant to the study of gender in the Muslim world. Thus, by the time students encounter these materials, they are able to problematize the issues in broader currents of understanding.

In conclusion, these eight modules facilitate bringing relevant materials around an organizing principle to the classroom context. Additional modules can be added as the instructor sees fit; and not all modules are employed each time the course is taught. The publication of new materials as well as the articulation of different questions with regard to the study and teaching of gender issues, both globally and in the context of Muslim societies, can and will lead to a reconceptualization of these models, making it evident that these are offered only as starting points for the instructor. There is obviously a great deal of material available, not all of which can be taught at any given time, and the Internet continues to be a promising resource as more academics take on the responsibility of placing trustworthy materials in the public domain. Unfortunately, an investigation and mapping of these materials is outside the scope of the present review; it is a task that needs to be undertaken, however. This review has not investigated the many audio-visual materials also available for classroom viewing and discussion; another area that merits research and comment. Still, the key benefit of the module approach, in my experience, has been to enable students to connect between scriptural and ideological materials to data that is gathered from the field so as to reveal the many complexities that obtain in the study of women and gender issues in the culturally diverse Islamic world.

NOTES

1. Beth Baron, "A Field Matures: Recent Literature on Women in the Middle East," *Middle Eastern Studies* 32, n. 3 (1996): 172.

2. Herbert L. Bodman, Jr., comp., *Women in the Muslim World: A Bibliography of Books and Articles Primarily in the English Language* (Providence, R.I.: Association for Middle East Women's Studies, 1991). The preparation of a much needed more current bibliography is already underway by AMEWS.

3. Arvind Sharma, ed., *Women in World Religions* (Albany, N.Y.: State University of New York Press, 1987), Introduction, 10–36.

4. Mary Daly, *Beyond God the Father: Toward a Philosophy of Women's Liberation* (Boston: Beacon Press, 1973), 1–12.

5. Deniz Kandiyoti, "Islam and Patriarchy: A Comparative Perspective," in *Women in Middle Eastern History: Shifting Boundaries in Sex and Gender,* ed. Nikki R. Keddie and Beth Baron (New Haven: Yale University Press, 1991), 23–42.

6. Leila Ahmed, *Women and Gender in Islam* (New Haven: Yale University Press, 1992).

7. See Ahmed, *Women and Gender in Islam,* n. 2, 250, and n. 8, 252.

8. Barbara Freyer Stowasser, *Women in the Qur'an, Traditions, and Interpretation* (New York: Oxford University Press, 1994).

9. Barbara Daly Metcalf, *Perfecting Women: Maulana Ashraf 'Ali Thanawi's* Bihishti Zewar; *A Partial Translation with Commentary* (Berkeley and Los Angeles: University of California Press, 1990).

10. Huda Lutfi, "Manners and Customs of Fourteenth-Century Cairene Women: Female Anarchy versus Male Shar'i Order in Muslim Prescriptive Treatises," in Keddie and Baron, eds., *Women in Middle Eastern History,* 99–121.

11. Eleanor A. Doumato, "Hearing Other Voices: Christian Women and the Coming of Islam," in *International Journal of Middle East Studies* 23:2 (1991): 177–199.

12. Amira El Azhary Sonbol, ed., *Women, the Family, and Divorce Laws in Islamic History* (Syracuse: Syracuse University Press, 1996); Mai Yamani, ed., *Feminism and Islam: Legal and Literary Perspectives* (New York: New York University Press, 1996).

13. Shahla Haeri, *Law of Desire: Temporary Marriage in Shi'i Iran* (Syracuse: Syracuse University Press, 1989).

14. Asghar Ali Engineer, *The Rights of Women in Islam* (New York: St. Martin's Press, 1992). See in this connection also John L. Esposito, *Women in Muslim Family Law* (Syracuse: Syracuse University Press, 1992).

15. Cassandra Balchin, ed., *A Handbook on Family Law in Pakistan* (Lahore: Shirkat Gah, 1994).

16. Asifa Quraishi, "Her Honor: An Islamic Critique of the Rape Laws of Pakistan from a Woman-Sensitive Perspective," in *Windows of Faith: Muslim Women Scholar-Activists in North America,* ed. Gisela Webb (Syracuse: Syracuse University Press, 2000), 102–135.

17. Deniz Kandiyoti, ed., *Women, Islam and the State* (Philadelphia: Temple University Press, 1991); Deniz Kandiyoti, ed., *Gendering the Middle East: Emerging Perspectives* (Syracuse, N.Y.: Syracuse University Press, 1996); Azza M. Karam, *Women, Islamisms and the State: Contemporary Feminisms in Egypt* (New York: St. Martin's Press, 1997); Suha Sabbagh, ed., *Arab Women: Between Defiance and Restraint* (New York: Olive Branch Press, 1996); Mahnaz Afkhami, ed., *Faith and Freedom: Women's Human Rights in the Muslim World* (Syracuse: Syracuse University Press, 1995).

18. See, for instance, Patricia Jeffery and Amrita Basu, eds., *Appropriating Gender: Women's Activism and Politicized Religion in South Asia* (New York: Routledge, 1998).

19. In this regard, some pertinent works are Yvonne Yazbeck Haddad and Jane Idleman Smith, eds., *Muslim Communities in North America* (Albany: State University of New York Press, 1994); Barbara Daly Metcalf, ed., *Making Muslim Space* (Berkeley and Los Angeles: University of California Press, 1996); Yvonnne Yazbeck Haddad and Adair T. Lummis, *Islamic Values in the United States: A Comparative Study* (New York: Oxford University Press, 1987); Yvonne Yazbeck Haddad and John L. Esposito, eds., *Muslims on the Americanization Path?* (New York: Oxford University Press, 1998), all of which have more detailed bibliographies.

20. While Edward Said's *Orientalism* (New York: Vintage Books, 1979) and *Culture and Imperialism* (New York: Vintage Books, 1994) are critical in framing the issues, there are works such as Sara Suleri's *The Rhetoric of English India* (Chicago: University of Chicago Press, 1992); Billie Melman's *Women's Orients: English Women and the Middle East, 1718–1918: Sexuality, Religion and Work* (Ann Arbor: University of Michigan Press, 1992, 1995); Kumari Jayawardena's *The White Woman's Other Burden: Western Women and South Asia During British Rule* (New York: Routledge, 1995) (this work deals largely with Hindu women), and Chandra Talpande Mohanty et al., eds., *Third World Women and the Politics of Feminism* (Bloomington: Indiana University Press, 1991) that explore colonial legacies with respect to women. More recently: Meyda Yegenoglu, *Colonial Fantasies: Towards a Feminist Reading of Orientalism* (Cambridge: Cambridge University Press, 1998).

21. Ahmed, *Women and Gender,* 167.

22. Kandiyoti, in Afkhami, ed., *Faith and Freedom,* 21.

23. Examples of such works might be Cynthia Nelson's article titled "Biography and Women's History: On Interpreting Doria Shafik" in the above-mentioned *Women in Middle Eastern History;* Fedwa Malti-Douglas, *Men, Women and God(s): Nawal El Saadawi and Arab Feminist Poetics* (Berkeley and Los Angeles: University of California Press, 1995). There is much more available in English on Middle Eastern (including North African) and Iranian women at present than there is on South Asian women, which is more so than on Central Asian, Southeast Asian, and sub-Saharan African women. Studies on European, Australian, and North American Muslim women's voices can be expected to emerge with greater vigor in the future.

24. Elizabeth Warnock Fernea and Basima Qattan Bezirgan, eds., *Middle Eastern*

Muslim Women Speak (Austin: University of Texas Press, 1977); Judith E. Tucker, ed., *Arab Women: Old Boundaries/New Frontiers* (Bloomington: Indiana University Press, 1993); and the classic work edited by Lois Beck and Nikki Keddie, *Women in the Muslim World* (Cambridge: Harvard University Press, 1978).

25. Attention to which has been drawn by Kandiyoti, ed., in *Women, Islam and the State;* and in *Gendering the Middle East;* as well as by Afkhami, ed., *Faith and Freedom,* among others.

26. Valentine M. Moghadam, *Modernizing Women: Gender and Social Change in the Middle East* (Boulder: Lynne Rienner, 1993), 27.

27. An essay engaging some of these issues is Margot Badran's "Toward Islamic Feminisms: A Look at the Middle East," in *Hermeneutics and Honor: Negotiating Female "Public" Space in Islamic/ate Societies,* Asma Afsaruddin, ed. (Cambridge: Harvard University Press, 1999), 159–188.

28. For selections, see chapter 2: "The Koran on the Subject of Women," in Fernea and Bezirgan, eds., *Middle Eastern Muslim Women Speak.*

29. Amina Wadud-Muhsin, *Qur'an and Woman* (Kuala Lumpur: Penerbit Fajar Bakti Sdn. Bhd., 1992).

30. Riffat Hassan, "Women in the Context of Change and Confrontation within Muslim Communities," in *Women of Faith in Dialogue,* ed. Virginia Ramey Mollenkott (New York: Crossroad, 1987), and "Muslim Women and Post-Patriarchal Islam," in *After Patriarchy: Feminist Transformations of the World Religions,* ed. Paula M. Cooey, William R. Eakin, and Jay B. McDaniel (Maryknoll, N.Y.: Orbis Books, 1991).

31. Fatima Mernissi, *Women and Islam: An Historical and Theological Enquiry,* trans. Mary Jo Lakeland (Oxford: Basil Blackwell, 1991).

32. Maysam J. al-Faruqi, "Women's Self-Identity in the Qur'an and Islamic Law," in Webb, ed., *Windows of Faith: Muslim Women Scholar-Activists in North America,* 72–101.

33. Such issues are discussed, as examples, by Riffat Hassan in articles such as "Muslim Women and Post-Patriarchal Islam," in Cooey, Eakin, and McDaniel, eds., *After Patriarchy;* by Barbara Freyer Stowasser in *Women in the Qur'an, Traditions, and Interpretation;* by Amina Wadud-Muhsin in *Qur'an and Woman,* among others.

34. Caroline Walker Bynum, Stevan Harell, and Paula Richman, eds., *Gender and Religion: On the Complexity of Symbols* (Boston: Beacon Press, 1986).

35. Vernon Schubel, *Religious Performance in Contemporary Islam: Shīʿī Devotional Rituals in South Asia* (Columbia: University of South Carolina Press, 1993).

36. Guity Nashat and Judith E. Tucker, *Women in the Middle East and North Africa: Restoring Women to History* (Bloomington: Indiana University Press, 1999).

37. Nabia Abbott, *Aishah: The Beloved of Mohammad* (Chicago: Arno Press, 1942); Denise Spellberg, *Politics, Gender, and the Islamic Past: The Legacy of 'A'isha bint Abi Bakr* (New York: Columbia University Press, 1994).

38. Ellison Banks Findly, *Nūr Jahān, Empress of Mughal India* (New York: Oxford University Press, 1993).

39. For example, see Afaf Lutfi Al-Sayyid Marsot, *Society and the Sexes in Medieval Islam* (Malibu: Undena Publications, 1979); Marsot, *Women and Men in Late Eighteenth-Century Egypt* (Austin: University of Texas Press, 1995); Gavin R. G. Hambly, ed., *Women in the Medieval Islamic World* (New York: St. Martin's Press, 1998); and Beverly B. Mack and Jean Boyd, *One Woman's Jihad: Nana Asma'u, Scholar and Scribe* (Bloomington: Indiana University Press, 2000).

40. Thus, from South Asia I have drawn upon Anees Jung, *Unveiling India: A Woman's Journey* (New Delhi: Penguin Books, 1987); Anees Jung, *Seven Sisters: Among the Women of South Asia* (New Delhi: Penguin Books, 1994); Ismat Chughtai, *The Quilt and Other Stories* (New Delhi: Kali for Women, 1994), Patricia Jeffery and Roger Jeffery, *Don't Marry Me to a Plowman!: Women's Everyday Lives in Rural North India* (Boulder, Colo.: Westview Press, 1996); Patricia Jeffery, *Frogs in a Well: Indian Women in Purdah* (London: Zed Books, 1979); Rukhsana Ahmed, trans. and ed., *We Sinful Women* (New Delhi: Rupa and Co., 1994). For Iran, Erika Friedl, *Women of Deh Koh: Lives in an Iranian Village* (New York: Penguin Books, 1991); Farzaneh Milani, *Veils and Words: The Emerging Voices of Iranian Women Writers* (Syracuse: Syracuse University Press, 1992); Franklin Lewis and Farzin Yazdanfar, comp. and trans., *In a Voice of Their Own: A Collection of Stories by Iranian Women Written Since the Revolution of 1979* (Costa Mesa: Mazda, 1996); John Green and Farzin Yazdanfar, eds., *A Walnut Sapling on Masih's Grave and Other Stories by Iranian Women* (Toronto: TSAR Publications, 1994). From Egypt, the novels of Nawal El Saadawi (among others, *Woman at Point Zero* [London: Zed Books, 1983]); Sherifa Zuhur, *Revealing Reveiling: Islamist Gender Ideology in Contemporary Egypt* (Albany: State University of New York Press, 1992); Lila Abu-Lughod, *Writing Women's Worlds: Bedouin Stories* (Berkeley: University of California Press, 1993). From the Arab world, Margot Badran and Miriam Cooke, eds., *Opening the Gates: A Century of Arab Feminist Writing* (Bloomington: Indiana University Press, 1990). From Africa, Charlotte H. Bruner, ed., *Unwinding Threads: Writing by Women in Africa* (Oxford: Heinemann, 1994); Sarah Mirza and Margaret Strobel, eds. and trans., *Three Swahili Women: Life Histories from Mombasa, Kenya* (Bloomington: Indiana University Press, 1989). From Canada and the United States, Nurjehan Aziz, ed., *Her Mother's Ashes and Other Stories by South Asian Women in Canada and the United States* (Toronto: TSAR Publications, 1994). From England/Egypt, Ahdaf Soueif, *The Map of Love* (New York: Anchor Books, 1999). From Afghanistan, Veronica Doubleday, *Three Women of Herat* (Austin: University of Texas Press, 1990).

41. Miriam Cooke, *Women Claim Islam: Creating Islamic Feminism Through Literature* (New York: Routledge, 2001). Two others: Fedwa Malti-Douglas, *Woman's Body, Woman's Word: Gender and Discourse in Arabo-Islamic Writing* (Princeton: Princeton University Press, 1991); Roger Allen, Hilary Kilpatrick, and Ed de Moor, eds., *Love and Sexuality in Modern Arabic Literature* (London: Saqi Books, 1995).

42. See, for example, Bouthaina Shaaban, *Both Right and Left Handed: Arab Women Talk About Their Lives* (Bloomington: Indiana University Press, 1991); Haleh Esfandiari,

Reconstructed Lives: Women and Iran's Islamic Revolution (Washington, D.C.: The Woodrow Wilson Center Press, in conjunction with Johns Hopkins University Press, 1997); Haideh Moghissi, *Populism and Feminism in Iran* (New York: St. Martin's Press, 1996); and Miriam Cooke, *War's Other Voices: Women Writers on the Lebanese Civil War* (New York: Cambridge University Press, 1988); Miriam Cooke and Roshni Rustomji-Kerns, eds., *Blood into Ink: South Asian and Middle Eastern Women Write War* (Boulder, Colo.: Westview Press, 1994); Miriam Cooke, *Women and the War Story* (Berkeley and Los Angeles: University of California Press, 1996).

43. On veiling, Ahmed, Stowasser, and Zuhur, already mentioned, as well as Fadwa El Guindy, *Veil: Modesty, Privacy and Resistance* (New York: Berg, 1999); on female genital mutilation (or modification/ cutting), Evelyne Accad, *The Excised* (Boulder: Three Continents Press, 1994); Noor J. Kassamali, "When Modernity Confronts Traditional Practices: Female Genital Cutting in Northeast Africa," in *Women in Muslim Societies: Diversity Within Unity,* ed. Herbert L. Bodman and Nayereh Tohidi (Boulder, Colo.: Lynne Rienner, 1998); and Esther K. Hicks, *Infibulation: Female Mutilation in Islamic Northeastern Africa* (New Brunswick: Transaction, 1996); as well as the film by Pratibha Parmar, *Warrior Marks* (1993), distributed by Women Make Movies. For honor killings, the CNN-aired film, *Honor Killings in Jordan;* the ABC Nightline-aired film, *A Matter of Honor;* Human Rights Watch, *Crime or Custom? Violence Against Women in Pakistan* (New York: Human Rights Watch, 1999); and the writings of Riffat Hassan.

Part Three

CONTEMPORARY ISSUES AND CHALLENGES IN TEACHING ISLAM AS A RELIGION

CHAPTER NINE

The Wedding of Zein
Islam through a Modern Novel

MICHAEL A. SELLS

THE NOVELS AND STORIES OF TAYEB SALIH are among the more widely read works of fiction within the Arabic-speaking world. They are also among the more internationally influential works of modern Arabic literature.

Salih roots his fiction in traditional culture as it encounters or is confronted with the disruptions of the modern world. He also ushers the reader into the interior conflicts and controversies over the nature of tradition itself. The reading of a work by Salih opens up central issues concerning religious culture, the diversity within tradition, different modes of being Muslim, and even as it articulates a common humanity that embraces the characters, their stories, and their predicaments.

Salih's five major novels and many of his short stories take place within a fictionalized locale in northern Sudan. The attention of literary critics and popular readership has focused on his novel, *Season of Migration to the North* [*mawsim al-ḥijrat ilā ash-shamāl*], at the expense of Salih's other, equally valuable works. The short novel, *The Wedding of Zein* ['*Urs az-Zayn*], fits a broad array of courses: introductory courses in world religions, midlevel courses on Islamic literature and civilization, and a class on cultural identity in modern fiction.[1] After seventeen years of reading *The Wedding of Zein* in classroom settings, I continue to discover—and continue to find my students discovering—new meanings, connections, and complexities within the story.[2]

From the first pages, the story challenges any reified or essentialist assumptions concerning what is normative in a religious tradition. The narrator begins by recounting the effect that the news of the impending wedding of Zein has upon the differing factions within the village. The controversy among the factions, intensified by the effect of the news of Zein's wedding, offers a microcosmic view of a dynamic Islamic world of competing perspectives and interpretations. It also helps overcome what can be a confining student expectation in courses on religion: the expectation that the instructor and the course will define the essence of a religion and definitively delineate its boundaries of belief and practice. If a living tradition is an extended argument over the meaning and boundaries of that tradition, then the goal of a course on Islam is not to settle the argument but to bring the student into the argument and help the student appreciate its passions and its complexities. The story format employed in *The Wedding of Zein* plunges us so quickly into a world of competing versions tradition, and so naturally, that the normal expectation for closed definitions is taken by surprise before it can harden into a demand.

The unpretentious quality of *The Wedding of Zein*, the vividness of the characters, the apparent simplicity of the village, the folksy tone of the narrative voice, and the absence of explicit doctrinal discussion allow immediate access to the book. These same qualities, however, can lead to a reading of *The Wedding of Zein* that remains oblivious to the subtler allusions that add dimension to the characters and depth to the story. Indeed, I find that my students have thoroughly enjoyed the work on first reading, but when probed about how the novel represents key controversies in Islam—concerning knowledge, authority, love, poetry, and sanctity—they draw an initial blank. Here opens up what has been one of the most consistently rewarding moments in my work as a teacher.

That what is most profound refuses to take itself too seriously is a central theme in *The Wedding of Zein*. In this essay, I examine how the novella's artistic combination of down-home unpretentiousness and cultural depth mirrors its interior themes of knowledge and pretension. To find access to the story's mythic and cultural subtext, I employ a series of questions about different aspects of the story. Examples of the questions and of some of the issues opened up by such questions are given below.

Diverse Worlds in a Single Village

Question: What are the different groups within the village and how do they interact with one another?

The story opens with the news, circulating through the village, that Zein is to be married. The narrative then backs up and displays the reasons why such an announcement is extraordinary. Zein is introduced as a kind of village fool;

physically deformed, outrageous in behavior, lacking in steady employment or strong family ties, and utterly ineligible to marry, let alone marry the most beautiful girl in the village. It is not that Zein isn't interested in women. To the contrary, he is constantly falling in love. When one of his beloveds is married to someone more eligible, he soon finds himself in love with another.

Zein's personality and behavior become a touchstone for the various factions within the village. The first faction consists of the Imam of the mosque and his followers. The Imam is a man with some formal training who views himself as an educated man among the ignorant, with strong opinions about what constitutes proper Islamic behavior. He supervises the mosque, attends to basic rites of passages such as weddings and funerals, and gives hellfire and damnation sermons during his Friday sermons. Most villagers (and the narrator) show little affection for the Imam and resent his intolerance and aloofness. A circle of particularly observant older men supports him, however, and comprises his more attentive audience.

Another faction is formed by a group of pragmatists called "the gang," led by a certain Mahjoub, who supervises projects central to village welfare, such as flood control, irrigation, and health care. This group supports the mosque and the Imam financially, although they themselves are not particularly observant of ritual obligations and mosque attendance. Further from the Imam's orbit is a group of rebels, mostly young men, but led by an old poet. This group uses a vocabulary sprinkled with revolutionary expressions such as "dialectical materialism." They also frequent the "Oasis," a bar and bordello on the edge of town.

Juxtaposed to the social order of males in the village is a group of young women, along with their mothers who enter the narrative through their efforts to secure a good match for their daughters. One of the young women, Ni'ma, "the most beautiful girl in the village," challenges expectations involving suitors and marriage, and by doing so, takes on a role that, although it is less public, is as important to the outcome of the story as that of Zein.

Finally, there is the "holy man" Haneen, a mystical personality who comes and goes mysteriously and wanders alone through the desert for months at a time. Haneen is both marginal to village life as it is normally perceived and central to the unfolding of the story. Because of the enmity between Haneen and the Imam, the reader may be tempted to generalize that Haneen represents an antiritual element in Islam. When I ask the class what Haneen takes with him on his journeys, the usual answer is a bit of water. When I ask what the water is for, most students reply with the assumption that it is drinking water, having missed the narrator's remark that Haneen's only provisions are a container for ablution water and a prayer rug. A discussion of this point allows a comparison with that tradition of Sufis who are both "lost" in meditation and at the same time observant of ritual—such as the classical Sufis who would know, from within their state of being "absent," to wake themselves at the proper time for performing the prayers, before going back into their trance once again.

The relationship between the Imam and the villagers is particularly important. The villagers are caught up in the rhythmic cycles of the Nile and the harvest—pastoral cycles that are portrayed in vignettes of masterful lyricism. Once a week the Imam's harsh sermons break the rhythmic spell and force each villager to confront mortality and the terror of the day of judgment or moment of truth, when what a person has made of his or her live is revealed, without the possibility of change. After the jolt of the sermon's apocalyptic urgency wears off, the villagers, to the Imam's frustration, revert back into the agricultural rhythms and daily preoccupations of their lives.

It is common for the reader to share the general dislike for the Imam they find in the narrator's tone and in the villagers' reactions. Yet those same villagers view him as indispensable, presiding over weddings, funerals, and over other central functions of life and death, a function they realize no one else could perform—a point easily lost, particularly in societies with a built-in bias against organized forms of religion and ritual.

The discussion can first hone in on how the tension among the different factions and personalities threatens to pull the village apart, as well as the agent and event that catalyzes their dramatic reconciliation. The portrayal of these issues of tension, diversity, and unity within the microcosm of a fictional village in northern Sudan can then be extended to a discussion of similar issues in the wider world of Islam as a religion and Islam as a civilization.

Faces of Zein

Question: What are the different aspects of Zein's personality and how are those aspects dramatized in the story?

Zein constantly transgresses the normal boundaries of village propriety and decorum. He enters the women's quarters at will. He is a glutton at wedding feasts. He laughs inordinately. His naiveté allows the mayor or Umda to exploit him with false promises that if he carries out tasks for him he will be able to court the Umda's daughter. Like a jinni, he can take on traits of various animals. His teeth were lost when he was riveted to the ground in a haunted area near a graveyard—probably an encounter (and perhaps an initiation by) the *jinn*. He has a deformed spine and long "ape-like" arms. His voice is compared to the braying of an ass.

Yet many of these same physical deformities are bound up with Zein's extraordinary, at times even superhuman, strength. He is known, for example, for his feats in swimming the Nile. The combination of a physical deformity with inordinate strength is found in folklore and mythic tales from a wide variety of cultures. Zein's inordinate strength, although it does not seem important at first, will play a central role in the climactic turning point in the story.

Like the hero with both a deformity and inordinate strength, the wise fool is a common feature in traditional literatures and here is given its own original twist. Despite Zein's foolishness, he is recognized as having some mysterious connection to the realm of sanctity and wisdom. Some of his physical defects are attributed to the moment when as a child he was violently possessed by a jinni; the jinn in Arabic tradition have both destructive and constructive roles, and can bring inspiration as well as evil. Zein's mother insists he is a blessed and chosen person. His interactions with the socially marginalized such as Ashmana the deaf and Mousa the lame bring him special regard. The deeper point here is not that he is kind or charitable to them in bringing them food and firewood; that would be seen as virtuous but not extraordinary. Rather, he alone is able to enter into a genuine relationship with them as human beings. With Ashmana, for example, who is terrified of all others—even those who are kind to her and bring her provisions—he establishes a friendship and is able to reach and be reached by her humanity. For the community, Zein's ability to touch the humanity of such characters is not the only clue that there might be something blessed about him. He is also the only confidant of the reclusive mystic Haneen. Haneen maintains personal relations with no one else, singling out Zein for sudden and unexplained visits.

Zein is also a lover. As he recognizes and falls in love with each new beauty in the village, he becomes a comic version of Majnun Layla, the poet and lover driven mad (literally "jinned") out of his love for Layla who ultimately perishes in unrequited love for her. Zein becomes the prophet of love. His histrionic proclamation, "I am slain out of love for so-and-so," becomes a treasure for each potential bride, raising her status and value. When the narrator refers to the women he is slain for as his "Laylas," it offers a perfect opportunity to lead the students into a discussion of allusion. (Even in classes where we have read poetry attributed to Majnun Layla, these allusions can pass by unnoticed on first reading).

Zein's remarkable ability to recognize beauty in a girl before it is apparent to others brings him the attention of the mothers of potential brides, each of whom wishes him to proclaim publicly the beauty of her daughter, thus increasing her status among potential spouses. His sensitivity to beauty reveals itself in other ways as well. Zein, for example, can recognize from afar the voices in a group of women ululating at a wedding and distinguish within the blend of voices, the individual style of each woman. A short recording of ululation can help students who have not heard ululation before to understand more vividly what Zein's unusual ability to parse it reveals about his heightened awareness.

Zein is both a boundary breaker and a boundary crosser. He has no fixed role in the village. He wanders from one place to another, sleeping in different parts of the town with a rock as a pillow. As mentioned earlier, he not only wanders physically but also socially, transgressing the class, gender, and group boundaries within the community. He is invited for tea to the women's quarters (a prohibited space for males outside the family)—in the hopes that he will recognize the beauty of a young woman, a place from which any male considered eligible for marriage would be strictly prohibited. Zein befriends the bedouin and attends their weddings, despite their uneasy and often mutually hostile relationship with the villagers. He also links different factions within the village, spending time with Mahjoub's gang, with Ashmana and Mousa, and with Haneen—with almost everyone, in fact, but the Imam.

At first, Zein is marginal to the community, without a respectable role and apparently ineligible for marriage and responsibility. Then, he is portrayed crossing boundaries, linking the various feuding factions together and bridging the male and female domains. By the end of the story, this marginal figure has moved to the center, becoming the axis around which the community turns.

Wisdom and Language

Questions: What is the effect of the interplay among dialect, formal Arabic, and words from Western languages? What is the attitude of each faction or major character toward language, authority, and wisdom? How are these attitudes dramatized in the story? In particular, what are the attitudes of Ni'ma toward learning and how does her commitment to learning put her in jeopardy?

Tayeb Salih is one of the pioneers in the use of Arabic dialect in the novel and short story. In the case of *The Wedding of Zein*, the use of dialect also reflects (and performs) a central theme within the story, the relation among language, authority, and knowledge. Before the work of writers like Salih, dialect had been used in comic theatre, but fiction (both narrative and dialogue) was composed entirely in Modern Standard Arabic. Gradually, authors and readers began to feel confined by dialogues composed in a language that no one would ever speak in such situations. They sensed that a fiction limited to Modern Standard failed to capture the difference in linguistic registers central to Arabic cultures, and in the subtlety, ironies, and social negotiations within

Arabic civilization. Yet the use of dialect in fiction carries risks, beyond offending the literary conservatives, who judged it too lowly a discourse for "high" art. One risk was that use of a dialect might limit the potential readership of the work to those speaking the dialect it employed. In contrast to the Cairene dialect of another dialect pioneer, Yusuf Idris which—due to the Egyptian radio, television, and film industry—is understood throughout the Arabic world, some expressions from the local Sudanese dialect of Salih's novels can be obscure even to many Sudanese, making his innovation particularly daring. The gamble paid off, however; not only were his books not marginalized because of the dialect, but they have also reached an unusually large and international readership.

The Wedding of Zein is grounded in the tensions and subtleties of Arabic diglossia (the double-language phenomenon characteristic of many cultures, including almost all Arabic-speaking cultures). The themes of diglossia in Salih's story, as well as the use of diglossia in his writing, exemplify the significance of polysemantic performance in a culture and the role of that performance in almost every aspect of a society in which it is embedded.[3]

The school headmaster dramatizes the relationship of dialect, knowledge, and authority within the novel. The headmaster prides himself on his education and his ability to read some words in foreign languages. His view of knowledge is instrumental; he uses knowledge as a weapon to put other people in their place, particularly his students whom he calls "dumb asses" and his friends to whom he is constantly condescending. His intellectual stance is exposed through his contextual misuse of classical Arabic, his use of formal Arabic (which only a school-trained person would know) in contexts where it is inappropriate, such as everyday conversation in the coffee shop of one of his friends. The headmaster's deflation, caused and deserved in part by his abuse of language, is performed with a play on the same language issues, even as it exemplifies and parodies his own attitudes toward knowledge and authority within the village.

Ni'ma is the headmaster's opposite in her conception of learning. Early on, she demands to be sent to school along with the boys. Her unusually strong commitment to learning and her academic excellence leads to expectations that she would pursue higher professional training in medicine or law. At this point, Ni'ma decides that instead of educating herself for a profession, she will aspire to another kind of knowledge. She devotes herself to the study of the Quran. The Surahs of the Compassionate (Q 55), Maryam (Q 19), and the Recounting (Q 28) are among her favorites.[4] Students who take the initiative to read and contemplate these surahs find clues to Ni'ma's behavior and character, as well as to the symbolic ramifications of her role in the village.

Ni'ma's devotion to learning leads her to refuse a succession of suitors who, in the view of the village, are more worthy than Zein in character and family stature. Her family is vexed. If she does not marry soon, gossip will start. In addition, her younger sisters will be delayed in their marriage plans. After one of her refusals, her father raises his hand to strike her. Then something holds him back, some sense that her refusal did not result from willfulness or rebellion. That deeper something protects her throughout the novel.[5]

Eiron and Alarzon

Question: What happens to the headmaster in the coffeehouse of Sheikh Ali? What are the various jokes involved? What is the big joke on the headmaster? What does the headmaster's increasing discomfort reveal about the struggle in the village over issues of stature, knowledge, language, and power?

The struggle over knowledge is performed in one of the story's comic vignettes. The mordancy of these vignettes is even easier to underestimate than the story as a whole. A particularly complex vignette takes place in the coffeehouse of Sheikh Ali where a friend, Abdul Samad, has come to try to extract a debt payment from Ali. Another friend Hajj Ibrahim is also present. The headmaster drops by and the conversation among the four turns to the upcoming wedding of Ni'ma—to whom, like many others, the headmaster had proposed, and by whom, like many others, he had been turned down.

It is never stated that Ali, Abdul Samad, or Ibrahim know that the headmaster had proposed to the parents of Ni'ma. When someone mentions the "news" everyone is talking about—the impending wedding of Zein and Ni'ma—the headmaster loses his self-control. He shouts his disbelief that Ni'ma could marry "that dervish of a fellow." The headmaster uses the term "dervish" as a pejorative, the equivalent to an American slang term (such as deadbeat) for a person without a job, a role, or status. Yet the term also applies in a sense which he did not intend—one who has renounced mundane preoccupations such as status and career to pursue the path of mystical devotion.

The headmaster's uncontrolled exclamations reveal his emotional investment in the issue of Ni'ma's upcoming marriage to Zein. Ali, Abdul Samad, and Ibrahim sense an opportunity to avenge themselves for countless putdowns by the headmaster. They expand on the tale of Zein's wedding, dwelling on every aspect of the strange news. Then they recount, at length, oral traditions from Arabic poetry and legend of similarly unusual marriage choices. Once they have impaled the headmaster on his own pretensions, they suggest to the headmaster that he himself might wish to take a second wife, a divorcée perhaps, who might be appropriate for the headmaster's advanced age. Then, seeing the headmaster's anger at the mention of divorcées, they proceed to twist the knife:

> "Do you mean to say that his honour the Headmaster, when wanting to marry another wife in addition to the mother of his children, should marry a 'second-hand' woman?" said Sheikh Ali, fanning the flames. "Really, Hajj Abdul Samad, you are a proper oaf." (p. 93/85)

Abdul Samad then picks up on the English expression used by Ali, "second-hand." He proceeds to berate Sheikh Ali for using foreign words. As throughout the vignette, however, the various barbs that Sheikh Ali, Hajj Abdul Samad, and Hajj Ibrahim hurl at one another are directed at and land upon the headmaster. After all, it was the headmaster who had so often used foreign vocabulary and overly formal Arabic to show off his learning and put his friends in their place. With wicked timing and an ironic self-deprecation, his interlocutors have turned the pretentiously formal language ("a proper oaf") and the foreign terms ("second hand") back onto the headmaster. Within the verbal mimicry of the headmaster is embedded a mimicry of the headmaster's values:

> Abdul Samad seized hold of the English word 'second hand', which Sheikh Ali had employed, and proceeded to tease him about it. "What's that you said, Sheikh Ali" '*Sakan Dahan*'—and he pronounced the words as if they were Arabic. "Wonders will never cease—Ali Wad Shayeb using foreign talk!" (p. 93/85)

As Abdul Samad repeats the English expression "second hand," he rubs salt into the wound to the headmaster's pride by mimicking the headmaster's view of women as objects that can be possessed and presenting them with analogies to new and used cars—all through a mock criticism of his friend based upon the headmaster's view of language.

Sheikh Ali then proceeds to expound on women in the past who married homely men, evoking figures from the past, such as Shajar al-Durr, on Kuthayyir Azza, as well as a famous marriage that occurred in the Ibrahimab tribe. The headmaster had always considered his three tormenters to be uncultured and ignorant because they had no formal education. Now, having exposed himself by his anger and disarmed by his own discomfort, he is confronted with the previously unsuspected erudition of Sheikh Ali, discoursing on classical heritage from a seemingly inexhaustible well of oral tradition. A new aspect of the tensions over knowledge and authority is revealed, as the oral tradition takes its revenge upon the pretensions of formal education and book learning.

At this point in a discussion, I ask the students about the literary roles of the headmaster and his three interlocutors. These characters offer parallels to the Graeco-Shakespearean comic tradition of *Alarzon* (a pretentious and puffed-up character) and the *Eiron* (a humble and common character who ultimately turns the table on the Alarzon). In Shakespeare, the Alarzon and Eiron characters can appear in side vignettes, as they do in *The Wedding of Zein*—where the *Alarzon* (the headmaster) is exposed and deflated by the seemingly naive and ignorant *Eirons*. The vignette becomes an occasion for the discussion of irony as an aspect of literature, an aspect that can be particularly difficult for many undergraduates to grasp. It also allows for a discussion of the distinctions between comic irony and other forms of the ironic.

Barakah

Question: What is the turning point in the story?

To raise the question of a turning point may seem out of fashion in view of much of modernist and postmodern subversion or deconstruction of plot. Yet as a work molded in part on traditional fable forms, *The Wedding of Zein* does indeed offer a clear and dramatic moment, when the entire set of tensions and factions within the village is transformed and realigned, a moment the significance of which is revealed only in retrospect, at the end of the story.

Earlier in the story, Seif ad-Din, an abusive young dissolute, had attacked Zein for behaving inappropriately at his sister's wedding. Zein was sent to the hospital where in addition to recovering from Seif ad-Din's attack, he was given a new set of teeth. The new teeth and his improved appearance allowed the villagers to see him and regard him as more of a person in his own right, one who might even be eligible for marriage.

When Zein later crosses paths with Seif ad-Din, he leaps upon his former attacker and begins to choke him. Zein's quasi-superhuman strength becomes apparent when Mahjoub's gang attempts but fails to pull him away from Seif ad-Din. When it seems inevitable that Zein will choke his adversary to death, the quiet, slight, gentle Haneen appears and places his hand on Zein's shoulder. At Haneen's touch and the sound of his blessing, Zein's iron grip softens and Seif ad-Din falls gasping to the ground. Haneen utters the phrase "Zein the Blessed" (*az-zayn al-mabruk*) (p. 65/63). Haneen uses the same occasion to announce that Zein will marry the most beautiful woman in the village. Zein and Seif ad-Din reconcile with one another on the spot. Then Zein kisses Haneen on the head, referring to him as our blessed shaykh, our blessed father (*shaykhuna al-mabruk, abuna al-mabruk*) (68/65). Haneen then pronounces blessings on all present, and by extension, the entire village, with a dual invocation: "May our lord bless you. May our lord bring about blessing for you" (*rabbina yibarik fikum. rabbina yaj'al l-barakah fikum*) (p. 68 / 65).

Haneen's miraculous intervention and its effects are given a textured narrative. Miracle after miracle is recounted, but with increasing narrative acknowledgment that with the passage of time some may recall these past events in an exaggerated fashion. First, the inhuman strength of Zein, that had thwarted the combined efforts of the gang, melts away with the soft touch and voice of Haneen. Furthermore, according to Seif ad-Din himself and another character (who, the narrator admits, has a tendency to exaggerate), Seif ad-Din was already dead, had already passed through the "alligator jaws" of death; Haneen's intervention had raised him from the dead. After the incident, the village harvested the finest crops in recent memory. Yields doubled and quadrupled. New development projects, such as the construction of a hospital, brought employment opportunities. This sudden prosperity, along with other unusual occurrences such as snowfall, was attributed to "the year of Haneen." As these miracles are recounted, the narrative voice shows a range of stances, from credulity to skepticism.

Meanwhile, not only are the mortal enemies, Zein and Seif ad-Din, reconciled, but also Seif ad-Din is converted, repents, and becomes the most zealous follower of the Imam. The voice of the former dissolute now can be heard wafting over the village five times a day as the new Muezzin, Seif ad-Din calls villagers to prayer. Seif ad-Din's newfound zeal is also shown through his attack on his old haunt, the Oasis, which, when it refuses his demand to close down, he burns to the ground. This "miracle" of Seif ad-Din's conversion is not without a certain ambiguity. Seif ad-Din (Sword of the Faith) has radically and miraculously changed his behavior and allegiance. In another way, perhaps, his personality has not changed at all. He is still an extremist, having moved from extremist rejecter of religion to zealous defender of the faith. As evidenced in his burning down of the Oasis, he is still violent. In view of the violence committed in the Sudan in the name of religion at the time of the writing of *The Wedding of Zein* and since, the violent implications in Seif ad-Din's zeal may offer a sense of foreboding.

Greater than all of these aspects of the miracle, is what for the village is the miracle of miracles. Ni'ma, the most beautiful woman in the village, had firmly refused the most eligible young men of good family, substantial means, and personal charm. She is now to marry Zein, the dervish of a man, considered a fool and a freak by many and an unlikely candidate for marriage to anyone, let alone Ni'ma (although, being Zein's cousin, it is acknowledged that there is no technical impediment to such a wedding).

The artfulness of the narration allows the barakah scene to proceed in a vivid fashion, without calling explicit attention to the conceptual world of popular Islam that underlies it. In the first discussion of the episode, I prefer to focus on the story proper. Then, with the vividness of the story on our minds, we can enter into an examination of the role of barakah as a quasi-tangible force residing in the body of shaykhs and in their tombs; of the miracles [karamāt] that barakah can bring about through the personality of the shaykh; and the local visit or pilgrimage [ziyārah] to the shrine of the holy person. From here, it is possible to briefly explore the inscription of barakah language within everyday idioms, from *barakat llah fik* (the blessings of God on you, thank you), *mabruk* (you've been blessed, congratulations), *allah yibarak fik* (God bless you, as equivalent to thank you or you're welcome).

Once the role of barakah in popular Sufism and popular Islamic culture (many who engage in ritual *ziyarah* do not consider themselves Sufis or categorize themselves as practicing any particular aspect of Islam) has been introduced, the controversies over Sufism and popular Islam can be engaged, from the early attacks of Ibn Taymiyya to the extreme anti-Sufi ideology of the Wahhabi version of Islam now dominant in Saudi Arabia. Indeed, the tension between practitioners and opponents of popular Sufism or popular Islam is at the heart of the tension between the Imam (with his connections to the larger world of officially recognized Islamic leadership) and Haneen.

The night of barakah contains two other aspects of the miracle that are only revealed at the story's end. At the wedding, the factions of the village that had been in tension and conflict with one another join in celebration. This is the moment when "opposites come together." And, as Zein leaves the final wedding in midcelebration, the reader begins to understand something else about Haneen's blessing that had been only obliquely raised earlier in the story.

Modes of Identification with Islam

Question: Discuss the religiosity of the gang. In what sense are they religious?

Just after the episode of the miracle and preceding the explosion of energy in the wedding, is a moment of calm. The "gang" is gathered outside Sa'eed's shop toward evening, after a day of hard work. Although they are ritually nonobservant for the most part, the gang both support and make possible the formal institutions centered around the mosque on the one hand, while reflecting on Islamic ritual patterns of time and space on the other. As the evening prayer time approaches, they are gathered together for their evening meal—a communal act that parallels communal prayer being performed by the observant Muslims in the village. After the meal, they turn meditative, citing aphorisms, proverbs, and other expressions from both the poetic and the

Islamic tradition, bearing on destiny in both its Quranic and its classical poetic contexts. The narrator depicts the moment of deepest calm as follows:

> By then the people would have finished the evening prayer. They would talk quietly and contentedly, enjoying their warm, tranquil feeling which is also experienced by the worshippers as they stand in a row behind the Imam shoulder to shoulder, looking at some faraway point at which their prayers will meet. At such times the vehemence in Mahjoub's eyes lessens as they idly roam along the faint, fading line where the light from the lamp ends and the darkness begins (where does the lamplight end? how does the darkness begin?) His silence takes on great depth at such moments, and if one of his friends asks him something he neither hears nor makes answer. This is the time when Wad Rayyis suddenly breaks out into a single phrase, like a stone falling into a pond: "God is living." Ahmed Ismaeel inclines his head a little in the direction of the river as though listening to some voice that comes to him from there. At this hour, too, Abdul Hafeez cracks his fingers in silence and Taher Rawwasi gives a sigh from deep within him and says: "Time comes and Time goes." (p. 114/105)

This passage opens up the range of ways, in which people can adhere to a religious tradition, and breaks the common assumption of two fixed and rigidly bound categories of religious and nonreligious. Taher Rawwasi's expression ("Time comes and Time goes") evokes the concept of time/fate [dahr] that grounds the poetic tradition and that is partially incorporated into Islam. Wad Rayyis "breaks out into a single phrase, like a stone falling into a pond: 'God is living'." His exclamation opens up a discussion of the relationship of the evocation of the divine name in the phrase "God is living" [Allāhu ḥayy] and the theme of life (represented by the wedding that is about to be announced) at the heart of the story. Wad Rayyis also exemplifies the effect of religious patterns on those who may not deem themselves religious or who may not appear religious or regularly observant to others. The gang responds not only to the cycles of pastoral life (the tranquil moment occurs after a day's work in the fields and a robustly enjoyed meal) but also to the rhythms of Islamic ritual life—in sustained and personal ways, even if by the standards of strict orthopraxis they are negligent.

Wedding as *Hieros Gamos*

The calm is broken by the ululation announcing the wedding. The wedding dramatizes in a particularly comprehensive manner the coming together of opposites that was said to be one of the signs of Haneen's miracle. The bedouin and the villagers offer one striking example of such a *coincidentia oppositorum*. The villagers had considered the Koz bedouin to be uncouth bumpkins, while the bedouin considered themselves to be the authentic upholders of the classical Arab ideals—illustrating in a local example a creative tension that has been the warp and woof of Arabic society for centuries. The simultaneous presence at the wedding of these two, normally mutually exclusive groups is paralleled by the marriage of Quranic religiosity with secular entertainment. A group reciting the Quran together is found next to a group forming a circle around an erotic dancer, with many moving back and forth between the two worlds. During the dance, the Imam happens to let his glance wander toward the cleavage (described in hyperbolic terms) of the dancer's breasts. His eyes "become cloudy as muddied water"—perhaps a moment of humanization of the otherwise self-righteous and rigid figure, who had shortly before exasperated the community with his grudging and insulting remarks at the wedding ceremony. The entire village (with the possible exception of Seif ad-Din) celebrates side by side, as Zein moves from one circle to the other, dancing at the center of each.

Ni'ma is a principal actor and agent of change within the novel. Ni'ma chose Zein for marriage and Ni'ma's choice precipitated the subsequent events that transformed the village dynamic. In depicting her choice, the narrator refers to her conviction that she had been chosen to make a sacrifice. Her readings of the Quranic passages on strong women (Mariam and the mother of Moses) have deepened her determination to follow her sense of destiny, wherever it should lead her, at whatever sacrifice. What exactly the sacrifice entails is never made explicit, although we can infer certain aspects of it. She sacrifices her professional possibilities by choosing to remain in the village and by choosing Quranic knowledge over technical training (a choice that is frequently a cause of discussion and argument among the students). She sacrifices possibilities of marrying a handsome and relatively wealthy suitor, who might have lifted her and her family several notches in social status. The name, Ni'ma [Na'ima], is based on an Arabic radical [$n/'/m$] with connotations of bounty, fertility, and lush life. And by marrying Zein, Ni'ma has clearly helped bring to the village these very qualities—which are evoked with such power in another of her favorite Quranic passages, the Surah of the Compassionate.[6]

Along with Ni'ma, Haneen is a major agent of change within the story. By announcing Zein's blessedness, by touching Zein, and through the miracle of overcoming of Zein's strength with his own gentleness, Haneen not only proclaims Ni'ma's choice of Zein as spouse but also saves Zein from destroying the prospect of the marriage. And Haneen plays a central role in the wedding. When Zein vanishes from the festivities, they search for him throughout the village. They follow him past the fields, past the mosque, past the residences, offering an intimate and closely knit last view of the important sites of the village, each of which evokes the characters and the drama associated with that site earlier in the story. In the end, Zein is found weeping at the tomb of Haneen. The tombs in the graveyard are described as standing in the darkness like ships on the ocean swells. Before this moment, the death of Haneen had been mentioned only in an artfully disguised parenthesis, so we arrive at the tomb of Haneen with a certain sense of surprise. Here we sense a final intimation in Haneen's touching of Zein's shoulder during the night of the miracle: the possibility that he was transferring to Zein the spiritual leadership along with his barakah.

Zein is persuaded to return to the wedding. Once again he enters the ring of dancing and stands in the heart of the circle, like the "mast of a ship" (p. 128/119). At this point, the class can discuss the classical Sufi idea of the *qutb,* the "pole" that holds the cosmos together, and then ask if Haneen and then Zein carry out an analogous role on the microcosmic level of the village. Zein—who had been the marginal character throughout the novel, hovering at the edge of the community, transgressing its conventions and boundaries but never having a role—now has been transformed into the very center of the community bond and life, the *axis mundi* of this fictionalized Sudanese village. At this moment, there are revealed two other aspects of the *coincidentia oppositorum:* the coming together of death (represented by the tombs) and life (by the circle of dancers), as well as the joining of celebration (the wedding) with grief (the graveyard remembrance of Haneen that occurs temporally within the wedding).

Haneen and Zein form yet another set of opposites brought together at this wedding. Haneen as a holy man is ascetic, gentle, restrained, mysterious, and slight of build. Zein is exuberant, uninhibited, gluttonous, large, and inhumanely strong. Yet Haneen chooses Zein as his only confidant and eventual successor. Similarly, Zein and Ni'ma represent two opposites, brought together in the *hieros gamos.* Ni'ma is both beautiful and the epitome of *'aql* (a quality that combines reason, judgment, and maturity). Zein is physically ugly, lacking in self-control and decorum. Yet, of course, Zein's name means "beautiful," and it was Ni'ma who sees beauty in the seemingly ugly connoisseur of the beauty of others. Ni'ma brings her seriousness and sense of destiny to the powerful, spontaneous, and unfocused energy of Zein. Ni'ma's sense of vision, destiny, and sacrifice lead her to determined action. She realizes the vision for herself (through her marriage) and for the community (through the marriage of the various factions and through the year of bounty), thus reflecting in subtle ways the themes of her favorite Quranic passages.

Meaning and Boundaries

In the blurb on the back-cover of the book, Kingsley Amis writes of Salih's characters that "the reader is invited to laugh at them, or at least to smile. And yet his humour is fundamentally kind; even at their most ridiculous, all the characters retain an essential dignity." Publishers are notorious for picking out the wrong quote to describe a novel, and it may be that Amis went on to deepen his comment. As it is, although grateful for his support of this work, I find myself in sharp disagreement with Amis's remark. The significance of *The Wedding of Zein* resides in what it reveals not only about a particular fictional village in the Sudan but also about community and human nature generally. And—unless we take the headmaster's condescending view of these villagers—when we laugh, we laugh at what we recognize in ourselves.

The Wedding of Zein presents a plurality of human types. Though the types may be sketched in the broad, artistic brushes of folklore and fable rather than filled out in sociorealistic detail, they nevertheless offer a supple sense of humanity, both local and universal, and a vivid portrayal of chance and growth within the protagonist Zein. In addition, they offer a complex yet accessible portrayal of "popular Sufism," or barakah Islam, and show the cultural agency of barakah by making it key to the turning point of the story. In their various stances toward religion, knowledge, and community, these types offer a microcosm of similar difference throughout the Islamic world. The story is a comedy, that is, it ends on the happy note of idealized community and an Islam that is vital, open, and not only tolerant but also celebratory of its diversity. This happy ending mirrors inversely the tragedy of *Season of Migration to the North*, where individual and community identity falls apart. Finally, the novel allows us to engage the characters as human beings and to see in them—whatever our own multiple religious, ethnic, and national identities—the reflection of a common humanity.

Wider Questions

1. Examine the role of knowledge in the novel. What are the various views of knowledge in the village, the sources of prestige and status, and competing worlds of knowledge? Relate these village positions to position in readings of classical texts.

2. What is the role of barakah in the novel and popular Sufism in general? Compare the function of barakah in *The Wedding of Zein* with its more explicit role in "The Doum Tree of Wad Hamid" which occurs in the same volume. View the film *Ways of Faith* ("The Arabs" series) on religion in the Sudan, and read Trimingham, *Islam in the Sudan,* on the tension between popular Sufism and self-declared orthodox Islam.[7] Read selections from Ibn Taymiyya's attack on popular Islam and modern Wahhabi criticisms of the same practices.[8]

3. Compare the presentation of popular Sufism in *The Wedding of Zein* to similar practices in other Islamic cultures, employing scholarly case studies, of a Sufi shrine in Tunisia, for example, or Sufi shrines in India, or the shrine of Bawa Muhayyidin near Philadelphia in the United States.

4. How do themes from classical Islamic and Arabic literature guide what seems to be on the surface a simple, country folk story? And how do elements of folk literature transform themes of the high literature of Arabic and Western classics?

5. How and why is Ni'ma able to act in a way that allows her to transcend what appears to be normal gender boundaries and limitations in the village? What quality validates her actions for the villagers and protects her from coercion or retribution?

6. The name "Zein" evokes beauty. Zein is initially portrayed as ungainly, even ugly. How is beauty defined and valued by different elements within the village, and what is Zein's role as the prophet of beauty?

7. Tayeb Salih worked as a drama critic for the BBC in London. Read the section on comedy in Northrop Frye's *Anatomy of Criticism.*[9] In what way does *The Wedding of Zein* correspond to the categories of comedy given by Frye for Western Shakespearean and Greek comedic traditions? How does he employ Islamic and Arabic classical tradition and more localized Sudanese culture and folklore?

8. Is Zein in any way a Trickster? Examine the Trickster literature in African and Native American cultures and explain in what ways Zein conforms with or diverges from the construction of the Trickster in contemporary scholarship.

9. Compare issues of barakah and popular Islam as presented in *The Wedding of Zein* to the two short stories by Salih, "A Handful of Dates" and "The Doum Tree of Wad Hamid" (published in the same English version) or to Naguib Mahfuz's story "Zaabalawi."

10. Reconstruct the village by taking out one of the principal groups or individuals: Haneen; the Imam and the observant elderly men; the gang; Ni'ma; or Zein. What would be the effect on the village? How might the removal of a character or group affect the village?

Appendix

NOTES ON OTHER MODERN WORKS OF FICTION

Below are some other selected works I have found useful in courses on Islam or, more specifically, Islamic Literature and Civilization. In a more general introduction course on Islam, I use only one or two selections. This sampling represents my own experience and my own priorities in teaching. It is not—emphatically—and does not attempt to be either comprehensive or representative. It is radically unbalanced in its focus on works written originally in Arabic, a focus that reflects my own scholarly background and literary focus and works that I have used successfully in the class-room. I look for modern works that combine a modern fiction-writing style—often heavy with irony and sometimes with disillusion—with significant allusions to the Quran, hadith, classical Islamic theology and philosophy, and the poetic tradition. Of the many novels written in the Islamic world, or written by Muslims, several have combined modern sensibility with a sustained grounding in the classical religious tra-dition. These works challenge students to find classical themes, where they might tend to focus simply on the psychology of the protagonist. They also demonstrate how the classical themes live within and inform the modern world. I'm sure to this partial list others could add some excellent suggestions from within or outside the Arab world.

1. The Heinemann/Three Continents edition of *The Wedding of Zein,* translated by Denys Johnson-Davies and illustrated by Ibrahim Salahi contains two outstanding short stories that work well with the long novel or novella. "A Handful of Dates" is the story of the disillusionment of a young boy, who had idolized his grandfather as the embodiment of Quranic values. The grandfather had taught his grandson the Quran, but by the end of the story was engaging in precisely the kind of predatory business practices most scathingly condemned in the Quran ("Do you think your wealth will make you immortal?"). This short story is filled with literary subtlety and the ending is complex. I ask the class to discuss both the grandfather and Masood, the romantic spendthrift who loses his property to the grandfather, in the context of Quranic val-ues of generosity, responsibility, and self-control. I have found particularly intriguing the metaphorical implications of the young boy's vomiting of the dates acquired by his grandfather from Masood to be a particularly rich discussion. Is one aspect of the boy's disillusion and nausea his realization that through, eating the date, he was par-ticipating with his grandfather in consuming Masood himself who had identified him-self with the date palms?

2. "The Doum Tree of Wad Hamid" offers a sustained portrayal of barakah Islam at the intersection of traditional, formalist, and modernist-development worlds. The *wali* Wad Hamid and the tree that contains his barakah are shown in dreams, mythopoesis, social practice, personal and collective psychology, political manipula-

tions, personal and communal understanding of healing, and the struggle to balance tradition and identity with progress and modernization.

3. Mahshid Amirshahi, "The End of the Passion Play."[10] Of the modern Persian stories, this story makes particularly effective use of a classical theme, in this case the *ta'ziyya* passion play reenactment of the martyrdom of Imam Husayn at the Battle of Karbala in 680 C.E. In her treatment of the *ta'ziyya,* Amirshahi uses the centrality of the event and the idealism associated with Husayn in a mordant exposé of hypocrisy and repression. The narrative voice is supple, shifting, and unreliable. Thus, the unwary reader may tend to accept at face value the narrative voice when it presents the common-sense judgment of the village concerning the central protagonist, Abu al-Canfoot. Abu al-Canfoot, who has a can (actually a rough piece of corrugated iron) replacing his amputated foot, is the stepfather of a young and idealistic boy. The central question is whether Abu al-Canfoot's severity, including beatings and practical enslavement, illustrates the tough love of a caring stepfather, as suggested at times by the narrator, or something else. The narrator hides a clue in cryptic comments on how Abu al-Canfoot appropriates the boy Taghi's inheritance.

For contextualization, I have found most useful the last section of the life of Husayn by Sheikh al-Mufid.[11] The account by al-Mufid of Husayn's passion and death offers a thick and challenging version of passion literature and sets a literary and mythic context for the discussion of the ritual of the *ta'ziyya.*

4. Naguib Mahfuz, "Zaabalawi."[12] This short story tells of an unnamed narrator who seeks the semi-mythical Shaykh Zaabalawi to cure him of an unspecified illness. The central story is taken up in the narrator's meeting with seven intermediaries, each of whom has a different perspective on where Zaabalawi might be, and—crucially— each of whom represents a different stratum of traditional society and *adab* (or lack thereof). The penultimate intermediary is a singer and poet who chants verses such as "I have a memory [dhikr] of her" until the walls "dance with ecstasy," and appears to exemplify the classical ideal of cultivation, hospitality, and artistic achievement. The last guide is a drunkard, Hagg Wanas, who insists the protagonist get drunk before he will speak to him. When the protagonist feels the effect of the wine, he goes through a series of Sufi-like states, ending in a state of bliss. He wakes up to find that while he had been sleeping, Zaabalawi had been there, sprinkling water on his temples.

The challenge for the student reader is to avoid focusing entirely on the protagonist—blaming him for not realizing he was already cured, accepting without further questioning the claim that "the search was the cure," or engaging in other purely psychological interpretations. Such a focus ignores the worlds represented by the various Cairene characters encountered in the quest and the cultural realms they represent. One reward in teaching such a work is to see students, when asked what each intermediary was like (what was his view of reason, what was his view of *adab,* what was his view of creativity?), come alive to the social and cultural aspects of the story. They can then entertain the thought that the alienation from traditional culture (or the ideals it represents) that is symbolized, in varying degrees, by the characters in the story, may be itself part of the illness. If Zaabalawi as healer represents ties to traditional culture and ideals, the fact that he is now being pursued by the police (for practicing medicine without a license, perhaps) may be an indication of the wider cultural aspect of the narrator's illness. After his ecstatic encounter with Zaabalawi during his drunken stupor, he wakes to find consciousness hitting him like a policeman's fist.

A second temptation is to read the last encounter with Hagg Wanas as pure Sufi allegory for mystical union. The problem, of course, is that Mahfuz has located Hagg Wanas with too much sociorealistic detail as a real drunkard, in a real tavern, in a real section of town, not in some mythical or symbolic tavern of a medieval Sufi poem. The Sufi themes are profound, but the portrait of the protagonist, waking up drunk to the concerned look of the bartender, carries with it an irony and a complexity beyond the one-for-one allegorization of wine.

For context, I use selections of Sufi writings, such as Qushayri's discussion of intoxication, absence, presence, and *fana'*. I also use samples of Mi'raj literature from the collection of Muslim and the Sufi Mi'raj of Bistami and ask the students to compare the protagonist's voyage through the seven circles of Cairo to the Mi'raj voyage through the seven spheres.

5. Tayeb Salih, *Season of Migration to the North*. This work is an inverted mirror image of *The Wedding of Zein*, a tragedy embodied in a protagonist (Mustafa Saeed) who is, among many other things, a self-created personification of Orientalist stereotypes about the East. Indeed, the work can be read in conjunction with Edward Said's *Orientalism*.[13] The tragedy Mustafa Saeed provokes is embodied in the fate of women in England and in the Sudanese village who are destroyed in the intersection of the different cultural worlds. The story raises issues from Shakespeare (with its explicit allusions to Othello) and the practice of clitoridectomy. The latter issue and the general portrayal of violence against women both in the East and the West can raise in the classroom sudden emotions in a manner that requires some pedagogical strategy. If the class or instructor is taken too much by surprise, the intensity of feelings can close down discussion rather than opening it up. The eerie relationship between the unnamed narrator and Mustafa (who collapse into one another at a particular moment), as well as the scene in which the narrator is paralyzed and cannot act to save the woman he loves, make the novel a particularly gripping read. There is a large critical literature on *The Season of Migration to the North*, allowing the student to explore various aspects of the novel as appropriate.[14]

6. Ghassan Kanafani, *Men in the Sun and Other Palestinian Stories*, translated from the Arabic by Hillary Kilpatrick (London: Heinemann Educational; Washington, D.C.: Three Continents Press, 1978); and *Palestine's Children: Returning to Haifa and other Stories*, translated by Barbara Harlow and Karen E. Riley (Boulder, Col.: Lynne Reiner, 2000). While not specifically grounded in religious themes, these novels offer

a deeply human portrayal of the Palestinian experience of *nakbah* and exile, an experience that has impacted not only the Arab world (both Christian and Muslim), but also the Islamic world as a whole. The novel humanizes the Palestinian, brings us into his struggles, dreams, and aspirations—without polemic and without generic demonizing Israeli Jews—in a way that can help dispel anti-Palestinian, anti-Arab, and Islamophobic stereotypes, which are often tied up, in part, with the Middle East conflict.

7. Cheikh Hamidou Kane, *Ambiguous Adventure,* translated from the French by Katherine Woods (London: Heinemann, 1972). This book offers a compelling account of a traditional Quranic education and the culture shock upon arriving in Europe of a Senegalese steeped in such a world.

8. Emil Habibi, *The Secret Life of Saeed, The Ill-Fated Pessoptimist,* translated from the Arabic by Salma Khadra Jayyusi and Trevor Le Gassick (New York: Vantage Press, 1982). Habibi's work is filled with subtle ironies, linguistic extravaganzas of dialect and pun, and a sense of the comic within the tragic.

9. Jamal al-Ghitani, *Incidents in Zaafarani Alley* (Cairo: General Egyptian Book Organization, 1986).[15] This novel contains within it a wide range of classical and modern culture. My understanding is that a more complete translation, better able to reflect the play and wit of Egyptian dialect, may be in the works.

NOTES

1. I refer to *The Wedding of Zein* as a novel, though it might also be called a novella. The categorization would depend upon the definition of the novel as opposed to novella, a question that does not concern the issues addressed in this essay. All page references include the pagination in the Arabic edition followed by that in the Johnson-Davies English translation. See al-Tayyib Salih, *'Urs az-Zayn* (Beirut: Dār al-'Awda, 1970); and Tayeb Salih, *The Wedding of Zein,* translated by Denys Johnson-Davies (London: Heinemann, 1969, 1982). I have used the spelling of personal names employed within the translation. The English edition of *The Wedding of Zein* also includes two stories by Salih: "A Handful of Dates" and "The Doum Tree of Wad Hamid," also translated by Denys Johnson-Davies, along with evocative illustrations by Ibrahim Salahi.

2. For a recent bibliography of scholarship on the works of Tayeb Salih, see Ami Elad-Bouskila, "Shaping the Cast of Characters: The Case of al-Ṭayyib Ṣāliḥ," *Journal of Arabic Literature* 19 (1998): 59–94. For the wider literary context, see Roger Allen, *The Arabic Novel: An Historical and Critical Introduction* (Syracuse, N.Y.: Syracuse University Press, 1995).

3. The use of dialect offers a special challenge to the translator. The local dialects of the host language (in this case English) contain a very different set of cultural associations. Thus, to choose a particular local dialect of English would reduplicate the tension between formal written language and spoken language, but the specific regional and cultural associations of the chosen dialect would be distracting. Denys Johnson-Davies used a variety of strategies to reflect the diglossia within the dialogues

of *The Wedding of Zein,* with various forms of overly formal or somewhat archaic English being used, for example, to represent the headmaster's inappropriate resort to formal Arabic in conversation. Of course, to say that dialect represents a special difficulty
in translation is not to suggest a work cannot be appreciated in translation. All literary
translation poses extraordinary obstacles and engaging such obstacles is not only a
difficulty but also a source of richness for both translator and reader.

4. Page 52 in both the original Arabic and the translation. The translation renders
sūrat al-qaṣaṣ as "The Retribution"; a mistake evidently resulting from a confusion between *qaṣaṣ* (story, narrative, recounting) and *qiṣāṣ* (the equivalency of punishment to
crime). The translation as "Retribution" is significant in that the English-reading audience will be thrown off track by the theme of retribution, a theme decidedly not one
of special interest to Ni'ma.

5. The difficulty posed, to herself and her family, by Ni'ma's continued rejection of
suitors reflects a reality faced by students in my classes whose families adhere to the
paradigm of arranged marriage. Whether Muslim or Hindu, for example, some of my
students of South Asian heritage will be facing similar pressures even as they read the
story, whether they are studying in the United States on a student visa or are the children or are of South Asian American background. Their families may expect them (if
they are women) to marry soon after graduation. In some cases, the marriage of
younger sisters will be put on hold until the older sister, about to graduate from college, is married—leading to increased stress on the student, her parents, and her sib-
lings. While Ni'ma's choices lead to a celebratory conclusion of the story, the story
does not offer (nor could it offer) a solution to the problems of young women in a similar predicament—but complicated by the differing mores and general societal expectations in the industrialized world.

6. Ni'ma's choice, while it results in the rebirth of the village, also strikes some students as unsatisfying from the point of view of women's role in society. While *The
Wedding of Zein* is a novel that features a female character, whose agency is central to
the story, the happy ending of the wedding finds her receding from public view into
the private space of the life of a married woman in a traditional village culture. Had
Ni'ma chosen to go north to Cairo to study medicine or law, she might have found
herself navigating the tides of gender and cultural difference that are the subject of
Salih's *The Season of Migration to the North.*

7. Ali el-Mek, *Ways of Faith,* in *The Arabs: A Living History* series (1990). This outstanding film centers on the religious center of Umduban. It focuses on issues of healing (both traditional and modern), Quranic schooling, popular education, and the role
of the sheikh as religious leader, all central themes in the works of Tayeb Salih. J.
Spencer Trimingham, *Islam in the Sudan* (New York : Barnes & Noble, 1965). Though
marred by gratuitous expressions of contempt for the alleged decadence of much of
Islamic popular belief and practice, *Islam in the Sudan* is nevertheless useful for its
wealth of detail, especially if used in conjunction with Constance Berkeley's fine arti-

cle, "Popular Islam in aṭ-Ṭayyib Ṣāliḥ," *Journal of Arabic Literature* 11 (1980): 88–104. Berkeley has also written one of the few articles in English dedicated solely to *The Wedding of Zein*. See her review article on the Denys Johnson-Davies translation: "El Tayeb Salih, *The Wedding of Zein*, trans. Denys Johnson-Davies," *Journal of Arabic Literature* 11 (1980): 104–114. See also Ali Abdallah Abbas, "Notes on Tayeb Salih: *Season of Migration to the North* and *The Wedding of Zein*," *Sudan Notes and Records* 35 (1974): 46–61.

8. Muhammad Umar Memon, *Ibn Taimiya's Struggle against Popular Religion, with an annotated translation of his Kitāb iqtiḍā' aṣ-ṣirāṭ al-mustaqīm mukhālafat aṣḥāb al-jaḥīm* (The Hague: Mouton, 1976).

9. In essay three of Northrop Frye, *Anatomy of Criticism: Four Essays* (Princeton: Princeton University Press, 1957).

10. Mahshid Amirshahi, "The End of the Passion Play," in *Modern Persian Short Stories*, trans. Minoo S. Southgate (London: Three Continents, 1980), 161–172. The story originally appeared as *Akhar-i taʻziyah* in Mahshid Amirshahi's collection of short stories *Baʻd az ruz-i akhar* (Tehran, 1969).

11. Muhammad b. Muhammad Mufid, *The Book of Guidance into the Lives of the Twelve Imams (Kitab al-Irshad)*, trans. I. K. A. Howard (Elmhurst, N.Y.: Tahrike Tarsile Qur'an, 1981).

12. Naguib Mahfuz, "Zaabalawi," in *Modern Arabic Short Stories*, selected and translated by Denys Johnson-Davies (London: Oxford University Press, 1980), 137–147; the Johnson-Davies translation also appears in *The Norton Anthology of World Masterpieces*, 2:1961–1965 (New York: Norton, 1992); and *The Harper Collins World Reader*, 2:1620–1627 (New York: Harper Collins, 1994). The original appeared in *Al-Ahram*, 12 May 1961, and was incorporated into Mahfuz's collection of stories, *Dunya Allah* (Cairo: Maktabat Miṣr, 1963), 135–150. For a recent critical study of the story, see Ami Elad, "Mahfuz's Zaʻbalawi: Six Stations of a Quest," *International Journal of Middle East Studies* 26.4 (November 1994): 631–644.

13. Edward Said, *Orientalism* (New York: Pantheon Books, 1978).

14. See the references in Elad-Bouskila (above, n. 2), especially Mona Takkieddine Amyuni, ed., *Season of Migration to the North by Tayeb Salih* (Beirut: American University of Beirut Press, 1985).

15. Jamal al-Ghitani, *Waqāʼiʻ Ḥārat al-Zaʻfarānī* (Cairo: Dār al-Thaqāfah al-Jadīdah, 1976). A second edition was published in Cairo by Maktabat Madbuli in 1985.

CHAPTER TEN

Teaching about Muslims in America

MARCIA K. HERMANSEN

THE TOPIC "MUSLIMS IN AMERICA" IS INCREASINGLY featured in the academic curriculum, occasionally as a course of its own within specialized programs or more often as a session or part of a session within an introductory course on "Islam," "World Religions," or "Religion in America." Depending on the context, various approaches to the topic could be productive. I would like to suggest some of these approaches as well as indicate some of the resources available for teaching about this topic. The strategies used for presenting this material will vary with the composition of the student audience and the overall focus of the course.

Since I am currently teaching "Islam" in an environment where a large percentage of the class is made up of American-born Muslims, I have become increasingly aware of the need to provide an American context to the course. Even in parts of the country where the audience is not so diverse, we should be cautious about exoticizing Islam by presenting it as a religion that is only practiced in archaic or alien sites. This is a powerful rationale for incorporating material about Muslims in America into a range of courses.

Initially, it might be noted for nonspecialists that the topic "Muslims in America" intersects with a number of cultural debates current in American society. One example of this is the increasing pluralism apparent in the general population and especially in the university population, as the first generation of students born since the immigration boom of the mid-seventies enters college. In addition, it may be observed that scholarly as well as popular writing about Muslims in America sometimes becomes politicized. One camp of commentators argues that Muslims, according to a "clash of civilizations" model,[1] are intrinsically conditioned to be undemocratic and reject the values of American life. Other scholars, such as Yvonne Y. Haddad, Jane I. Smith, John Esposito, and Earle Waugh have studied Muslims in America with more attention to their constructive adaptations and contributions to the new environment. In fact, Yvonne Haddad's books and articles represent the largest corpus of work specifically devoted to Muslims in America.[2]

Periodically, political and cultural events raise issues related to the study of the Muslim presence in the United States in a provocative way, examples being the World Trade Center bombing, the refusal of a Muslim-identified basketball player to salute the American flag, child marriage, female circumcision, and so on. All of these may be sensationalized but are very much a part of the public consciousness. Since I initially formulated this paragraph, the terrorist attacks of Sept. 11, 2001 have thrust these issues even more into the foreground.

This background of troubling political and cultural confrontation will inevitably become part of classroom discussion of issues related to Islam and Muslims. Such discussions may in turn lead to broader discussions of issues such as the role of immigration in American society, whether there should be one set of normative values for Americans, what is it like to have multiple identities/affiliations, how far can one extend cultural relativism, race in American society, and so on. In summary, the instructor incorporating material on Muslims in America will need to be prepared not only with material specific to this topic but also ideally will have a broad acquaintance with contemporary social and cultural theory and issues.

Immigration

Since immigration is the context of much of the Muslim experience in America, some discussion of the history of the Muslim presence in America is appropriate to set the stage for this topic. Yvonne Haddad and Adair Lummis have proposed models of stages or waves of immigrants characterized by diverse concerns, ethnic backgrounds, and religious attitudes.[3] A synopsis of this model is that there have been some five stages of Muslim immigration to America. "The first wave, 1875–1913, was composed mostly of uneducated and unskilled young men (some as young as thirteen years old) from the rural areas of what now constitutes Syria and Lebanon, then under Ottoman rule. The second wave, 1918–1922, followed World War I. By the time of the third wave, 1930–1938, American immigration laws confined immigration primarily to relatives of those already in the country who were naturalized citizens."[4]

According to Haddad and Lummis, "The fourth wave, 1947–1960, reflects America's assumption of its leadership role in the world. Immigrants began to include such people as North Africans and displaced groups from Eastern

Europe fleeing communism, as well as children of the educated elites in various Arab countries, mostly urban in background, educated, and Westernized prior to their arrival in the United States."[5] These immigrants, who included many South Asian Muslims, perceived themselves as permanent settlers and often came in pursuit of higher education or career opportunities. It is this cohort that founded many of the more permanent Muslim institutions in America, for example, the Islamic Society of North America (ISNA) and the Muslim Student Association.

The change of immigration laws in the mid-1960s opened the doors to what might be considered a fifth wave, although diverse backgrounds and causes for immigration characterize these later Muslim immigrants. The wars and upheavals of this period gave rise to their own ethnic waves of immigrant Iranians, Afghans, Somalians, Bosnians, and so on.

In addition to profiling these immigrant Muslims, interest has also been taken in the fact that a significant proportion of the Africans brought to the New World as slaves may have been Muslim.[6] Middle Eastern and South Asian Muslims only came in sizeable numbers during the present century. Depending on the location of one's academic institution, there may be local connections to the earlier history of Muslim immigration to the United States. The "immigration" aspect of Muslim history in America can be used in classroom lectures and student projects associated with local history. Students from Muslim immigrant backgrounds might become interested in tracing the history of their own family and the Islamic institutions in which they participate. For example, the West Coast was one site of immigration by Punjabi farmers, including Muslims, studied by Karen Leonard in *Making Ethnic Choices*.[7] Detroit and the automobile factories attracted both Arab Christians and Muslims. Often large educational institutions attracted Muslim students, who during a later stage of immigration founded Islamic institutions such as the Islamic Society of North America and the Muslim Student Association. In the southern states there are still a few traces of the earliest African Muslim immigrants, for example, handwritten religious texts preserved in memory.[8]

The history of immigration policies in the United States provides a backdrop for understanding the increase of Muslim immigration in the 1960s, roughly corresponding to the era of the Civil Rights movement. If a class has many students from immigrant backgrounds, various aspects of this history can tie in to a productive discussion, for example, issues of assimilation, adaptation, the myth of return, and so on. The recent history of Muslim societies and events such as the turmoil in Palestine, the Iranian revolution, the Afghan war, Somalian, Bosnian, and Kosovar crises may also be brought into the presentation when discussing recent Muslim immigration patterns.

The population of Muslims in North America is a matter of some discussion, with the striking popular observation being that the current estimate of roughly 6 million indicates that Muslims are the largest non-Christian minority religion in the United States.[9] Statistics are difficult to obtain, but the total population is thought to be between 3 and 8 million, and the three major groups are African American (indigenous) Muslims, Arab Muslims, and South Asian Muslims. One estimate puts African Americans at 42 percent, South Asians at 24.4 percent, and Arabs at 12.4 percent (with smaller groups of Africans at 6.2%, Iranians at 3.6%, Southeast Asians at 2%, European Americans at 1.6%, and "other" at 5.4%). Another estimate puts "Americans" at 30 percent, Arabs at 33 percent, and South Asians at 29 percent. There are other differences, between the majority Sunni and minority Shi'i groups, smaller sectarian groups like the Isma'ilis, Zaidis, and Khojas, and sects like the Ahmadiyyas and Druze, whose Islamic identity is contested.[10]

Diaspora Religion

The consideration of the immigrant Muslim community also permits classroom discussion on the topic of diaspora religion, a subject that is coming under closer academic scrutiny.[11] The theory of religious adaptation and persistence in diaspora is still in the developmental phase, as one scholar commented, "the earlier literature on South Asians in the West focused on social concerns and neglected religion, reinforcing a stereotype of the migrants leaving their religion in the old country."[12] Creative adaptation in the diaspora is a topic for which scholarly and pedagogical resources are increasingly available. For example, the Pluralism Project at Harvard under the direction of Diana Eck produced a CD-ROM entitled "On Common Ground," which features images and text relating to the new religious communities taking root on American soil. In order to create this resource, graduate students in religion from Harvard, representing various regions of the United States, studied their local immigrant religious communities. One adaptation of this type of student project is Karen Leonard's assignment for a graduate class in the Los Angeles area to study the burial customs of various immigrant religious communities and how they have adapted to American laws and facilities.[13]

African-American Islam

A survey of the Muslim population in the United States today discloses that between one-third and 42 percent of American Muslims are African-Americans, who have accepted the Islamic religion. The study of African-American Islam is in itself a rich and complex topic. My experience is that students have awareness of names such as Malcolm X and the Nation of Islam[14] but are not clear of the relationship between movements such as the Nation of Islam and mainstream Islam, leading to much initial confusion. The instructor has to decide how to frame the relationship of certain proto-Islamic movements to mainstream Islam. To label such movements "non-Islamic," as many Muslims might, would violate the self- understandings of the participants in them. At the same time, it is clear that theological aspects or political or social positions taken by some of the new religious movements are unacceptable from the standpoint of traditional Islamic teachings. Attempting to define Islam as "orthodox" is in itself problematic, as scholars such as Wilfred Cantwell Smith have argued that Islam is in any case "orthoprax," primarily defining adherence through performance rather than the assertion of particular dogmas or creeds. In any case, basic historical background about the period in which these movements emerged will be helpful in explaining their appeal in the African-American community. Helpful resources are Aminah Beverly McCloud's *African American Islam,*[15] and Richard Brent Turner's work, *Islam in the African American Experience.*[16] Alex Haley's retelling of Malcolm X's biography is a classic in its own right, and excerpts of Malcolm X's dramatic conversion experience while on the pilgrimage could be used in a class reader.[17]

I have occasionally found aspects of Nation of Islam theology to be difficult for an unsophisticated student audience. Some of the teachings, for example, the myth that whites are blue-eyed devils created by an evil scientist called Yacub,[18] can be very disturbing for students in terms of their reactions and their reactions to each other's reactions. For example, white students may laugh or ridicule the material or become very offended. I have experienced presentations of this material both by white students and by African-American students and have come to realize how sensitive it is. My caveat is that the level of the students and their sophistication must be taken into account. If the instructor is not willing to spend the necessary time unpacking the material, then it may be preferable to avoid some details.

On the other hand, in a student group with more sophistication, Nation of Islam theology offers opportunities for understanding the shaping of theology and the dynamics of new religious movements. An instructor in the "Introductory Theology" course at my current institution uses the book, *The Nation of Islam: An American Millenarian Movement* by Martha F. Lee,[19] as a text in order to confront students with just such issues. Understanding the relationship of the Nation of Islam to mainstream Sunni Islam is also complex, since many American Sunni Muslims either do not take a particularly confrontational stance to the Nation of Islam or else condemn it virulently. I suggest explaining the reticence to condemn as emerging from a tolerance of gradualism. After all, taking the long perspective, Malcolm X and Wallace Muhammad are ex-members of the Nation of Islam, who ultimately became mainstream Muslims. While many Muslims have clear differences with the teachings of the Nation of Islam—for example, on the teaching that Fard Muhammad is an incarnation of the divine—often they refrain from excessive condemnation in the hope that even this branch of the movement will eventually mainstream.

The popular association of Islam with African-American celebrities in the media should be considered in the light of broader patterns in American culture such as the representation of African Americans as predominantly sports stars, musicians, or criminals.[20] More generally, the issue of the often negative representation of Islam and Muslims in American popular culture may become a topic for discussion. Recommended sources on this sort of stereotyping are studies by John Woods[21] and Laurence Michalak.[22]

Urban Geography

Another approach to the study of Muslims in America is to highlight issues of urban geography. Students living in New York and Chicago can be shown maps of their urban areas with the changing patterns of Islamic centers indicated at various historical periods. Questions that can be pursued include: Where do Muslims usually live, how are neighborhoods influenced by ethnicity? How can Muslims create sacred space in America, what is essential to a mosque? Sources of articles on various urban centers include Haddad's *Muslim Communities,* which considers Seattle, upstate New York, and San Diego. Raymond Williams compares Chicago and Houston in the 1980s (including maps).[23] If a given region has not been previously studied, this topic could become the basis for an assignment, in which students do some mapping of their own locality in terms of the history and current locations of Muslim institutions and presence. Paul Numrich studied the patterns of Buddhist and Muslim settlement and religious institutions in Chicago over the last fifty years, and the maps in his article might provide a model for similar presentations involving your local area.[24] Another helpful source for understanding the creation of a "new Muslim space" by immigrants is Barbara D. Metcalf's edited volume, *Making Muslim Space in North America and Europe.*[25]

As an example of new configurations of Muslim space in North America, the Christian Science Monitor video "Muslims in America" shows the mosque in Cedar Rapids, Iowa, where an innovative approach to separate seating areas for males and females situates them in sections beside each other rather than having the males placed in front. If one conducts a class visit to a local center, students might be asked to consider how the building's use of space and symbolism reflect its situation. Is it an adaptation of a previous structure, for example, churches in New Jersey where the figures in the stained glass windows have been covered over, an ex-movie theatre in Chicago where the seats have been removed, or are they attempts to represent Islam in America from the foundation up.[26]

The environment within the United States in which Muslim immigrants live may, in turn, influence their religiosity. The question may be asked, does this diversity arise from immigration patterns, local American subcultures, or a combination of factors. Canadian readers of this article should be aware of specifically Canadian aspects of Muslim identities in North America. A starting point are some of the publications of Earle Waugh. A comparison of Canadian multiculturalism and postcolonial experience with the context of Muslims in the United States could be instructive as well.

Muslims' Identities and American Culture

One avenue of access for students to appreciate the Muslim presence in the Unites States is to point out Islamic elements in mainstream American culture. This can be especially helpful in making connections for Hispanic and African-American students. For example, a connection to the Spanish heritage can be made through a presentation on Islamicate architecture. This works especially well in Southern California and Florida. While teaching in Southern California, I began my slide presentation on Islamic architecture with an image of a window at San Diego State University, where some of the older buildings featured Hispano-Mauresque architecture. I would ask students to guess which Muslim society the image came from, and after many tries I would finally tell them that it was as close as the next campus building. This really brought home the point about the connections of Islam with histories closer to their own experience.

At the same time, Islamic cultural influences on contemporary pop culture in the West and in the United States, in particular, can be brought into the classroom. Examples are Islamic influences on rap music,[27] collaboration of rock and alternative groups with Islamic musicians,[28] and John Moyne and Coleman Barks's translations of Rumi's poetry.[29] A number of scholarly studies of American Muslim identity and "Americanization" may provide material for consideration of this topic.[30]

Living in America presents Muslims with many questions that would not arise in traditional, more homogenous contexts, for example, the applicability of Islamic law within the American system,[31] the accommodation of practice of Muslims from various legal schools and ethnic backgrounds within a single Islamic center. I have found a useful entry piece to this topic to be an article in Steve Barboza's collection, *American Jihad: Islam after Malcolm X.*[32] This selection, narrated by Professor Ali Asani of Harvard, points out many issues faced by American Muslims, including diversity within the community and the challenge of overcoming stereotypes which Muslims themselves may participate in perpetuating.

Speaking comparatively, it is possible to imagine that American Muslim institutions of worship may come more and more to sort themselves out along lines of practice so that one may come to speak of liberal, conservative, and "orthodox" mosques and Islamic centers, just as American Jews have come to constitute Reform, Conservative, and Orthodox (among other) congregations. Within mosques, one index of this is the means for separating males and females. Some centers use partitions and curtains while in other cases where the structure has been designed to be a mosque, women may occupy a balcony. In some centers women do not attend or sit in a completely separate room connected only by a remote loudspeaker.

One debate occurring within the American Muslim community concerns the place of women. While liberal or modernizing mosques, centers, and associations integrate women into teaching and decision-making positions, other mosques, centers, and associations minimize women's participation or are uncertain how to include them. Women in South Asia traditionally did not pray in mosques,[33] while in the Arab world they did, and practices in the United States vary (and depend partly on the physical structures). Women's access to mosques for meetings of their own is regulated by the Imams, men who are usually immigrants trained outside the United States and not necessarily sympathetic to meetings about, for example, family counseling or domestic abuse. At the same time, the websites and e-mails issued by Muslim organizations, such as Sound Vision in Chicago, are increasingly airing these debates from a Muslim perspective.[34]

Muslims, in a similar manner to Jews, face the issue of whether there can there be a "cultural" Muslim, someone who identifies with the Muslim identity without being religious. In this context, a class might discuss comparative Christian, Jewish, and Islamic concepts of religious identity in confessional and legal terms.

Today, due to the emergence of English as a Muslim lingua franca and the role of the West in projecting Cyberspace Islam, American Muslims are becoming more influential in establishing norms and identity for the community [ummah] as a whole.

Conversion

Yvonne Haddad has at times configured the categories of American-Muslim experience as that of settlers, sojourners, and converts. This model could provide yet another way to present aspects of Muslim identity in North America.

It may be that a course offers an opportunity to discuss the angle of conversion to Islam in America. The major study of this is Larry Poston's *Islamic Da'wah in the West: Muslim Missionary Activity and the Dynamics of Conversion to Islam.*[35] Poston's analysis suggests that conversion to Islam in the West may not replicate the pattern of William James's model of a sudden adolescent snapping, emerging in many cases from an unstable personality. Rather, many converts to Islam are adults who spent much time researching and reflecting on religious issues. The experience of American women converts can also provoke interest and challenge the stereotype that Muslim women are oppressed by religion.[36] Catalogues from Muslim publishers such as Kazi Publications in Chicago offer a range of convert literature[37] and video testimonials.

The prisons as sites of conversion is also a fascinating aspect of Islam in America.[38] Metcalf's collection on *Making Muslim Space* features a particularly interesting chapter by Robert Dannin on Islam in the prison system as a "counter discipline." Dannin explains how Islam for prisoners can offer "an autonomous source of education and discipline in all aspects of life."[39] Dannin notes how "Islam's popularity in the prison system rests in part on the way in which Quranically prescribed activities structure an alternative social space that enables the prisoner to reside, as it were in another place within the same confining walls."[40]

The phenomenon of prison conversion is significant. Dannin offers the statistic that in New York State alone, the Department of Corrections counted 10,186 registered Muslim inmates in 82 different prisons in 1992. African-American Muslims were 16.9 percent of the prison inmates and one-third of incarcerated African Americans in New York State.[41] American institutions such as the military and the prison system increasingly accommodate the religious requirements of Muslims and provide them with Islamic chaplains.

Institutions

The consideration of Muslim institutions in America allows students to observe religious history and adaptation in the making. Articles are already available which consider issues like the Islamic Center as a necessary response to the situation of Muslims in diaspora, the changing role of the Imam, whose duties now come to include what might be considered "pastoral" functions such as family counseling and mediation,[42] Islam in the American military, the participation of women, and a growing Islamic schooling movement. A large project founded by the PEW Charitable trust and conducted by Sulayman Nyang and Zahid Bikhari at Georgetown University is studying the interface of emerging Muslim institutions in the United States with American organizational patterns. Research findings can be followed on their web site.[43]

Sufism and Sectarianism in America

Yet another way of trying to understand the scope of the American Muslim community is by its members' attraction to forms of religiousness, whether liberal, conservative, or Sufi.[44] The Muslim community itself is internally diverse and Shi'i, Nizari Isma'ili, and Ahmadi communities add their diversity to the American landscape.[45]

In some parts of the country, students may have come in contact with popular American Sufism such as Sufi dancing. Sufi movements provide examples of the adaptation of Muslim practices to an American setting. An article describing many of these movements is my article "In the Garden of American Sufi Movements: Hybrids and Perennials."[46]

Internet Searches

There are many informative web sites featuring material relevant to the study of Muslims in America. In undergraduate teaching, Internet materials offer not only a valuable source of up-to-the-minute data but also present information in a format that levels the canons of authority that might help students to assess the reliability of sources from which they are drawing. On the Internet students will be made aware of some of the contestations of identity and legitimacy among various groups.[47] Related web-based assignments might involve comparing a number of American Sufi websites, comparing the Nation of Islam with the Warith Deen Muhammad web site, or exploring how the ISNA web site represents Muslim identity.

A suggestive article on this new frontier explores American Muslim youth on the Internet and focuses on the idea of fatwas (Islamic legal opinions) being issued in new contexts.[48] A good starting place for discovering Web sites with Islamic materials is the Web page of Professor Alan Godlas of the University of Georgia.[49] This page has links to sites relating to a whole range of topics in Islamic Studies. I have referenced a number of other links to material found on-line in the course of this article. For bibliography, I would recommend Jane I. Smith's *Islam in America*.[50]

NOTES

1. Samuel P. Huntington, *The Clash of Civilizations and the Remaking of World Order* (New York: Simon and Schuster, 1996).

2. Yvonne Y. Haddad, ed., *Muslims of America* (New York: Oxford University Press, 1991), ed. with Jane Idelman Smith, *Muslim Communities in North America* (Albany: State University of New York Press, 1994), and *Mission to America: Five Islamic Sectarian Communities in North America* (Gainesville: University of Florida Press, 1993).

3. Yvonne Y. Haddad and Adair Lummis, *Islamic Values in the United States: A Comparative Study* (New York: Oxford University Press, 1987).

4. Yvonne Y. Haddad, "Make Room for the Muslims!" in *Religious Diversity and American Religious History,* ed. Walter H. Conser, Jr. and Susan B. Twiss (Athens: University of Georgia Press, 1997), 219.

5. Haddad and Loomis, *Islamic Values,* 219.

6. Sylviane A. Diouf, *Servants of Allah: African Muslims Enslaved in the Americas* (New York: New York University Press, 1998).

7. Karen I. Leonard, *Making Ethnic Choices: California's Punjabi Mexican Americans* (Philadelphia: Temple University Press, 1992).

8. Diouf, *Servants of Allah,* 129–30.

9. Fareed H. Nuʿman, *The Muslim Population in the United States* (Washington: American Muslim Council, 1992). Useful material and charts from this population are available on-line at *http://www.amermuslim.org/publish/bo/population.html*

10. Karen Leonard, "American Muslim Discourse and Practice," forthcoming.

11. For example, Harold Coward, *The South Asian Religious Diaspora in Britain, Canada, and the United States* (Albany: State University of New York Press, 2000).

12. John R. Hinnells, "The Study of Diaspora Religion," in *A New Handbook of Living Religions* (Cambridge, MA: Blackwell, 1997), 820.

13. Karen Leonard, "Mourning in a New Land. Changing Asian Practices in Southern California," *Journal of Orange County Studies* 3/4 (Fall 1989/Spring 1990): 62–69.

14. On-line at *http://www.noi.org/main.html*

15. *African American Islam* (New York: Routledge, 1995).

16. *Islam in the African American Experience* (Bloomington: Indiana University Press, 1997).

17. Malcolm X, *The Autobiography of Malcolm X* (New York: Ballantine Books, 1992).

18. Martha F. Lee, *The Nation of Islam: An American Millenarian Movement* (Syracuse: Syracuse University Press, 1996), 28–29.

19. Ibid.

20. As in Vincent F. Rocchio, *Reel Racism: Confronting Hollywood's Construction of Afro-American Culture* (Boulder: Westview Press, 2000).

21. John Woods, "Imagining and Stereotyping Islam," in *Muslims in America: Opportunities and Challenges,* ed. Asad Husain et al. (Chicago: International Strategy and Policy Institute, 1996), 45–77.

22. Laurence Michalak, *Cruel and Unusual: Negative Images of Arabs in American Pop-*

ular Culture (Washington: American-Arab Anti-Discrimination Committee, Issue Paper 15, 3d ed., 1988).

23. Raymond B. Williams, *Religion of Immigrants from India and Pakistan: New Threads in the American Tapestry* (Cambridge: Cambridge University Press, 1988), chapters 7 and 8.

24. Paul Numrich, "Recent Immigrant Religions in a Restructuring Metropolis: New Religious Landscapes in Chicago," *Journal of Cultural Geography* 17:1 (1997): 55–76.

25. *Making Muslim Space in North America and Europe* (Berkeley: University of California Press, 1996).

26. Gulzar Haidar, "Muslim Space and the Practice of Architecture: A Personal Odyssey," in Metcalf, ed., *Making Muslim Space*, 31–45.

27. While most influence occurs through the Nation of Islam contacts in Black America and even a particular sect called the "five percenters," there is also a genre of Islamist rap, for example, the group "Soldiers of Allah."

28. On this see Carl Ernst, *The Shambhala Guide to Sufism* (Boston: Shambhala, 1997).

29. *We Are Three. Open Secret: Versions of Rumi,* translated by John Moyne and Coleman Barks (Putney, VT: Threshhold, 1984). Barks's renditions have been featured as part of a public television special hosted by Bill Moyers, *The Language of Life: A Festival of Poets* (New York: Doubleday, 1995), also available on videocassettes from Public Affairs Television, 1995.

30. Yvonne Y. Haddad and John L. Esposito, *Muslims on the Americanization Path* (New York: Oxford University Press, 2000), and a forthcoming collection edited by Karen Leonard, *Muslim Identities in North America.*

31. See Katheen Moore, *al-Mughtaribun: American Law and the Transformation of Muslim Life in the United States* ("Albany: State University of New York Press, 1995).

32. "Allah at Harvard," an interview with Ali Asani, in Steven Barboza, *American Jihad: Islam after Malcolm X* (New York: Doubleday, 1994), 36–42.

33. Regula Qureshi, "Transcending Space: Recitation and Community among South Asian Muslims in Canada," in Metcalf, ed., *Making Muslim Space*, 46–64.

34. SoundVision.com

35. *Islamic Da'wah in the West* (New York: Oxford University Press, 1992).

36. Marcia K. Hermansen, "Two-Way Acculturation: Muslim Women in America," in Haddad, ed. *Muslims of America*, 188–201, and Carole Anway, *Daughters of Another Path: Experiences of American Women Choosing Islam* (Lee's Summit, MO: Yawna Publications, 1996).

37. For example, the works of Jeffrey Lang, *Struggling to Surrender: Some Impressions of an American Convert to Islam* (Beltsville, MD: Amana Publications, 1995) and *Even Angels Ask: A Journey to Islam in America* (Beltsville, MD: Amana Publications, 1997).

38. Aminah B. McCloud and Frederick Thaufeer al-Din, *A Question of Faith for Muslim Inmates* (Chicago: ABC International Group, 1999).

39. Robert Dannin, "Island in a Sea of Ignorance: Dimensions of the Prison Mosque," in Metcalf, ed., *Making Muslim Space*, 131–46. Quote cited is on page 131. This article is available on-line at *http://www.nyu.edu/classes/crisis/prison.html#intro*

40. Ibid., 132.

41. Ibid., 131.

42. Earle Waugh, "Muslim Leadership and the Shaping of the Umma: Classical Tradition and Religious Tensions in the North American Setting," in *The Muslim Community in North America*, ed. Baha Abu Laban and Regula Qureshi (Edmonton: University of Alberta Press, 1983).

43. *http://www.projectmaps.com/*

44. Links to American Sufi websites are found at *http://world.std.com/~habib/sufi.html#websites*

45. On some of the sectarian communities, see Haddad, ed., with Smith, *Mission to America*.

46. In *New Trends and Developments in the World of Islam*, ed. Peter Clarke (London: Luzac Oriental Press, 1997), 155–78.

47. For background on Internet Islam, see Jon W. Anderson, "The Internet and Islam's New Interpreters," in *New Media in the Muslim World*, ed. Dale F. Eickleman and Jon W. Anderson (Bloomington: Indiana University Press, 1999), 45–56, and Gary Bunt, *Virtually Islamic: Computer-Mediated Communication and Cyber Islamic Environments* (Cardiff: University of Wales Press, 2000).

48. Emily Wax, "The Mufti in the Chat Room: Islamic Legal Advisers Are Just a Click Away From Ancient Customs," *Washington Post*, July 31, 1999, C1.

49. *http://www.arches.uga.edu/~godlas/*

50. *Islam in America* (New York: Columbia University Press, 1999), 219–26.

CHAPTER ELEVEN

Incorporating Information Technology into Courses on Islamic Civilization

CORINNE BLAKE

S TUDENTS IN MOST COLLEGES AND UNIVERSITIES in the United States have access to the Internet and other information technology, either through campus computer labs or their own personal computers. While sitting at a desk, students can "travel" to a wide variety of Internet sites to access vast amount of information about Islam, Islamic civilizations and societies, and contemporary issues in the Muslim world. Students can click to an Internet site in Britain to read the Quran in Arabic or English, jump to Japan to read translations of Persian poetry and literature, and go back to the United Kingdom to go to hear different Quran recitations. They can check out the latest news from the Iranian news agency, read hadith in translation at the University of Southern California, view pictures of mosques and historical buildings in Isfahan, read perspectives on the veil [ḥijāb] written by Muslims in different countries, jump to Turkey to read Sufi poetry in translation, then return to the United States to view pictures of Islamic miniatures, calligraphy, and carpets.

Internet material can enrich undergraduate courses on Islamic religion, history, and civilization by providing students with access to primary sources, multimedia, and research material that is often unavailable at smaller institutions. Through the Internet, students can gain exposure to the perspectives of Muslims and Muslim governments on contemporary news events. Students who have never had the opportunity to talk with a Muslim suddenly have access to a global community where different points of view within the Muslim community are expressed and debated. Professors can use material located on the Internet to develop assignments that encourage students to think critically and allow them to pursue their particular interests within the general theme of the course. The purpose of this chapter is to provide faculty interested in using information technology with ideas and suggestions about how to locate relevant material and incorporate it into courses.

Locating Relevant Material

A number of different types of material are available on the Internet. Perhaps the most useful material for courses on Islamic civilization is translations of religious texts and literature. One can locate at least eight different full text translations of the Quran, as well as translations of hadith collections such as Bukhari, Malik's *al-Muwaṭṭa'*, and hadith qudsī in complete text and partial collections of Muslim and Abū Dawud. A number of legal texts have been put on-line, including selections from *al-Maqāsid* of Imam al-Nawawī, al-Shāfiʿī's *Risālah*, and numerous Shiʿi texts. There are translations of documents, including the Pact of ʿUmar, various edicts [farmān], and nineteenth- and twentieth-century treaties, as well as selections from manuscripts such as Busbecq's *Turkish letters*, Ibn Battuta's travels, Usmah b. Munqidh's *Autobiography*, and al-Tanukhi's *Ruminations*. One can find full text translations of Arabic, Persian, and Ottoman literary classics, such as *1001 Nights, The Perfumed Garden*, the *Gulistan* of Saʿdi, the *Shahnameh* of Firdausi, and the *Book of Dede Korkut*. There is also poetry: the Hanged Poems, Ghazels by Hafiz, poetry by Jalal al-Din Rumi, etc. A wide range of full text and selections from the writings of twentieth-century authors such as Sayyid Qutb, Taha Hussein, and Ayatollah Khomeini can also be found. While the translations of these texts vary in quality, in my view, most are adequate for use in survey undergraduate courses such as "Islamic Civilization." Professors interested in using this material for more specialized upper-level courses can, of course, point out problematic passages.

In addition to massive amounts of translated primary source material, other useful material is available through the Internet. A number of Middle Eastern scholars have posted articles at various sites. There is a good deal of multimedia material: Quran recitations, music from various Islamic countries, poetry recitation, and photographs of Muslim art, architecture, and modern cities. Reference material such as detailed contemporary and historical maps and systems to convert Gregorian and Hijri dates can also be found on the Internet. For courses that deal with the contemporary era, news sources with detailed news written about and by Islamic countries and governments can be very useful. Students can access thousands of pamphlets and articles written about contemporary issues from various points of view.

The most time consuming part of using information technology for teaching is searching the Internet to locate material valuable and relevant to one's course. By now, most people have a favorite search engine that they use to search for specific topics and subjects on the Internet; popular and established search engines include Yahoo (*http://www.yahoo.com*), Dogpile (*http://www.dogpile.com*), AltaVista (*http://www.altavista.com*), and Google (*http://www.google.com*). Since search engines may locate thousands or even millions of mostly useless sites, this approach can be frustrating. A search of "Turkey" on Google in March 2002 yielded 6,810,000 responses (some of them with recipes for stuffing!), "Shiite" produced 37,300 responses, and "Quran" produced 399,000 responses.

Unless one is looking for a very narrow topic, I suggest beginning at one of the large Web pages that act as gateways, organizing links to sites related to Islam. There are many excellent gateways; those listed below are established sites that can act as a starting point to find links with other gateways as well as specific sites.[1] The Internet Islamic History Sourcebook (*http://www .fordham.edu/halsall/islam/islamsbook.html*) is an invaluable Web page that contains links to a large amount of material useful for courses on Islamic history. This site, which is drawn from the Ancient, Medieval, and Modern History Sourcebooks, includes links to material about Islamic religion, art, culture, and history from pre-Islamic Arabia to the modern period. There are links to articles by prominent scholars, as well as extensive translations of primary source material. There are also links to Quran translations, hadith collections, and historical maps of the Middle East.

To find useful material about virtually any topic related to Islam, Islamic history, the Middle East, and Middle Eastern countries, try looking at a well-organized site maintained by Columbia University (*http://www.columbia .edu/cu/libraries/indiv/area/MiddleEast*). This site, which is organized by region, country, and a wide range of topics—religion, language, literature, minorities, food, music, water, political violence, electronic journals and newspapers, etc.— serves as a gateway to massive amounts of information about Islam and the Middle East. The Middle East Center at the University of Texas also maintains a comprehensive site (*http://link.lanic.utexas.edu/menic*) organized by country and topics, including business/finance/ economics, government/country profiles, and oil/energy/natural resources.

A site at the University of Georgia entitled "Islamic Studies, Islam, Arabic, and Religion" (*http://www.arches.uga.edu/~godlas*) contains links to numerous sources for Islam, Islamic law, Sufism, Muslim women, Islamic art, Shi'ism, etc. and includes annotations about most sites. It also includes a collection of articles about the events of September 11, the Taliban, and Osama bin Ladin, as well as links to other large gateways. An article I wrote entitled

"Teaching Islamic Civilization with Information Technology" (*http://www. albany.edu/ jmmh,* click on "past issues," then "Vol. 1, 1998"), published in an on-line journal, *Journal for Multimedia History,* also contains numerous links to sources relevant for courses on Islamic civilization. The Ahlul Bayt Digital Islamic Library Project (*http://www.al-islam.org/organizations/dilp*) and the Shi'ah Homepage (*http://shia.org*) are good places to begin searching for information about Shi'ism. In addition to the wealth of information available over the Internet, another option is to use some of the CD-ROMs published with sources on Islam and Islamic civilization. There are numerous CD-ROMs with translations of hadith and Quran and recitations of the Quran. A CD-ROM entitled "Alim," for example, published by the ISL Software Corporation,[2] includes the Quran in Arabic and in three translations, with simultaneous translations for comparative purposes, 30 hours of Quran recitation, and Syed Mawdudi's introductions to the surahs. It also includes complete texts of hadith from Bukhari, Muslim, and others, biographies of Muhammad's companions, and a chronology of Islamic history. The Islamic Computing Center in London (*http://www.ummah.org.uk/icc/*) carries a Windows and Mac product on disc entitled "Islamic Law Base" that contains volumes of fiqh about different law schools and translations of other legal material. They also have a CD-ROM entitled "WinSeera" that includes translations of four early biographies of the Prophet that can be searched chronologically or by theme. To find other useful CD-ROMs, try linking to the Islamic Computing Center or some of the on-line Islamic bookstores from one of the pages mentioned above.

The problem with CD-ROMs is that it can be difficult to discover what is available, and then they have to be purchased. It can also be problematic to make CD-ROMs available to students. They can be put in the computer lab, but it may not be convenient for commuting students to come to the lab, and the CD-ROM could be lost or stolen. One CD-ROM is not adequate for a large survey class, and it may be expensive to purchase more. At some universities, it is possible to put CD-ROMs on a universitywide server, often through the library, but not all companies allow their CD-ROMs to be networked and others charge high fees. Because of these problems, I tend to assign students material from the Internet and list CD-ROMs (available through the computer lab) as a backup for students who are having difficulty accessing sites.

Internet Assignments and Assessment

Once relevant material has been located, the next step is to decide what to use and how to use it. Locating material on the Internet can be time consuming, but the real challenge, as always, is deciding what to use and creating assignments based on the texts. Since most of the material listed above is primary source material, it can be used as any printed texts. With the Quran translations, for example, students could read specific surahs and note what they reveal about Islamic concepts such as the nature of God, Heaven and Hell, prophecy, righteous behavior, either in class discussion or in an essay. Students could be required to read specific hadith, or translations of Arabic, Persian, or Ottoman poetry or literature, and asked to discuss the material in class or respond to questions about what they read. Students could read articles written by Middle Eastern scholars on the Internet, instead of in-class handouts or library reserve. They could read several pamphlets on contemporary topics and compare the authors' views. There are a number of sites on women in Muslim societies, for example, with numerous pamphlets that could be used for this type of assignment.[3] In other words, any assignments that one would use with printed primary, secondary, or reference material can be used for material found on the Internet.

Some of the Internet material—chronologies, maps, biographies, photographs, etc.—can be assigned as reference to enrich students' understanding of topics treated in class. After learning about Sufism, for example, students could be asked to explore one of the Sufi sites and write about or discuss what they learned. For a class on the Quran, students could listen to Quran recitations, look at the Quran in Arabic, or read Mawdudi's introductions to surahs. For other classes, it may be appropriate to have students listen to Middle Eastern music or view photographs of Islamic art, architecture, and/or cities, then discuss or write about what they learned. Students could also be asked to look at historical maps and discuss or write about the expansion of the early Muslim empires.

The advantage of using the Internet in these cases would be ease of access, for both the professor and the student. Instead of ordering several books, finding tapes of Quran recitation or music, putting books and articles on library reserve, and/or laboriously photocopying a course packet, professors can simply type the links into the course syllabus.[4] Students don't have to buy translations of the Quran, Arabic or Persian literature, or expensive translations of hadith collections. They do not have to depend on library reserve or photocopied course packets; they do not have to listen to tapes in a lab. Instead, they can read or listen to assigned material on their computer at home or in the lab. Another advantage of using the Internet is access to material that is not available in the libraries of many smaller colleges. Most libraries have translations of the Quran and classics such as *1001 Nights,* but they may not have translations of hadith collections, Persian literature, Islamic legal texts, newspapers from Muslim countries, contemporary pamphlets, etc. Learning about the wide variety of web sites related to Islam also encourages students to become lifelong learners. I had cynically assumed that once my students finished the course, they never looked at these sites again. After the terrible tragedy of September 11, however, several former students approached me to let me know that they had accessed some of the sites to gain a broader perspective on the events. One student said that he had directed friends who wanted to learn more about Islam to sites where they could read the Qur'an, newspapers from Muslim countries, opinion pamphlets, etc.

Using the Internet provides more than ease of access, however; it also allows professors to create assignments that give students more flexibility to pursue their own interests. Students can be directed to a site with news about a particular country, for example, and asked to read whatever stories they find interesting; they can be sent to a site with lots of opinion papers and choose papers on subjects of their interest. They can search hadith collections to find information about a topic of their choice. Students can be directed to a site with translations of many classics of Persian and Arabic literature, where they can choose to read whatever looks interesting to them. The whole class could read the frame story to *1001 Nights,* then each student could be assigned to read a different story within the text. This individualized approach serves to enrich class discussions, as students in the class contribute different perspectives and approaches gained from reading a variety of materials on a common topic.

With the Internet, professors can also design assignments to develop critical thinking that would be difficult or impossible to complete with printed material. All the Quran translations and hadith collections on the Internet, for example, have search functions. Instead of using a concordance, which may not be available in the more affordable translations or in the library, students can use the search function to find passages about an assigned topic or a topic of their own choice. Since several hadith collections with search functions have been put on-line, students can be asked to locate hadith from two or three different collections about a particular topic, or a topic of their choice, then compare what they read. A site at the University of Southern California (*http://www.usc.edu/dept/MSA/quran*) enables students to compare different translations of the Quran easily. When students click on a surah, it comes up verse by verse in three translations: M. H. Shakir, Yusuf Ali, and Marmaduke Pickthall.

Using the Internet also allows students to compare material about specific topics from different sources. Students could choose one pillar of Islam— prayer, fasting, hajj, etc.—or any other topic and search for relevant passages in the Quran and hadith about that pillar or topic. They could then write an essay or engage in a class discussion about how hadith material compliments and elaborates on information from the Quran. Or one could pose a legal question and have students search the Quran, hadith, and other legal material to find relevant information and write their own fatwā. Similarly, students could be assigned or pick a legal issue and asked to search Sunni and Shi'i hadith collections and other legal material to compare approaches to their issue in Sunni and Shi'i traditions. In addition, there are a number of Internet sites that offer translations of the Bible with extensive search functions. Students could search for particular stories or prophets—Adam, Noah, Joseph, Moses, Jesus, etc.— mentioned in both, and compare Quranic and biblical approaches to these stories. They could also compare recitations of surahs by different shaykhs.

Some of the material on the Internet takes the form of sites dedicated to a particular topic—Sufism, Islamic art, Muslim women, contemporary news, opinion pamphlets, etc.—with extensive links. Students could be asked to develop answers to specific questions, using material from this site, or they could be directed to "explore" the site, that is, follow a specified minimum number of links. The question here is how to assess students' work, how to determine whether they perfunctorily followed one or two links or thoroughly examined the site. One approach is to have students submit notes which include a record of the links they followed and any comments or reactions to the material. If students need to explore a number of sites, it may be easier to have them record comments and reactions in an Internet journal that is submitted periodically. Students could also discuss the site in class or prepare a formal presentation about it for the class. For a more formal assessment, students could be asked to write critical reviews of assigned sites. In addition to writing about their comments and reactions, the review could include analyzing who sponsored the site and wrote the articles, checking references cited, assessing biases, etc. This assignment is particularly useful in terms of encouraging students to approach information from the Internet critically.

Some professors use a listserv for their courses—private e-mail discussion groups available only to students enrolled in the course—for assessment. To set up such a list, contact Academic Computing or the webmaster at your college. These lists are useful for recording information about any changes in upcoming assignments; they can also serve as a "discussion section" for the course. Students are required to check the list regularly; they are also required to participate by submitting material to the list. Students can be asked to submit questions and comments about printed, CD-ROM, or Internet material, for example, on a regular basis. Students can be asked to explore different sites about particular topics—each student could look at the web pages of a different Sufi order, for example, or each student could find news from different Muslim countries—and write to the listserv about what they found. Students could also read different sections of a large document—large literary works such as *1001 Nights,* Shi'i legal texts, etc.—and submit critical reviews of what they read to the listserv. Students could then engage in an e-mail "discussion" about the topic, using the wide variety of material provided by the whole class. Students can be graded on their contributions to the list-serv, in terms of quality and, perhaps, quantity. If using a listserv seems too technologically challenging, of course these assignments could also be given as the basis for in-class discussion or as writing assignments.

Web Pages and Problems

I have tried to demonstrate that there is a lot of material about Islam and Is-lamic history available to students through the Internet. When I first began using these materials, I directed students to the various sites by typing web ad-dresses in the syllabus. Students often had difficulty reaching the sites; they would not understand all the symbols, type the address incorrectly, and, in general, became very frustrated. A better approach is to develop a Web page for the course, with links to the required readings or sites. From this page, which can be a complete on-line syllabus as well, students simply click to reach the sites.

Developing a Web page used to be a complicated process that required knowledge of HTML. With the Web-authoring programs available now, any-one who can use a word processor can author a Web page. Links can be cre-ated on word processing programs such as Microsoft Word by clicking "hy-perlink" under "Insert," then typing in the Internet address. When the rest of the syllabus is complete, the document is saved as an HTML file. Many fac-ulty members also have access to Netscape Navigator or other easy-to-use programs for writing Web pages. The truly technically challenged can hire student workers. Once the syllabus is complete and saved as an HTML file, the students need to learn how to access the syllabus. Most colleges and uni-versities put on-line syllabi either in department Web pages or in a section for faculty Web pages.

In my experience, most students react positively to Internet assignments: with a few clicks of the mouse, they can access material that would take hours to locate in the library. Nonetheless, relying on technology can present prob-lems. Even with the help of a course Web page, it is still sometimes difficult for students to access sites; the university's system could be overloaded, there could be problems at the site itself, or there could be a traffic jam on the In-ternet "superhighway." Students, especially those using computers at home that are not hooked up to high-speed modems, may become frustrated wait-ing for large sites with photographs and other multimedia material to down-load. Links that worked when the syllabus was first put together could be changed or even gone by the time students need to complete the assignment. Students at some colleges have difficulty accessing computers and have to wait in long lines, especially during midterms and finals.

Not all of these problems can be solved, but it is possible to avoid some problems and provide alternative solutions for students who are having difficulty. Check the links, of course, the week before the assignment is due. Advise students where to find additional open computer labs in the engineering school, the library, the business school, their local library, wherever. When the same material is available at several sites or through different entry points, as is often the case, put links to alternate locations in the syllabus to improve the chances that at least one of them will be working. There are a number of sites that include Quran and hadith translations, for example, and many literary classics are available through different sites. News about Muslim countries and contemporary pamphlets are also available at several locations. A CD-ROM with some of the material could be put in the computer lab or on the library server for backup. If the material is available in the college library, put copies on reserve for students who are having trouble accessing the sites. If the material is not available in the library, consider printing it out when writing the syllabus and putting it on reserve. In addition to providing backup in case of computer failures, students who dislike reading on a computer screen or prefer to read the material in print will benefit from having access to printed copies of the material.

The unreliable nature of technology and the problems discussed above can give students more—or at least different—excuses not to complete assignments. Some students may view assignments from the web as optional supplementary assignments rather than as required reading. I learned this the hard way when I gave an in-class writing assignment based on an Internet text, and 28 out of 35 students tried to claim that they had not read the material because their computer was "down." In addition to providing alternative sites and paper copies of assigned material, giving written assignments, as always, helps ensure students actually complete the reading. Students also can respond in different ways—in a journal, a formal essay, or a submission to the listserv. They can also be assessed through writing short paragraphs in response to the material in class or through class discussions and presentations.

In conclusion, using information technology in undergraduate courses on Islamic Civilization—or any other subject—requires an initial commitment of time to locate relevant material, create assignments based on the material, and write an on-line syllabus. In return, students have access to primary sources and other material that used to be available only at larger institutions with developed research libraries. They now have flexibility to choose topics and explore their own interests related to the assigned subject, and they can continue to access this material even after they graduate and move away. Through written assignments and class discussion, they learn to approach the material critically and analytically and develop their ability to think critically. Students not only gain access to massive amounts of information about Islam and Islamic history, but they also become aware of the wealth of information (and misinformation) about almost any topic that can be found through the Internet.

NOTES

Some portions of this article were published in an on-line journal entitled *Journal for Multimedia History* at *http://www.albany.edu/jmmh*

1. Because of the ephemeral nature of Internet sites and addresses, I have included only a few sites that have been stable for several years. If the address listed becomes out of date, try to find the site with a search engine, putting the title of the site in quotation marks.

2. Their phone number is (800) 443–3636.

3. One of the most comprehensive and established sites is the Muslim Women's Homepage, at *http://www.jannah.org/sisters.*

4. See below for more information about on-line course syllabi.

CHAPTER TWELVE

Teaching Religion in the Twenty-First Century

TAZIM R. KASSAM

The Lure of Religious Studies

What drew me into the study of religions? Chantings of the *Rig Veda;* the Buddha's smile in serene meditation; the smoke and smell of incense at shrines; the *muezzin's* piercing call to prayer at the crack of dawn; flickering candles and quiet gestures offered before the altar; shining black bodies leaping in wild dance to the beat of pounding drums; funeral processions of mourners crying, *"Allahu Akbar"* and *"Rama Rama."*

The rich liturgy, pageantry, and aesthetics of religious life lured me into the study of religions. These surfaces of enchantment extended an invitation to delve deeper into the mysteries of life as they were felt, expressed, and celebrated by different people. The desire to understand the evocative songs of Mirabai and the breathtaking dances of *Bharata Natyam* led to a study of Vedic scriptures, Indian philosophy, and Hindustani classical music. The exquisite design of Islamic art and architecture, the scintillating touches of Quran manuscripts, the rapt whirling of Turkish dervishes inspired a study of Islamic Civilization and the poetry of Sufi mystics such as Jalalludin Rumi and Ibn al-Arabi. The cryptic sayings and *koans* spoken by David Carradine in the popular television series *Kung Fu* kindled an interest in Zen Buddhism, the *Analects* of Confucius, and Lao Tzu's *Tao Te Ching.*

Philosophy, art, architecture, music, ritual, literature, poetry, mysticism, metaphysics, cosmology, myth, community, culture, ethics, sacrifice, self-realization—religions appeared to encompass all of these. As William Scott Green says, "unlike art, politics, or even philosophy, religion tends to expand its reach, to be comprehensive in scope, and to exhibit an enormous range of expression. It makes demands on the entire human person and claims to provide definitive answers to the urgent questions of life and death."[1] Thus began a journey of a thousand steps.

Specializing in the History of Religions

When I set out to study religions, I did not want to focus on a particular religion but to study several religions concurrently. Specialization in Comparative Religion or what is now called History of Religions enabled me to do so. Looking back on my years at McGill University's Faculty of Religious Studies in Montreal, I enjoyed three vital conditions: (a) to be able to encounter the diversity of religious expressions in terms of their own intrinsic interest; (b) to do so within an academic, nonsectarian, and multicultural context; and (c) to be required to entertain interdisciplinary perspectives and engage in critical reflections on the nature of religion.

To be able to study several religions in depth is to get an appreciation of the marvelous array of symbols, stories, rituals, and insights produced over the course of human history. It permits an enlarging experience of human cultural diversity in indigenous terms through rigorous language study and cultural immersion. At the same time, studying religions together helps raise fundamental theoretical questions. For instance, it complicates the meaning of the term "religion" which means different things to a Christian, a Buddhist, or an American Indian. Indeed, the particularity of meanings led Wilfred Cantwell Smith to assert that there is no such thing as religion in the abstract, only specific instances of religious practice, persons, places, and so on. The very concept of religion was a stepchild of the Enlightenment constructed as the antithesis of reason and the enemy of science. Religion as a field of study and as a caption of academic departments is of relatively recent coinage. Although the term religion falsely suggests an entity that is stable, definable, homogeneous, self-contained, what we call World Religions—Islam, Christianity, Buddhism—are not static but dynamic, evolving, mutually influencing traditions. Thus, the study of any one religion often entails a study of the many cultures in which it developed and through which it found self-expression.[2]

The opportunity to learn about religions in an academic, nonsectarian, and multicultural context is a gift of democracy, liberal education, and the American Constitution. William Scott Green notes that "by mandating both freedom of and freedom from religion, the First Amendment guarantees religion as a legitimate, legally protected form of difference in American society"[3] and argues that the status of religion as a privileged cultural category makes it a highly relevant subject in this society deserving formal study. But the Enlightenment ethos of higher education continues to marginalize the study of religions as a serious academic endeavor. Colleagues in other departments often confuse teaching about religions with doing theology and inculcating faith. It is precisely the fact that the academic study of religions necessitates a deliberate, self-conscious analysis and, to the extent possible, suspension of preconceived notions and personal beliefs that makes it such a promising intellectual enterprise. Apart from learning to respect, understand, and deconstruct religious life by utilizing native categories, academic study makes many conceptual demands germane to a liberal arts education: searching for themes and patterns; formulating theories to account for rites and rituals; investigating the social and intellectual history of sacred texts; and so on.

Teaching to Learn and Learning to Teach

"But why do I need to know any of this stuff?" a student asks. "All these myths about Hindu gods are cool but some dude with an imagination made them up, right?! So Muslims like to pray five times a day and fast for a month but that isn't my business. Isn't religion kind of private anyhow? What difference does it make to me what other people believe in?! I don't care if my doctor goes to Church on Sundays or meditates in a Zen temple so long as she can fix my cold." It's like New York University law professor Burt Neuborne said: "When you accept public office, you're not a Catholic, you're not a Jew. You're an American."[4]

The primary reason I wanted to teach about religions and cultures was to share my own enthusiasm and fascination with these subjects and to rediscover and reconsider with students their history, role, and complexity. Hence, it came as a rude shock to read this student's journal entry that considered even basic information about world religions to be irrelevant. Of what use, I wondered, would s/he find intricate philosophical debates over concepts such as *sunyata* or *nishkamya karma yoga* or *tawhid?* As scholars and teachers smitten by the love of learning, it may be easy to dismiss the student's attitude as parochial, but this demand to know of what use it is to be well-versed on a particular subject is both legitimate and prudent.

When I first began to teach, I had the notion inculcated by graduate studies that my primary responsibility was to transmit a body of knowledge and its critical apparatus to my students and to turn them into mini-experts, as it were, thoroughly acquainted with the historical, conceptual, and cultural intricacies of the religions which I taught. In such a framework subject matter and the unfettered search for knowledge reigned supreme. The truth is that most academics went through graduate school and became scholars because they have a passionate interest in their fields of specialization. The quest for knowledge and the thrill of research and discovery is not to be belittled. But in our enthusiasm for our subjects, legitimate and proper in one context, we develop what M. Robert Gardner has aptly termed the "furor to teach." Ironically, he says: "True teachers want too much to teach, want to teach too much, and want too much to teach what they want to teach whenever, however, and to whomever they want."[5] So keen and earnest is our desire to convey to students what we think they ought to know that we forget the pedagogical necessity to find a fit between what teachers want to teach and what students want to and are ready to learn. We overlook the educational imperative that scholarship and learning needs to be meaningfully connected to the realities of our students. In fact, by venturing to see through the eyes of students we gain an opportunity to take a fresh look at our own enthusiasms and conceptions and thereby revitalize them.

Taking the cue from the students' remarks, I would like briefly to consider the contemporary living and learning context of North America and the relevance of teaching about religions in the twenty-first century.

Teaching Religions in North America

Several decades ago, Marshall McLuhan drew our attention to the fact that the natural and the built environment are coded with messages and together they form a crucible for shaping individuals. Learning environments include home, schools, churches, malls, food courts, video arcades, city centers, the Internet, sporting events, parks, and so on. Popular culture, television, mass media, and the entertainment industry are powerful instructional settings, all the more so because their messages are covert and subliminal. The truth that human development occurs within the total milieu of life is encapsulated in the African saying, "It takes a whole village to raise a child." The artificial segmentation of life into education, work, and leisure belie the fact that the formation of the individual takes place not only in educational institutions but also in the myriad situations of life made possible within a given society. While McLuhan makes his point with reference to the habitat created by the burgeoning electronic and communication technologies of this century, the truth in his pithy phrase, "the medium is the message," has wider application. All humanly constructed environments, regardless of their scientific and technological advancements, are richly programmed with messages. Terms such as culture, heritage, or civilization are pressed into service to convey this notion of meanings (or messages) socially constructed and encoded within any given society's living techniques, symbol systems, behavioral codes, and organizational patterns.

What, then, are some of the broader contextual factors that need to be borne in mind when thinking about teaching religions and cultures in the twenty-first century? What conditions and forces shape the learning habitat of our students? Numerous factors condition the character of our times, including the constantly changing nature of the American population; the impact of media in all its variety; the growth of multiple family structures and relationships; escalating violence and insecurity in schools and neighborhoods; the impact of global technologies and communications on employment and lifestyle; serial careers in the work force; protection of the environment and natural resources; inequities and divisions of race, gender, and class; development aid and the push for capitalism, democracy, and a global economy; and so on. Changes in all these areas occur so rapidly that one of the ongoing challenges of education and the curriculum is frequently to test and validate its prevalent representations of these social, political, and technological realities.

The present discussion of our students' living and learning environments is by no means extensive. It merely intends to draw attention to a few areas that have a bearing on the broader educational aim of preparing students to build their future. The idea is to respond seriously to the student's question, "Why does it matter to me to know about religions and cultures?" How would knowledge of and sensitivity to other religions and cultures assist students in effectively dealing with their current and evolving realities? As a teacher of religions and cultures, it seems essential to grapple with this issue of relevance and to articulate how such knowledge might serve the students' self-interest. How does one make a convincing case to students that as they assume the responsibilities of adulthood and are called upon to solve problems and to make decisions, they would do well to take into account deeply embedded religious and cultural patterns of societies as carefully as economic, political, and geographic facts and figures? Unless one can convincingly build this case, what we teach in departments of religion will remain "elective" subjects—exotic, abstruse, and interesting, but inconsequential in the larger scheme of things. These questions also serve as a provocation for thinking about how to advance the appreciation of religions and cultures among the many publics beyond the college campus.

HISTORY, MODERNITY, AND THE EXPERIENCE OF TRANSIENCE

In *Future Shock*, Alvin Toffler identifies four defining characteristics of the highly technological post-industrial society: the death of permanence, signifying a decisive break with the past; transience—the psychological counterpart of acceleration and high turnover; novelty— the escalating ratio of new material goods and products to old; and diversity—a surfeit of choices, variety in lifestyles, and social differentiation.[6] Bearing out his predictions, in the few decades that have passed since his work was published the world has quite literally changed: innovations in science and technology have occurred in leaps and bounds; revolutions and wars have reconfigured national boundaries and sociopolitical structures; and the cold war, which polarized and paralyzed the world in a deadlock of superpower maneuvers, is over. Yet, it is startling to find, on rereading his work, that many of Toffler's insights into the nature of the future continue to be germane. His main point in the seventies was that Western society was hurtling toward a future that was much different from anything it had known in the past. Unless societies deliberately anticipated and prepared themselves to adapt to the future, they would go into "future shock" and experience disorientation and confusion similar to the "culture shock" felt by visitors when they set foot in unfamiliar cultures.

One of Toffler's most provocative ideas pertains to the altered nature of time and change. Change itself is not new. What is unprecedented about change in this century is its acceleration. As Neil Postman puts it: "Change changed."[7] Whereas in the past, the lag between human response and the pace of environmental change was manageable, now "change occurs so rapidly that each of us in the course of our lives has continuously to work out a set of values, beliefs, and patterns of behavior that are viable, or *seem* viable, to each of us personally."[8] And just as soon as a working solution is developed, it becomes irrelevant because so much has changed in the meanwhile. Toffler refers to this situation as "the perishability of fact. Every seasoned reporter has had the experience of working on a fast-breaking story that changes its shape and meaning even before his words are put down on paper. Today the whole world is a fast-breaking story."[9]

The hallmark of the experience of reality in a highly technological society is transience. Speaking of life as a series of experienced situations, Toffler indicates that not only is the flow of situations faster but also the similarity between situations decreases as novelty increases. He identifies five components in any given situation: things, place, people, organization, and information.[10] As such, as long as some of these components remain relatively stable while others change, societies are able to cope. But what happens when change occurs in every component? Toffler endeavors to show that each one of these once dependable pivots of orientation and stability have come loose. Things are disposable; dwellings are temporary; relationships are short-lived; organizational structures mutate; informational maps of reality become obsolete the moment they are drawn. This "death of permanence" is likely to create acute disorientation in societies, whose experience of slower times and steadfast tradition have provided an enduring source of comfort.

As they adapt, technological societies begin to live with an expectation of transience, novelty, and speed. Generation X, even more so than their baby boomer parents, take it for granted that reality is highly variable, fast-paced, and ever-shifting. Toffler refers to durational expectancies, that is, how long individuals expect their relationships, jobs, things, interests, and so on to last.[11] In highly technological societies, these expectancies and attachments have shortened dramatically. Recycling emphasizes the quality of impermanence and the reality of "morphing." What was newspaper yesterday is a paper cup today and a cabinet tomorrow. The death of permanence signifies a break with the past both literally and psychologically.

This zeitgeist has important ramifications in terms of attitudes toward history and identity. History, it is felt, can no longer serve as a guide as it did in more stable societies, where tomorrows repeated yesterdays and traditional systems of knowledge could be counted upon to transmit effective patterns of survival. Being dislocated from the past does not only mean that it cannot be looked upon for help in meeting the unprecedented problems of today but also that the past is a strange and different place. It has become foreign territory. Dramatic changes have caused a rupture, signifying the end of history. Breaking with the past conjures up the idea of being free from custom and tradition. Americans hold dearly to the belief that they founded a new society unencumbered by the baggage of centuries of tradition of their European ancestors. This love of progress at times belies a kind of prejudice toward the past. Consequently, "the inhabitants of the earth are divided not only by race, nation, religion or ideology, but also, in a sense by their position in time."[12]

For educators, the fact of unprecedented change has many implications. What is old, ancient, and in the past has lost its cultural caché and hold over the imagination and teachers have to work harder at restoring a sense and love of history.

TRUTH PARADIGMS: THE DOMINATION OF SCIENCE AND TECHNOLOGY

In many ways bias against the past is understandable. To some extent, it is rooted in modernity and the experience of the comforts, amenities, and freedoms afforded by developments in industry, science, and technology in the last century. Advancements in many sectors of life including health, communications, transport, automation, and construction have vastly benefited modern society. Through an alliance of capitalism, democracy, global politics, and scientific progress, Americans have created a wealthy superpower, and they live privileged lives relative to a vast majority of the world's population. What is distinctive about contemporary students is how very thoroughly their identity is located in and constructed by situations—things, places, instruments—that have come into existence only in the last few decades. Certain about the powers of science and technology, students have a future positive mentality and optimism that things can only get better and better. This confidence, however, which is deeply rooted in and reliant upon the conditions of modern life can be a source of estrangement not only from the past, as we have seen, but also from less-developed societies and nations.

It is important to put the advances of modern life into historical perspective. Using a clock metaphor, Postman says if sixty minutes of the hour represent three thousand years of civilization then each minute represents fifty years. On this scale, there were no significant media changes until nine minutes ago. At that time, the printing press came into use in Western culture. About three minutes ago, the telegraph, photograph, and locomotive arrived. Two minutes ago: the telephone, rotary press, motion pictures, automobiles, airplane, and radio. One minute ago, the talking picture. Television has appeared in the last ten seconds, the computer in the last five, and communications satellites in the last second. The laser beam . . . appeared only a fraction of a second ago.[13]

In the area of medicine, open-heart surgery arrived about ten seconds ago; more discoveries have occurred in the health sciences during the last minute than in the previous fifty-nine. This "knowledge explosion" is happening in every field. The microchip which appeared a millisecond ago will make possible new technologies in genomics, biotechnology, and smart products that will continue to boost living standards and lead to unimaginable new products and services.

The issue at stake for students and coming generations is that such extraordinary developments will also spawn unprecedented problems and dilemmas. Even though technological society is barely in its infancy, it already faces perplexing ethical decisions such as whether or not to permit human cloning. Einstein once said that we would never be able to solve the problems of the world from the level of thinking that we were at when we created them.[14] What is noteworthy is that as dependence on technology increases, so too does the unconscious and uncritical acceptance of scientific norms of truth and veracity. Modern Western cultures have thoroughly assimilated scientific values, attitudes, vocabulary, and techniques. In his study of the historical significance of science in Western culture, Richard Olson asks, "Has modern culture become so scientized that it is on a course toward a kind of stasis characterized by a monotonous but benign totalitarianism of scientific and technological reality?"[15] Scientific efficacy and mastery of physical reality, however, need not invalidate the aesthetic and intimate search for order, underlying form, and universally valid knowledge also to be found in religions and the arts. As Elizabeth Newman effectively argues, students need to challenge the objectivist framework of scientific knowledge and recognize that what and how we know cannot be separated: "scientific knowledge does not simply hang in midair, describing the real world 'out there.' Rather, as has been noted for some time, scientific knowing is rooted in the beliefs, judgments and commitments of the scientific knower; and thus is temporal and dynamic."[16] By examining the constructed axioms and circumscribed practices of scientific thinking, students can cultivate the intellectual independence to question its premises and to entertain multiple modes and methods of perceiving and relating to reality.

SECULARISM, PLURALISM, AND THE PROTECTION OF RELIGIOUS FREEDOM

So persistently is the point made in public discourse that the Constitution separates church and state that it leaves the impression that Americans are a faithless people. Hugh Hewitt asks, "When did many of us begin to believe that most of us had ceased to believe?"[17] The "us" refers to the "chattering class, the editorial writers, the TV producers, the professionally opinionated, and a large swath of the Academy."[18] In truth, Americans are a deeply religious people. According to Jacob Neusner, 92.5 percent of the American population professes belief in God and prays regularly. Most agree that "in God we trust" and "explain what happens in their lives by appeal to God's will and word and work, and they form their ideal for the American nation by reference to the teachings of religion: 'one nation, under God.'"[19] Hewitt hosted a radio talk-show in Los Angeles for five years (1990–1995) during which time he set aside an hour a week to talk about faith. His purpose was to highlight questions of everyday faith rather than to go after hot-button controversies. Of his experience, which frequently drew a full board of callers, he says: "I have to conclude that a great many Americans want to hear about, talk about, think about God in a serious way."[20]

Americans are not only religious, but they are also a people of many religions. Almost every living religion in the world is represented in the United States. The statistics of believers are as follows: Protestants: 60 percent; Roman Catholics: 26 percent; Muslims: 2 percent; Jews: 2.5 percent; Hindus: 1 percent; Buddhists: 1 percent.[21] In addition, it is home to followers of Zoroastrian, Shinto, Taoist, Sikh, Native American, and Latin American religions. Neusner aptly remarks that not only does this religious diversity make North America an opportune place to study religions; but also that religions in the United States are more interesting to study because they are multiracial, multinational, and multicultural. For example, in addition to having various types of European Christianity in America, there are Christians from Africa, South Asia, and the Far East.[22] Quite literally, the United States has become a microcosm of the diversity of ethnicities, religions, and cultures around the globe.

What holds this nation together is the American ideal that a person of any creed, color, race, language, gender, and country of origin can become a good citizen under the American Constitution and Bill of Rights. In recognizing religion as a native and unquestioned category of American life, the First Amendment guarantees that America will be home to more than one religion. The Constitution deliberately names and sets religion apart for special consideration, regarding it to be a legitimate, legally protected form of difference in American society. It declares freedom of religion to be a fundamental civil right of all its citizens, a liberty as basic as the right to free speech, free press, and free assembly. The First Amendment has two clauses that stipulates the government's role (or lack thereof) with respect to religious life: (a) the Establishment Clause and (b) the Free Exercise Clause. The Establishment Clause asserts that the government may not set up a church nor pass laws that aid or give preference to any particular religion nor force religious belief upon its citizens nor punish disbelief. The Free Exercise Clause inhibits the government from controlling or restricting people's religious beliefs or behavior.[23] In other words, the American Constitution is highly tolerant and protective of religious diversity.

It is important to recognize the fact that "America is multireligious by design and not because of an accident of history or immigration."[24] The "disestablishment" principle commonly referred to as the separation of church and state detaches civil authority from the sphere of religious activity in a way that puts restraints upon the former. It also forbids the oppression of one religion by another through means of the juridical system. Such measures were advocated by religious minorities such as the Quakers, who wanted to protect their religious life from the control of majority denominations. William Scott Green notes that "the United States was the first nation in history to apply the separation of church and state as a practical political principle, the first nation to make disestablishment of religion a foundation for its national life."[25] What often gets obscured in the religious rhetoric against secularism is that it is these very secular principles that have enabled and safeguarded religious pluralism. As a basic civil right, the freedom to practice religion is a secular and not a religious principle. Given that the term secular is commonly (mis)understood as irreligious, it is ironic that secular principles enable different religions, races and cultures to flourish in America in a manner that lets them "be true to themselves and to the American vision of a diverse society."[26]

CULTURES OF DISBELIEF: LAW, POLITICS, ACADEME, AND THE MEDIA

As Stephen Carter endeavors to show in *The Culture of Disbelief*, despite the fact that most Americans believe in God and seek moral instruction and personal inspiration from their faith, American law and politics trivializes religious devotion and presses the faithful to act "as though their faith does not matter to them."[27] For a nation whose Constitution protects religious freedom on the one hand and whose people are predominantly religious on the other, Hewitt argues that it is ironic that "the overclass is laced with a deep-seated assumption: that Americans do not really believe in God anymore."[28] He defines the "overclass" as the culture-defining, talk-show intellectuals in the spheres of law and politics, academe, and the mass media, who shape public perception on most issues. In his work, Carter shows how the legal and political establishment belittles religion through the message that faith is suspect and something to be ashamed of, as it "represents a kind of mystical irrationality, something that thoughtful, public-spirited Americans would do better to avoid."[29] Persons who frankly express that their faith influences their thinking run the risk of ridicule and contempt.

Similarly, the mass media look upon religious commitment as a troubling curiosity. Individuals who argue a political or ethical position based on religious formulations are worrisome; those who hold the tenets of their faith to be superior to social and political convention are suspect. Psychiatrists and cult specialists are called upon to explain their "strange" behavior. In general, the media and press only take notice of religion in the context of political conflicts, "a convenient substitute for a searching look at believers' beliefs."[30] The entertainment and film industry is more subtle in its rejection of religion, making light of it simply by ignoring its existence. "This near total removal of God from the vast amount of media we consume has an effect of gradually diminishing the relevance of the Divine to ordinary life."[31] Avoiding the "G" word is practiced by talk-show hosts, television producers, news makers, editors, and journalists. Attitudes percolate. Religion is an awkward, indelicate, and sensitive topic in everyday American conversation. Hewitt says, "Nervous laughter and sidelong glances will greet any watercooler talker who broaches even as ordinary a subject as prayer."[32]

Green attributes this reluctance to converse about religion to the fact that "historically, too few Americans have had the opportunity to study it and learn how to think about it."[33] In her 1991 presidential address to the American Academy of Religion, Judith A. Berling offers the following reasons why American culture and the academy are "skittish about religion as a topic of public conversation": (a) statements about religions are assumed to be in favor of a particular religious position; (b) learning about other beliefs might undermine one's own faith; (c) the legal separation of church and state is interpreted to mean that religion is a private matter unfit for public discourse; (d) statements about religion cannot contribute to the common good because they are sectarian; and (e) religions can only encounter each another within a competitive framework.[34] These undisputed preconceptions play a major role in dissuading cordial, frank, and intelligent conversation about religion. The net effect is that Americans are shy to talk about their own faith and remain ignorant about other faiths. If allowed to persist in a highly multireligious and multiracial society, such mutual incomprehension is likely to create conditions ripe for conflict and unrest.

Of the many problematic assumptions that prevail among the elite, culture-defining class is that religion is fundamentally anti-intellectual, irrational, and archaic. This attitude is especially evident in the academy. The antipathy toward religion in academe is chronicled in George Marsden's *The Soul of the American University*.[35] Marsden makes the case that religion is marginalized and excluded as a credible conversation partner in the academy's intellectual life. Indeed, religion as a legitimate field of study and as a discerning, substantive and rigorous intellectual orientation "hangs on the academy's perimeter."[36] Joshua Mitchell suggests that this dismissal of religion in higher education stems from the fact that religions admit a transcendent dimension which, naturally, cannot be proven by conventional scientific means. To admit such a thing in the Enlightenment tradition of academe is to "risk one's credibility as a rational being."[37] Scholars in modern universities are thus either oblivious to or intolerant of religion: it is either irrelevant or dangerous. "Straussians worry that religion is a species of un-reason . . . postmodernists are too busy showing the instability of all things social to be concerned about religion, which is but one mode of oppression among many. Liberals and democratic theorists treat beliefs as "preferences," and so mock anything approximating real belief."[38] Carter identifies this incongruity to be a problem of epistemology. Rules of evidence and justification in the humanities, social sciences, and natural sciences differ. Scientific claims can be tested and verified but there are no settled rules to assess aesthetic, moral, and religious claims. Hence, the general impatience among academics and policymakers with any talk of "higher things."

Given the cacophony of messages beamed from their various living environments, it should not surprise teachers of religions that students feel confused, indifferent, ambivalent, alarmed, and curious about studying religions. Scholars and teachers of religion should, however, be deeply concerned over the degree of hostility, ignorance, and discomfiture that exists about religion(s) in the public square. The task of teaching religion is at times exhausting, given the dominant and influential cultures of disbelief working against serious and respectful intellectual engagement with religious data. "If religion comes to be taken seriously within the academy, it will be because it has become a large enough presence in the world that it can no longer be ignored."[39]

Teaching Goals: Tolerance, Creative Encounter, and Critical Thinking

The function of education, T. S. Eliot said, is to help us to escape not from our own times, for we are bound by them, but from the intellectual and emotional limitations of our times. In the preceding section I have attempted to highlight a few of these limitations and paradigms. We live at an extraordinary historical juncture. Technological advances have sped up the pace of life and shrunk the globe. Telecommunications, satellites, and computers transmit information instantly everywhere in multiple formats: textual, aural, visual, and virtual. Contact among cultures has escalated. Encounters and exchanges of every kind—material, social, cultural, political, artistic—are commonplace.

Cultures in the past were able to flourish and preserve their integrity because of their relative isolation and distance from each other. Such seclusion is no longer possible. The travel and leisure industry has made visiting the remotest places on the earth economical, quick, and effortless. Not only are Americans highly mobile, but also many executives and consultants lead transcontinental lives. Commuting, traveling, and regularly relocating for work or leisure has become second nature. But Americans do not have to go abroad for cultural exposure. The United States is a land of immigrants, refugees, foreign students, investors, and visitors from almost every country in the world. Sizeable ethnic enclaves exist in all its major cities.

The demise of geography has meant severing the enduring connections between community and place. The disruption of traditional life and its customs has resulted in anxiety and instability in many societies. As the Aga Khan observed in a recent address to a gathering of international press owners: "Wherever we look, we find people seeking refuge from the disorienting waves of change in the tranquil ponds of older and narrower loyalties, in the warmth of familiar memories, in the comfort of ancient rituals."[40] The threat to cultural and social identity is experienced not only physically in terms of border struggles and conflicts over land, but disorientation and social instability is also precipitated by the cultural invasion of hitherto isolated societies. Ideas, newspapers, toys, movies, music, cars, and grenades are transported into these environments by communications, travel, and international trade. Capitalizing on the profit motive, tourism across the world has turned cultural heritage into a commodity.

What is the impact of these encounters? How are they shaping us and our societies? Rapid acceleration of contact among cultures has unleashed the twin forces of multinational homogeneity and cultural particularity. Globalism has begotten tribalism and a reclaiming of ethnic and national identity.

Resisting the bland homogeneity of the melting pot, Americans too reassert their particular identities. This is palpable in American life: divisions of class, race, religion, gender, ideology, and sexual preference. But when groups within a society define themselves primarily in terms of differences, the climate becomes one of chronic strife and conflict. The mere fact that cultures have been thrust face to face with each other does not mean that they will instinctively understand each other. In major cities of the United States, many groups of different origins and backgrounds collide on a regular basis at work and in subways, malls, and theatres. Their meetings occur at the safe level of a nominal American identity, but the deeper layers of religious, racial, and historical identities remain hidden and privatized.

Teaching and learning about religions is an opportunity to turn the experience of diversity and difference into a creative encounter. This cannot be done merely by transmitting information. "Data flows in greater volumes, at higher speeds, over greater distances to larger audiences than ever before. And yet the result has not been greater understanding or enlightenment. In fact, it has often been just the reverse."[41] The information explosion has proven that understanding and wisdom are still hard won. Developing the capacity to hear the dreams and stories of the rainbow of people who make up the daily workaday world takes deliberate effort. Rather than increasing cultural sensitivity, workshops in diversity training often exacerbate conflicts by confirming what teachers of religions and cultures already know: learning to respect what is truly different and to understand what we do not embrace is hard work, takes time, and demands a great deal of intellectual and imaginative perception. Cultural sensitivity means much more than good-natured tolerance or gracious etiquette. "In truth, cultural sensitivity is far more rigorous, something that requires a deep intellectual commitment. It requires a readiness to study and to learn across cultural barriers, an ability to see others as they see themselves."[42]

In the United States, pluralism and diversity have evoked more conflict than cooperation. Programs and policies under the banner of these terms have often resulted in finger-pointing and segregation instead of mutual appreciation and exchange. One observes a troubling trend of politicization, antagonism, and division among groups on campuses. Encouraging self-expression of different ethnic and racial identity has bred more—not less—insularity, intolerance, and prejudice. People's diverse histories and cultures, instead of being an occasion for broadening the resources of society at large and for seeking solutions to common human problems, have become an occasion to blame, censure, exclude, demand special rights, and so on. This situation can and must be ameliorated. A strong case can be made that learning about religions and cultures provides a favorable context for the respectful and rigorous study of difference.

CROSSING BOUNDARIES: LEARNING ABOUT THE UNFAMILIAR

Our commitment as teachers and learners of religions is to treat our subjects fairly, incisively, and with balanced perspective. Students need to develop the capacity both to appreciate and to critique the data that comes under the rubric of religions. Anthropology and the History of Religions often take a phenomenological approach to understanding cultural materials. A primary goal is to enter a culture or religious tradition and attempt to understand it from within. This means discovering the set of meanings participants themselves attach to a particular symbol, ritual, or myth. Embracing the Kantian notion of "enlarged mentality," the exercise of empathetic encounter involves taking the standpoint of the other person seriously enough to challenge one's own worldview, thereby pushing back the limits of one's own horizons.

Crossing over familiar boundaries to visit the worlds of the strange and unknown takes courage, awareness, and discipline. This important journey can be frightening and frustrating for students. Many experience the discomfort, resistance, and shock felt by travelers to foreign lands. Exercising the self-restraint of epoché, namely, temporarily suspending judgment and bracketing out one's own assumptions, makes the experience emotionally and intellectually demanding. But as Merleau-Ponty said of phenomenology: "This is a remarkable method which consists in learning to see what is ours as alien and what was alien as our own."[43] It is not possible truly to observe a culture in and of itself without also learning anew how to observe one's own. Empathetic participation thus goes hand in hand with detached self-observation, a curious combination of Buddhist mindfulness and Ricoeur's hermeneutics of suspicion.

Self-scrutiny and diligent attentiveness to cultural particularity takes hard work. Because assumptions are by nature unconscious and deeply buried, much effort must go into helping students learn to observe and trace the etiology of their own thinking. Often students in college get to investigate and confront their assumptions for the very first time when they take a course in religion. Exercises to help students accomplish this process include journals, simulations, and case studies. Personal involvement and freedom of expression allow them to surface or vent their views, to examine their assumptions and to verify information. When successful, they learn to appreciate that how one sees an issue can vary immensely and to own the fact that much of what persons perceive and defend is deeply linked to where they are, who they are, their history, culture, intellectual and natural environment.

LETTING GO: UNLEARNING THE FAMILIAR

Facing diversity and confronting differences are unsettling experiences. Students of diverse backgrounds who are assigned to work on a group project will try very hard to ignore or hide the fact that they have racial and cultural differences. When questioned about this, students will deny that they are covering up their differences. They interpret their silence about their own particular backgrounds as a sign of tolerance. By not needing to focus on differences, they feel this shows that they have transcended them. Rather, they participate in an amorphous American identity that erases the particularity of being a Jew or Christian. Since many students in cosmopolitan settings already enjoy ethnic foods, attend multicultural fairs and festivals, listen to world music, and experiment with clothing and customs of other cultures, they feel they have successfully accepted and incorporated them into their worldview. But beneath this attitude lies hidden a combination of romanticism and resistance.

Minnich speaks of the "the stubborn temptation to turn diversity into something familiar that does not challenge systems of privilege and power."[44] This is an understandable impulse. To honor another's culture or heritage may involve a probing of one's own that threatens cherished beliefs and celebrated heroes. There is great pressure in college life to get socialized into the status quo and deeper understanding can be subversive and threatening to this goal. It may raise the possibility that existing structures of authority need to be changed, reformed, or resisted. True comprehension may mean a frank facing up to and resisting of an oppressive social custom or misleading narrative that one's own forebears have collectively constructed. A far less unsettling route to dealing with diversity is by good-heartedly incorporating its exterior and exotic aspects. The weakness of superficial phenomenology is that a sympathetic apprehension of cultures may lead to romanticism and domestification. As Aziz al-Azmeh pointedly explains, "Exoticism, frivolous or aesthetic admiration, is of course premised on an unreflected notion of utter otherness; it is a mode of consuming an object, of employing it for decorative and other purposes, in a context other than its own. Exoticism is a pleasant way of subjugating one's contrary."[45]

Students who get beyond this mark begin a sustained process of self-awareness. They start to ask: How come I never questioned this before? They begin to see familiar situations, reactions, and behaviors anew. Their entry into foreign territory has extended their reach. They alight upon what Tylor describes as the "possibilities of one another."[46] For instance, when I deal with the oral nature of religions, so accustomed are students to thinking that only textual or written information is trustworthy that they are struck by the notion that in some cultures truly valued esoteric knowledge is only transmitted orally. They learn to recognize that just because something is published or posted on the Internet does not mean it is true, accurate, or reasonable. With skepticism begins a deliberate process of thinking for themselves. This independence of thought is a critical goal of intellectual endeavor. An essential part of one's task as teacher is to cultivate students' capacity for reflection and critical analysis: to help them become self-conscious of what they know; to question and observe their own epistemological activity; to pay attention to how ideas and artifacts are historically coded; to repeatedly investigate the data until they have done it full justice; and to appreciate the disciplined rigor of intellectual work.

SKEPTICISM: UNDERSTANDING CRITICALLY

Thus far, I have treated the subject of religions and cultures in an appreciative perspective and emphasized that this heritage contributes to the richness, beauty, and insights of human civilization. But no discussion of beauty is complete without a discussion of its opposite. Martin Marty puts it bluntly: "Religion motivates most killing in the world today."[47] The cumulative historical evidence indicting religions and cultures for causing oppression, hatred, conflict, and war is incontestable. This is another potential pitfall of the phenomenological method. Suspending personal biases and restraining premature judgment is dangerous if it entails total abdication of thinking. Withholding judgment to enter another's worldview does not mean relinquishing the exercise of all judgment. Otherwise put, the role of criticism and analysis in the study of religions remains as important as in any other academic discipline. Students often equate tolerance and understanding with acquiescing or agreeing with. To "make sense" of a ritual or belief means to see it as au courant or to use the jargon "just cool."

This raises a number of ethical dilemmas. For instance, my students view a film that has a segment showing Hindu worshippers bathing in the river Ganges. The commentator explains that Hindus regard the water of the Ganges to be pure and to have healing powers. He follows this with the scientific observation that, in fact, the water of the Ganges is highly polluted and many bathers contract diseases. Students will often ask how they can be expected to respect the bathing ritual and the Hindu belief in the miraculous nature of Ganges water when they know it is filled with bacteria and ashes of the dead. For some, this proves that religion entails blind faith. Others take the attitude that since truth is relative, the Ganges could have curative powers for the Hindu.

What is the way out of this conundrum? One wants to avoid the twin pitfalls of instant denunciation and blithe relativism. This issue offers an opportunity to explore with students what Carter calls "epistemic diversity." There is the language of faith and the language of science. Each appeals to different systems of value, truth, and human experience. To drive this point home, Rabbi Kushner says, "In that sense the Bible is truer than the daily paper, because the stuff in the daily paper really happened but it's irrelevant."[48] He adds, "Asking what a prayer means is like asking what a flower means."[49] Even if Hindu worshippers were to accept the scientific assertion that Ganges water is polluted (and many do), this does not diminish the religious significance of this body of water. The literalism of science obscures the imagination and symbolism of religious life. In the religious landscape of Hindu myth, poetry, art, and ritual, the Ganges is the great source of life, the mother that replenishes and purifies and embodies the powerful flow of existence. Indeed, for some Hindus, any river into which a drop of Ganges water is poured has the power of the Ganges because ultimately all rivers are but manifestations of her. The point is that meaning is not static and singular and that since human experience of reality has multiple dimensions (emotional, cognitive, aesthetic, practical), each generates and expresses itself through its own language and symbol system.

ADVOCACY IN THE CLASSROOM

This leads me to the question of advocacy and identity issues in the classroom. There is no escaping the fact that we are largely constructed out of where, who, when, and what we are. Being teachers and scholars makes our ideas and understanding no less subject to external conditions and forces. It bears reminding that scholarship "is inseparable from the cultural politics of its day, and knowledge never was, and will never be, an innocent endeavor, but was, and is, utterly sullied."[50] So that students learn to recognize the socially constructed nature of their own knowledge and experience, whenever possible, I disclose the standpoint from which my own views are constructed. But contrary to Donald Wiebe's view, one endeavors to practice the *academic* study of religions and not the theological or ideological study of religions.[51] Teaching about religions is not identical to propagating religions. If advocacy means inculcating a particular faith, then it belongs outside the secular classroom.

Sympathetic appreciation may constitute a first step to approaching religious data, but it must be balanced by detached analytical, theoretical, and interpretive tasks. Students can learn what it means to Muslims to perform the hajj. (And there is not one meaning, of course, but at least they ought to be encouraged to look at the many meanings of the hajj expressed by Muslims.)

But by itself, this information is insufficient. The hajj needs to be analyzed from a number of perspectives: its historical origin and precedents; the social function of this ritual for Muslims; the political and symbolic role of Mecca as the orienting point of Islamic prayer and mosque architecture; the modern hajj industry of travel agents and tourism; hajj in context of pilgrimage patterns in different religions. To bring to bear the range of theoretical and critical perspectives by which the hajj can be analyzed requires sufficient detachment and disengagement from the primary religious meanings attached to it by adherents. Faith commitments, in my view, can and often do inhibit such analysis.

Commending one or another faith, apart from being inappropriate in academic institutions, also works against the cultivation of multiple viewpoints that is essential for intellectual development. Advocacy excludes genuine consideration of alternative worldviews. Advocating faith also means assuming for oneself the authority of being a representative of a specific religious tradition. An individual teacher's presentation and interpretation of a faith is thus communicated as normative. No matter how well-informed, erudite, and convincing that interpretation is, to advance a particular interpretation as normative is polemical and has political implications. One has to look critically at the question of representation. Attempts to authentically represent the voices of hitherto victimized and marginalized groups often result in reification. Religious and cultural groups are not homogeneous but have their own internal distinctions, and attempts at representation inadvertently privilege one over another. It is for this reason that the argument that religions ought to be taught by scholar-adherents because they provide "authentic" interpretations of the tradition is inherently flawed. Authenticity is a claim to authoritative discourse and such testimony is part of the religious data that gets studied. However, the ability to advance respectful and critical understandings of religions is a learned and cultivated capacity that walks a fine line between sensitivity and discernment.

Concluding Thoughts: Religion Matters

Teaching and learning about religions is a challenging task to attempt today. Apart from the disputed role of religion in a highly technological and secular society, there is a deeply imbedded skepticism and even contempt of religion in academe, the media, and the legal and political establishment. Their faith in the ultimate authority of science and the Enlightenment legacy of rationalism is pervasive and often unconscious. Religion as a subject matter is felt to be anti-intellectual and thus unworthy of intellectual attention. Even though literature deals with fiction and imagination, it is still considered to be a worthy subject to study because students get to explore the themes of life. But religion, which is such an integral part of the lives of most citizens in America, is viewed as passé and inconsequential to the functions of society.

The fact is that religions are thriving and they are a sine-qua-non of contemporary American life, and indeed, of life on this planet. According to the organizers of the first Millennium World Summit held at the United Nations in 2000, "83 percent of the world's population believe in some formal religious or spiritual belief system."[52] Individuals and societies are shaped and guided by religious ideas and activities. In turn, they alter and develop the manifold aspects of religious life and thought. Furthermore, it is far from true that religious identity, because it is a personal choice, is irrelevant in secular life. Religion matters to people and bears upon their choices and actions. For many, religious values are more real and vital than the nation or the opinion of others. Declaring that the state and church are separate institutions does not thereby preclude the values of one from influencing the values of the other. In fact, often there is common ground. The attempt to restrict religion to the private domain does not mean it is inconsequential to civic life. Carter notes that the "religious devout hold principles that they will not surrender to societal demands."[53] Because religion matters so much to followers, it remains an ever-present subversive force in society. The autonomous authority of religious creeds and the commitment of believers to this authority remains a permanent source of instability for the status quo. "One way of coping with the fear is to try to brush off the religiously devout as fanatics, as is done with depressing regularity. Another way to deal with the fear of the subversive independence of religions is to try to domesticate them."[54]

A fundamental goal of education is to prepare students to face and recreate their world. Perhaps our solutions for today will not work for their tomorrows. We may not be able to provide ready answers, but we can ensure that they will have recourse to the cumulative insights and failings of all our yesterdays. Studying the cultures and civilizations of the world offers them this resource. It also helps to place them and their own society on a time continuum, providing necessary perspective and knowledge. When we turn to examine the pivotal and enduring legacy of world cultures and civilizations, we consistently encounter the crucial role of religions. The foundational "texts" that have shaped and sustained society include among others the Babylonian creation myth, *Enuma Elish;* India's *Rg Veda;* Plato's *Republic;* the *Analects* of Confucius; the Bible and Quran; the *Bhagavad Gita.* Is it impossible to discuss cultures and civilizations without talking about their art, aspirations, scriptures, celebrations, and patterns of life. Students thus appreciate how profoundly religions, however defined, permeate the self-understanding and development of human civilization.

Finally, I would like to address the question of how our learning and teaching about religions contributes to society from the point of view of my own area of specialization, Islamic Studies. Samuel P. Huntington in his work, *The Clash of Civilizations and the Remaking of World Order*,[55] suggests that Islam will replace communism as the enemy of the West. With the end of the Cold War, "the next substantial opponent of the West may be the Islamic world, partly because of its opposition to the materialistic side of western capitalism."[56] If the Cold War taught us anything, it should have taught us how these kinds of polarizations lead to dogmatism, escalation of war machines, and at the individual level, hatred and demonization of strangers as well as neighbors.

The point here is not to get into Huntington's thesis but to emphasize the importance of developing student's critical thinking skills. Neil Postman calls this ability "crap detecting."[57] In this case, students must learn to see the flaw in the idea of "civilizations" as homogeneous, static, and monolithic entities and to question a model that juxtaposes civilizations as adversarial and self-contained blocs. To construct an argument of civilizations clashing with each other is to essentialize the highly complex and variegated conglomerate of societies which have ancient ties of exchanges in goods, genes, ideas, and skills. Thus, for instance, if we assume Western civilization to be solely the creation of the peoples of Europe (as if Europe itself can be viewed in monolithic terms), one may ask: "Is Beethoven's Ninth Symphony, which includes Turkish marches, a part of Western civilization, or the late nineteenth- and twentieth-century French paintings, whose creators were influenced by Japanese art? And what of the cubists, through whom the influence of African art changed modern painting?"[58] Such dualistic thinking reduces reality to the following kind of rhetoric which breeds further misunderstanding:

> More than a clash of cultures, more than a confrontation of races, the collision between the global civilization emanating from the West and Islam is a straight-out fight between two approaches to the world, two opposed philosophies. Under the layers of history and the mosaic of cultures, we can simplify in order to discover the major positions. One is based in secular materialism, the other in faith; one has rejected belief altogether, the other has placed it at the center of its world-view. [59]

Students, journalists, and even scholars need to understand why this kind of writing does not inform or educate; why it does not illuminate what tensions exist, where they exist, what their true scope is, and precisely, what groups within the mosaic of the West and the Islamic world are involved in creating such hostile representations of each other. Teaching and writing about the Muslim world in an environment filled with sensationalism complicates the task of cultural translation and criticism. Sloganism, stereotyping, and oversimplification leads to defensive postures that result in a dialogue of the deaf. Hence, taken together, the fact of living in a multireligious society and given the surfeit of conflicting data received from the media, Internet, and print literature, it is particularly important for students to learn how to judge sources and think critically and constructively.

The religious heritage of humankind has much to say about the making and managing of the affairs of this world, including human relations, the exchange of goods, the arbitration of disputes, the organization of labor, and the celebration of life and nature. Historically, religions have played a central role in the task of building civilizations. Cultural and religious pluralism need not be an occasion for division and conflict but can be turned into an opportunity for creative encounters to work toward building common ground and an enabling environment for tolerance, cooperation, reconciliation, and an ethic of inclusion and respect. From the richness of American diversity, students can knit together a viable and vibrant society for tomorrow, which strikes partnerships that draw on the best accomplishments of individual cultures, and still learn from the latter's defects and mistakes. It would be an achievement if their academic encounter with religions left them feeling as Ari Goldman did after his Harvard Divinity School experience:

> Today, when I go on assignment to a church, a synagogue, mosque, or temple, I no longer go as a stranger, an outsider. The ideas preached and the rituals practiced are familiar, unthreatening, and ultimately, enriching to me. The amazing dialogue that began at Harvard between the Judaism within me and other faiths I encountered continues at St. Paul Community Baptist Church in a black section of Brooklyn, at St. Patrick's Cathedral on Fifth Avenue, at a Reform temple in Cincinnati, at a Zen retreat center in Los Angeles, at a Sunni mosque in Detroit. . . . In each case I leave as a Jew, rooted in the richness of my own faith but nourished by the faith of others.[60]

NOTES

This essay was originally written for a consultation on *Teaching and Learning in Religion and Theology* sponsored by the American Academy of Religion and the Lilly Foundation held in Santa Fe on April 18–20, 1997. The purpose of the consultation was to explore various topics, including the teacher's life and vocation; primary goals for teaching religion; the tension between advocacy and objectivity in the classroom; specialist versus interdisciplinary discussions of religion in college contexts; and what the study of religion and theology contributes to society and goals of good citizenship.

1. William Scott Green, "Religion within the Limits," *Academe* 82/6 (November–December 1996): 28.

2. Stephen D. Crites, ed, *The Religion Major: A Report* (Atlanta: American Academy of Religion, 1990), 9.

3. Green, "Religion within the Limits," 27.

4. The law professor quotes this from Stephen L. Carter, *The Culture of Disbelief: How American Law and Politics Trivialize Religious Devotion* (New York: Basic Books, 1993), 63.

5. M. Robert Gardner, *On Trying to Teach: The Mind in Correspondence* (London: Analytic Press, 1994), 5.

6. Alvin Toffler, *Future Shock* (New York: Random House, 1970), 6.

7. Neil Postman and Charles Weingartner, *Teaching as a Subversive Activity* (New York: Dell, 1969), 11.

8. Ibid.

9. Toffler, *Future Shock,* 4.

10. Ibid., 33.

11. Ibid., 42.

12. Ibid., 37.

13. Postman and Weingartner, *Teaching as a Subversive Activity,* 10.

14. Marianne Williamson, *Illuminata: Thoughts, Prayers, Rites of Passage* (New York: Random House, 1994), 25.

15. Richard Olson, *Science Deified and Science Defied: The Historical Significance of Science in Western Culture, from the Bronze Age to the Beginnings of the Modern Era* (Berkeley: University of California Press, 1982), 5.

16. Elizabeth Newman, "Teaching Religion and Science: The Challenge of Developing a New Conceptual Landscape," *Religious Studies News: Spotlight on Teaching* 4/1 (February 1996): 2.

17. Hugh Hewitt, *Searching for God in America* (Dallas: Word Publishing, 1996).

18. Ibid.

19. Jacob Neusner, ed., *World Religions in America: An Introduction* (Louisville: John Knox Press, 1994), 1.

20. Hewitt, *Searching for God in America,* xv.

21. Neusner, *World Religions in America,* 2.

22. Ibid., 4.

23. William Scott Green, "Religion and Society in America," in Neusner, *World Religions in America,* 295–297.

24. Ibid., 299.

25. Ibid., 296.

26. Ibid., 300.

27. Carter, *Culture of Disbelief,* 3.

28. Hewitt, *Searching for God in America,* xiii.

29. Carter, *Culture of Disbelief,* 6.

30. Hewitt, *Searching for God in America,* xiv.

31. Ibid., xiii.

32. Ibid., xv.

33. Green, "Religion and Society in America," 297.

34. Judith A. Berling, "Is Conversation about Religion Possible?" *Journal of the American Academy of Religion* 61/1 (Spring 1993): 1.

35. George M. Marsden, *The Soul of the American University: From Protestant Establishment to Established Nonbelief* (Oxford: Oxford University Press, 1993).

36. Green, "Religion within the Limits," 26.

37. Joshua Mitchell, "Of Answers Ruled Out: Religion in Academic Life," *Academe* 82/6 (November– December 1996): 30.

38. Ibid.

39. Ibid., 31.

40. Aga Khan IV, "Keynote Address at Commonwealth Press Union Conference in South Africa," *The Ismaili, Canada* (March 1997): 44.

41. Ibid., 45.

42. Ibid.

43. Cited by Elizabeth Kamarck Minnich, "Resisting Reality: Critique and Creativity," *Religious Studies News: Spotlight on Teaching* 2/2 (September 1994): 3.

44. Ibid., 2.

45. Aziz al-Azmeh, *Islam and Modernities* (London: Verso, 1993), 128.

46. Cited by Berling, "Is Conversation about Religion Possible?" 8.

47. Martin E. Marty, "You Get to Teach and Study Religion," *Academe* 82/6 (November–December 1996): 14.

48. Hewitt, *Searching for God in America,* 43.

49. Ibid., 47.

50. Al-Azmeh, *Islam and Modernities,* 126.

51. Charlotte Allen, "Is Nothing Sacred?" *Lingua Franca* 6/7 (November 1996): 33.

52. "World's Religious Leaders in New York without Dalai Lama," New York, August 28, 2000 (Reuters). Available: *http://www.tibet.ca/wtnarchive/2000/8/28_3.html*

53. Carter, *Culture of Disbelief,* 42.

54. Ibid., 43.

55. Samuel P. Huntington, *The Clash of Civilizations and the Remaking of World Order* (New York: Simon & Schuster, 1996).

56. Frank Whaling, ed., *Theory and Method in Religious Studies* (New York: Mouton de Gruyter, 1995), 5.

57. Postman, *Teaching as a Subversive Activity,* 1.

58. Ishmael Reed, "America: The Multinational Society," in *Multi-Cultural Literacy:*

Opening the American Mind, ed. Rick Simonson and Scott Walker (Saint Paul, Minn.: Graywolf Press, 1988), 157.

59. Akbar S. Ahmed, "Media Mongols at the Gates of Baghdad: The West's Domination of the Media—Civilizations at Odds," *New Perspectives Quarterly* 10/3 (June 1993): 10.

60. Ari L. Goldman, *The Search for God at Harvard* (New York: Random House, 1991), 282–283.

INDEX